Steve McNeil is a stand-up comedian and creator of Dara O'Briain's *Go 8 Bit*, the most successful videogaming TV show of the last 15 years. He has appeared on more video gaming shows than anyone else in the UK. He has written for *Time Out*, *Shortlist*, *Den of Geek* and more. His live show 'WiFi Wars' has a residency at the Royal Insititution in Mayfair. He is a Twitch streaming partner, and in 2018 was nominated for streamer of the year at the UK ESPORTS awards.

'An informative, accessible romp through the early years of the games industry. All hail Il pirata pallido; the gaming hero we never knew we needed.' **Adam Rosser, BBC Radio 5Live**

'Steve McNeil is funny, knowledgeable, and a massive, shameless, nerd. His brilliant book reminded me just how much of my life I've wasted. **Paul Rose (aka Mr Biffo),** *Digitiser*

'The *À La Recherche du Temps Perdu* of the gaming community. The "À La Recherche du Temps Pew-Pew-Pew", as it were.'
Dara Ó Briain

'Taking us on a historical journey from the very early days all the way through to the late 1990s the book tells the stories of the men and women behind some of the most wonderful (and occasionally awful) games of the golden age, the fierce rivalries, bizarre business practices and downright bonkers risks taken during the pioneering days of computer and video gaming . . . A thoroughly enjoyable read!'
Mark Howlett (aka Lord Arse)

'Hugely funny, and full of fantastic facts about the history of video games. But enough about me; Steve's book is also quite good.' **Ellie Gibson (Eurogamer)**

STEVE McNEIL

A journey through the
golden era of video games

HEADLINE

First published in 2019 by
HEADLINE PUBLISHING GROUP

First published in paperback in 2020 by
HEADLINE PUBLISHING GROUP

4

Cataloguing in Publication Data is available from the British Library

ISBN 978 1 4722 6135 9
Ebook ISBN 978 1 4722 6134 2

Designed and typeset by EM&EN
Printed and bound in Great Britain by Clays Ltd, Elcograf S.p.A.

Headline's policy is to use papers that are natural, renewable and recyclable
products and made from wood grown in well-managed forests and other
controlled sources. The logging and manufacturing processes are expected
to conform to the environmental regulations of the country of origin.

HEADLINE PUBLISHING GROUP
An Hachette UK Company
Carmelite House
50 Victoria Embankment
London EC4Y 0DZ

www.headline.co.uk
www.hachette.co.uk

For Tina and Ella

Contents

Foreword

by Dara Ó Briain

I take a pretty strong line on nostalgia. Actually, it would be more accurate to say that I have a pretty strong line on nostalgia in the sense that I have a great joke I tell onstage about nostalgia and I sell it with the conviction that would imply that it is my personal philosophy.

'Nostalgia,' I say, sternly, to the audience, 'is heroin for old people.' And then I tap my veins, and roll my eyeballs into my head, mumbling, 'I remember when everything was better . . .' like a seventy-five-year-old complaining about the delay in Brexit, while sitting in the *Question Time* audience.

And then I finish up my show and drive home to my house, pour myself a glass of fine vintage scotch, put on some early nineties dance music, fire up the free-standing arcade machine and play Pac-Land until bed.

Some things to take from this. Firstly, stand-ups are never to be taken literally, even when they're telling you 'this is a true story'. It might have been once, but we've probably tidied it up a bit. Or probably just made the whole thing up. Let's not be naive here, there were never three men walking into a bar. That chicken never crossed the road.

The main lesson, though, is that sometimes nostalgia is great and correct and perfectly justified, depending on what it's for and what you expect to get out of it.

If you ache for that feeling you had when you were eighteen, but you think that the way to get that feeling back is to consistently vote against progress, close the borders and whine about not being able to call minorities by the same names you used in the army back in the 1960s, then step away from the ballot box, buster, you're messing things up for the rest of us.

But if you think the key to getting the rush of youth back is to invest in a palm-sized plastic model of the console you got for Christmas in 1989 and play Alex Kidd for an evening, then put me down as player two, buddy! You're hurting no one!

Although not Alex Kidd, to be honest. I'm just a little older than that, so the golden ages of video games had already passed by then. I will not brook any dissent in this matter. The greatest music ever made was the music when you were nine-teen; the greatest era of games was whenever you were twelve. That pitches me right into the battle between Sinclair Spectrum and Commodore 64, and, for the record, I was on the side of the Americans. Of course I was! Sprites! A speech synthesiser! Its cavernous 64K memory (effective memory: 38K)! Plus, I was in Ireland, not Britain, and thus under no national obligation to support the weird, rubber keys of the underdog.

And what a golden era it was! Eighteen-minute-long loading times! Controllers with one button so you could *either* jump or shoot! And if you ran out of games, you could buy a magazine with the code of a game printed out, and you could spend hours and hours typing it all in.

You would probably say that things are better now but every time I try to play a quick game of FIFA these days I'm informed that I need a 6GB update and it takes two hours; and the controllers have seventeen buttons and the other people in Fortnite seem to able to jump *and* shoot and why can't they just stay still so I can shoot them and now I'm dead and have to start again. And there is less typing, but at least in the old days I didn't have to spend an hour before the start of a game selecting which nose my character should have.

So let's not mock the beautiful simplicity of the old days. And while there may be many other fine themes in this book, let's also acknowledge that nostalgia is perfectly reasonable when it's about your life.

Proust wrote an entire book about the rush of memories he got from eating a small cake; imagine how much material he would have got from the load screen of Manic Miner. Proust would have wept all the way through Track and Field, if he could have got past the javelin bit.

And yes, I'm saying this book is like Proust. You are holding in your hands the *À La Recherche du Temps Perdu* of the gaming community.

The 'À La Recherche du Temps Pew-Pew-Pew', as it were.

Try not to weep too much.

INTRODUCTION

Oh, hey guys!

If you know me at all, you probably know me as the pale, geeky one from the TV show I created, *Go 8 Bit* or, to give it its full title, *Dara Ó Briain's Go 8 Bit*, so called because he's much more famous than me and my co-creator Sam Pamphilon, so they put Dara's name at the start so people would actually watch it. I imagine if Dara was writing a book about video games, people would buy *that* one, but thankfully he's far too busy to write anything longer than a foreword, so they've asked me to write one instead. Maybe think of this book as *Dara Ó Briain's Big Book of Video Games, written by Steve McNeil* if that helps.

Let's not get bogged down in Dara's absence. Rest assured, you're in safe hands. I'm currently on a train on the way to a gig. The journey's only an hour (and I'm meant to be writing this) but in my bag I've got a Nintendo Switch that I'm mopping up Mario Odyssey moons on, a laptop that's halfway through a game of Tropico, and a phone on which I'm playing Cooking Fever with the zealousness of a crack addict that's just discovered a delicious new flavour of crack. Need more proof? I'm the guy who took a Nintendo Wii on his honeymoon.

Yeah.

In my head, the Wii was an acceptable 'gateway console' for my non-gamer wife, and I figured we could have fun with its intuitive controls and casual gaming. In retrospect, it was actually the most inappropriate item possible to take on what many would regard as 'snuggle week'.

As this book's subtitle states, we'll be taking 'a journey through the golden era of video games', which is, of course, a subjective opinion. Essentially, the guys that let me write this book (Hi, guys!), liked that phrase, and it's very hard to explain to people who don't know anything about games why referring to any era of video game history as the definitive 'golden era' isn't really appropriate. Still, we are where we are. I needed the money, and they presumably needed a book in their portfolio for 2018/2019 that covered 'youth culture' to meet some sort of strategic objective (we all know how much kids love playing Pong on their smartphones).

At the very least, this is *my* golden era. After a brief introduction where we take a look at when video games first crawled out of the sea, we begin our journey proper with the first breakthrough video game, Pong. My earliest memories of gaming are on a home Pong console – the black and white Adman Grandstand TV-game 2000 no less. Throughout my childhood, I can't remember a time where gaming wasn't a huge part of my life, only putting the controller to one side for several years, as many did, when I turned eighteen and the excesses of living on a university campus distracted me. This is where we end our journey in this book too, with the last game I fully immersed myself in – The Legend of Zelda: Ocarina of Time. Widely recognised as the best video game of all time (as if that's something that can be objectively true) it felt like an appropriate place for this nostalgia-fuelled volume to end. From then on I was simply too busy talking to girls. Mainly about other boys they fancied but, as I always say, a chat's a chat.

I rediscovered my love of gaming in my late twenties, after I settled down with my graciously tolerant wife, and I'm now lucky enough that my job allows me to play games on a pretty much daily basis. I've stopped taking games consoles on romantic breaks away with my wife, though. What clearer demonstration could there be of a man's love for a woman?

Okay, full disclosure . . . a few years ago on a holiday in Italy I did end up spending all night playing a game on my smartphone while my wife slept next to me*. Unfortunately, doing that in the dark with the screen in close proximity to my face gave me eye strain. I was in so much pain, and my vision so blurry, that I had to go to a local doctor and attempt to explain in Italian why my eye hurt. He prescribed an eye patch to allow my eye to rest and heal, which led to the locals referring to this pasty British mess as *il pirata pallido*: The Pale Pirate. If only they'd been aware of my childhood propensity for bootlegging games on my twin cassette deck for

---

* Kairosoft's Mega Mall Story, if you must know.

classmates, they'd have realised how apposite that nickname really was. Now that *Go 8 Bit*'s been on telly, you could maybe understand why someone *might* be willing to put up with being married to me, but this eye patch incident happened in 2010. Back then, I looked like a potato with a face drawn on it just like I do today, but I also worked in marketing.

One thing worth saying before we get stuck in, is that this book is a whistlestop tour of gaming. We could spend a whole book talking solely about the Nintendo-Sega rivalry, or the legal disputes that tied up Atari throughout its troubled existence. Indeed, many have, and they did a far better job than I could ever hope to in this silly book*. Having said that, unlike many other titles out there, I have attempted to cover *all* areas of gaming, including computer games (which tend to get sidelined in favour of console gaming) and a bit more about what was going on outside of the USA and Japan though, of course, console gaming in those two territories tends to dominate, due to its prevalence in mainstream culture.

Anyway, no more stalling. Here we go. I hope you enjoy reading this book. Writing it really ate into my playing-games-in-my-pants time.

Steve McNeil (The Pale Pirate) x

---

* For those who want to go deeper, I've included a bibliography at the end with some further reading.

1

THE LAND BEFORE PONG

Like all good stories, ours begins with Bagatelle. For the few of
you reading this that aren't well-versed in obscure billiard
sports*, Bagatelle is a bit like snooker but the aim is to whack a
bunch of balls up a slopey table with a cue stick and then hope
they plop in some holes scattered around it on their way back
down. Bagatelle also has influences from bowling: early versions had 'pins' which could be knocked down to score points.
Placing these upright again after each turn must have proved
too time-consuming for the players (who, based on what
little I know about history, were probably short-tempered due
to being riddled with pox and sozzled on gin) and so they
replaced the free-standing pins with hammered-in pins for
the balls to bounce and rest on, while the holes became the
primary targets. This combination of pins and balls is how
these games would eventually become known as pinball
games. This is an interesting fact you can tell at parties so that
people will find you impressive, and we're only on the first
paragraph. Want another? Slot machines have cherries and

* Shame on you.

5

melons on them because the early ones used to reward players with flavoured chewing gum instead of money, to side-step gambling laws. You are going to blow people's minds with your awesomeness by the time you've finished reading this book. You're welcome.

We've got distracted.

Bagatelle had existed for well over a hundred years when, in 1931, Chicago-based David Gottlieb released a coin-operated version, called Baffle Ball. It released seven balls to the player in exchange for one shiny penny and, rather than a cue stick, had a springy 'plunger' which you'd pull and release to launch the balls, one-by-one, into the arena. Gottlieb didn't invent coin-operated amusements; gambling 'slot' machines, for example, had been around since the turn of the century. He didn't even invent the springy plunger; that had been used in one form or another on Bagatelle tables since the late 1700s. There had been other coin-op bagatelle cabinets prior to Baffle Ball too, but Baffle Ball was the one that really took off. Lucky for him, really, given he didn't seem to have an original thought in his head.

I'm being unkind. He clearly got something right, as over 50,000 units were sold to drugstores and taverns across the United States; the additional source of income was simply too tempting to resist. When one of Gottlieb's distributors, Ray Moloney, was unable to get his hands on enough Baffle Ball tables to keep up with demand, he founded a new company, Lion Manufacturing, and created his own pinball table, Ballyhoo. It was so successful that he soon renamed the company from Lion to Bally, a name which, alongside Gottlieb and (Harry) Williams, still lives on today as a gold standard in pinball.

Williams had initially entered the market around the same time by refurbishing other people's cabinets and reskinning them with new 'playfield' designs to make them his own, as he realised he could do this far more cheaply than buying new tables, a bit like when Rover tried to relaunch the Mini Metro as the Rover 100, but far more successfully*. It wasn't long, though, before he began to innovate, firstly with the introduction of the now ubiquitous tilt mechanism, which discouraged people from being overly aggressive with his cabinets when trying to manipulate the ball's path. You may have been under the impression that something that could detect excessive force might require a high degree of engineering, but Williams' solution was to balance a ball on a little shelf and, if it fell off when people rocked the cabinet, the game stopped. Hardly rocket science, but it worked. The following year, Williams introduced electricity to pinball in his 1933 table, Contact. The pockets on the table would register a 'contact' (see what he did there?) with the metal ball, add points to a tally, then release them back into the field of play. Bells could also be triggered to ring, to reward the player, and it wasn't long before manufacturers started adding flashing lights to the mix as well and, clearly, this new ability of pinball tables to bombard the player's senses was intoxicating.

---

* As with so many things, I am indebted to a Mr. A. Partridge for this insightful reference point.

While Gottlieb was no doubt less than delighted there were so many new companies muscling in on his territory*, the far bigger threat came from 'payout' machines. These were versions of pinball where, based on your success on the table, you could win cash. States began to crack down on these as a form of gambling, but failed to make the distinction between payout pinball tables, and those that were purely for fun†. New York's mayor at the time, Fiorello LaGuardia, chose to announce this to the press by, quite sensibly, smashing the machines up with hammers and throwing them in the sea. It seems hard to believe now but, back then, political leaders sometimes did extreme things to feed their pathological lust for attention. Imagine! Not long after, World War Two also took its toll on the progress of pinball, as many of the cabinets were taken and melted down for the war effort.

However, once the war ended, the general population were keen to inject some fun back into their lives, and pinball manufacturers set about finding solutions that could demonstrate their game was more a matter of skill than luck, in the hopes of removing their ban. The big innovation that changed everything in 1947 was . . . wait for it . . . flippers! Yes, all the pinball tables you've been picturing in your head so far have been wrong because, for the first sixteen years, the balls just fell to the bottom and there was nothing you could do about

---

* Just one year after Baffle Ball, there were over 150 pinball manufacturers, mostly in the Chicago area.

† In fairness, coin-operated amusements was a one hundred per cent cash business, and so really lent itself to money laundering.

it. Knowing this raises more questions than it answers, most obviously – why did anyone find that fun?

Gottlieb's Humpty Dumpty, the first table to feature flippers (known then as 'bumpers'), had six: two at the top, two in the middle, and two at the bottom. The following year, Steven Kordek at Genco reduced this to just the two at the bottom for one of their tables, in no small part due to the fact that a pinball table with just two flippers is cheaper to make than one with six. That's maths! This quickly became the industry standard, and the demonstrable introduction of skill to the game led to some states relaxing the laws around them, although in New York it remained banned until the 1970s. All was not well though as, in the early 1950s, a new set of laws were passed that further restricted the distribution of 'payout' machines (including slots), which was obviously still a big part of many of these companies' business. But the USA's loss was Japan's gain . . .

The company Service Games was formed in May 1952 by Marty Bromley and his father who had, until then, been managing games rooms with slot and pinball machines on Hawaiian military bases. When the new restrictive laws came into force, Service Games bought the machines cheap and exported them to Japan, to set up games rooms for servicemen there. Seemingly it was fine to exploit American soldiers, but only on foreign soil.

They soon expanded into jukeboxes, which offered great potential distribution networks and had rapidly spread much like pinball had two decades earlier, and it wasn't long before they also merged with another company run by a guy, David

Rosen, which was in the similar business of importing electro-mechanical games (more on those in a moment). You may wonder why I'm telling you all this, but Service Games at this point became Sega Enterprises Ltd, a name you will no doubt be familiar with if you've ever played games. They weren't the only future games company beginning to move into the coin-operated amusements market, either. Originally, Sega's merger was intended to be a three-way deal with Taito, who were in the business of peanut vending machines – yes, that was a thing, the past is even more twee than you imagine. Taito pulled out of the deal, presumably because they felt feeding elephants in zoos was going to be bigger business than electrical amusements. Two other companies you may have heard of, Nintendo and Namco*, were also around at this time, with similarly tangential activities. Nintendo sold playing cards and toys. Namco distributed children's rides, beginning with just two mechanical horses stuck on the roof of a department store because all the good locations were taken by the competition. Less Disneyland, more travelling funfair on an industrial estate.

Sega eventually began creating their own games to sell back from Japan to the US and European markets, with games such as Periscope† (1966) – an electro-mechanical submarine

---

* Namco began life as the Nakamura Manufacturing Company – hence NA-M-CO.

† Side note: The origins of the game have been debated but it all gets REALLY confusing (even on the sites by REAL fans who've analysed EVERYTHING available) and, I'll be honest, I got bored. It's amazing how much of this relatively recent stuff is so hard to pin down though. Much

shooter simulator. Periscope was absolutely massive (three times the size of other attractions), costly to produce and certainly not intended to be shipped internationally. To combat this, Sega suggested operators charge twenty-five cents for it rather than ten cents, making it the first arcade game to cost a 'quarter' (the equivalent of nearly two dollars today!).

Electro-mechanical games were very popular novelty attractions around this time, and grew in tandem with pinball, jukeboxes and so on. Gottlieb had a very successful 'strength tester' grip prior to the release of Baffle Ball. Seeburg did well with light gun games, with cabinets like Six Gun, where you could have a shoot-out with a full size cowboy-slash-shonky-mannequin, or Shoot The Bear (1947) where you had to shoot at a moving statue of a bear to make it rear up and change direction. If you're struggling to picture that, imagine a woodland scene ripped from an Asterix comic and a figurine of a bear I had made in three minutes from whatever I could find at a car boot sale running around in circles while you tried to shoot it. Seeburg also distributed jukeboxes and vending machines. Another popular game was Speedway (1969) from the Chicago Coin company, which featured a projection on a screen of racing cars which you would manoeuvre between to increase your position in a race. It came complete with steering wheel, throttle, milometer and more – all the ingredients of what would recognisably be a modern car racing video game, but achieved through mechanical, non-computing

---

of it simply wasn't documented as it was viewed as inconsequential at the time. I mean, arguably, it still is. The planet's dying, guys.

methods. Chicago Coin were in pinball prior to this, and would make Pong clones in the years that followed.

In Japan, Pachinko was another popular pastime. It is similar to pinball, but with vertical cabinets rather than flat ones. The player flips tiny metal balls to the top which then tumble into holes which pay out more balls, and these can then either be reinserted for further play, or cashed in. Although gambling machines were banned, these, and Pachi-suro machines (like standard fruit machines but where each wheel can be stopped individually), gave the player just enough control to be deemed not merely a matter of chance and luck although, unless you've taken a lot of blows to the head, I'd struggle to convince you that Pachinko involves skill any more than blindfolding yourself and attempting a hole in one on a golf course. There might be a couple of people on the planet with poor enough social skills that they choose to put in the hours required to get good at it, but for most of us it's as much a game of skill as the lottery.

What all the above tells us is that there was a growing appetite for novelty attractions in public spaces, where people were willing to exchange money for an amusing diversion. The introduction of coin-mechanisms allowed various companies to automate and monetise these amusements, whether it was music via jukeboxes, ball games like pinball, snacks and drinks from vending machines, slot machines for gamblers, or electro-mechanical novelties emulating anything from shooting to racing cars. All of these could be distributed to similar locations to allow businesses to create additional revenue streams, hence many companies operating in several of these markets simultaneously. Within this context, it perhaps seems unsurprising that 'video games' would soon take off – and that many of these companies would attempt to ride that wave – but, before they could, technology had to reach a point where it was financially viable for computers to replace these more low-tech (but equally fun) solutions found at piers and fairgrounds.

So, let's whizz back through time and find out how that happened.

The first programmable computer was at the University of Pennsylvania in 1946. The Electronic Numeric Integrator and Calculator (ENIAC) weighed thirty tonnes, took up sixty-three square metres of floor space (due in no small part to its 17,000 vacuum tubes), and couldn't even run solitaire. Although, given how much it cost to build ($400,000 – over $6,000,000 in today's money), that would have probably seemed frivolous.

The following year (1947 – the year pinball discovered flippers), a patent was filed for a Cathode-Ray Tube Amusement Device – essentially a machine that you could plug into your television and then interact with on-screen using controllers, seemingly firing 'shells' at overlaid plastic transparent targets affixed to your screen via static electricity. You might think 'Ooh, that's the first home gaming system, right there!' – but sadly, other than a handmade prototype, it was never developed any further. It also fails on several key criteria. While it is an 'electronic' game, it only used analogue circuitry, nothing digital. It couldn't remember whether you hit a target or not, or keep score, because the targets weren't actually in-game, they were just stuck to your telly. It's not a 'computer' game as it wasn't built on a computer and it's not a 'video' game because it didn't produce its graphics through a video signal[*]. As a result, it often gets ignored or sidelined when talking about 'the first video game'. I'll be honest, I don't really care about any of that. With a bit of imagination, it could give the user a similar experience to what we would recognisably call a video game. Semantics pedants be damned.

Another that often gets overlooked is Bertie the Brain (1950) – and, yes, you're right, that *is* an awesome name for an early computer. Bertie was four metres tall and challenged oncomers to compete against him at noughts and crosses[†] (aka tic-tac-toe). I'd always assumed when the giant robots finally rose up to battle us, the fight would be more violent, but I'm bold enough to admit I misjudged the extent to which machines would enjoy shenanigans. A 3x3 grid of buttons allowed you to choose your spot, and this would then be played out on a huge grid of lights before you. Incredibly, it even had an adjustable difficulty setting. While it was fun, it was built by Josef Kates primarily to demonstrate his 'additron tube', a mini version of vacuum tubes, which were essential in the creation of early computers, though soon to be surpassed

---

[*] I'll level with you – even I don't understand what that one means.
[†] Noughts and crosses was a popular game in early programming experiments due to the relatively limited number of possible outcomes.

by smaller transistors. We could talk about what all those things are, but we won't, because it's boring.

Some people argue Bertie wasn't a computer game, because it didn't have moving graphics. If writing this book has taught me one thing, it's that historians of video games *really* want to find reasons early attempts don't count. This one wasn't even in any books, I just stumbled across it on Wikipedia so, in fairness, there's every chance it's not even true. My Wikipedia page frequently gets hacked to describe me as 'the future face of Bovril'.

So far, we've spent most of our time talking about North America, but it was actually in 1951, at the Festival of Britain (an event organised to celebrate the prospect of a better future after World War Two) that the world first 'played' a 'computer' 'game' (inverted commas included to appease games historians, you petty psychopaths).

John Bennett, an Australian employee of the UK computer company Ferranti, managed to put together a system that could play a digital version of Nim – an ancient game where players had to pick up objects and either be left with the last one, or avoid being left with the last one (the computer could play both versions). Dubbed the 'Nimrod', the machine measured 12ft x 9ft x 5ft, though only a tiny fraction of that was the computer itself. As with ENIAC, the machine consisted of vacuum tubes, which in this instance were used to display lights that represented the game's matchsticks, or 'rods'.*

---

* Nimrod was a biblical king associated with being rebellious against God, so this computer's name was not only wordplay on the game Nim

Again, this wasn't created to be fun, although the crowds drawn to it proved it undoubtedly was. Instead, the aim was to demonstrate the computer's ability to handle complex mathematical problems, this being Ferranti's core business.

Ferranti had two close encounters with gaming that year, as Christopher Strachey managed to create a draughts (aka checkers) game which ran on the Manchester Mark 1, a forerunner of the Ferranti Mark 1*. Throughout these early years of computers, there were various versions of checkers and chess developed or posited, as part of an ongoing exploration of Artificial Intelligence†. Alan Turing, a key figure in the breaking of German codes during the World War Two‡, wrote a chess program so advanced in fact, that no computer was sufficiently powerful to run it. Determined to demonstrate the program, Turing played a match against a friend where he acted as a proxy for his computer program, behaving as its logic would dictate, were there a machine capable of delivering it. After many hours, in which Turing painstakingly calculated each individual decision his program would make, I'm delighted to inform you that, eventually, he lost. LOL.

---

and its matchstick 'rods', but the existence of artificial intelligence in a religious context. Exceptional wordplay. Wordy footnote.

* The world's first commercially available electronic computer.

† Give Claude Shannon, Arthur Samuel and Alex Bernstein a google if you want to really go down the rabbit hole on this.

‡ Based at Bletchley Park, where I got married. Strangely, the museum there still tends to lean more on Turing than my big day in its marketing, but I'm sure that'll change once this book comes out.

Turing's overambitious attempt aside, it was clear here that computers *could* be used for games, but the cost was simply prohibitive. Yet, it went on. In 1952, Alexander Douglas created a version of noughts and crosses, often referred to retrospectively as 'OXO', on the University of Cambridge's Electronic Delay Storage Automatic Calculator (EDSAC) as part of his PhD thesis on human–computer interaction. This computer was of note in that it was the first computer with memory you could read, add to and remove information from – essentially RAM, as we would now know it. Fast forward a few more years, and we meet William Higinbotham, who had worked on the Manhattan project during the war, building the timing switches that made sure bombs exploded at the best possible moment. Of course, the definition of 'best possible moment' depended very much on which side of the bomb you happened to be. Post war, Higinbotham found work at the Brookhaven National Laboratory, which opened its doors to the public each year. In 1958, Higinbotham made the decision to offer something more engaging than the usual static exhibits, and set to work on a version of a tennis game on an oscilloscope screen. With a side-on view of a tennis court (complete with net in the centre), a ball would move between the two sides. Each player had a dial to change the angle of their 'racket', and a button they would press at the moment they wished to hit the ball. As with Nimrod, Tennis for Two was a big hit, and got another airing the following year but, after that, the exhibit was dismantled so the parts could be used on other projects.

While recognisably a representation of tennis, there is yet

again some debate over this qualifying as our first game. As with the Cathode-Ray Tube Amusement Device, the system had no memory of events – it didn't keep score, so the game would never be won or lost. Really, all that was happening was the oscilloscope was being manipulated to draw a trail behind a 'ball' instead of its usual curved lines, and would change its direction/angle when triggered by one of the player's controls. But who cares?! People's brains can contextualise and remember things. This was a game of tennis, on a screen! Why do games historians hate joy so much?!

I believe by this point I've made it clear that a bunch of terrible human beings have spent far too much time arguing about which, if any, of the above games qualify for the title of 'first video/computer game', but the next one is never disputed. So, if you take it that everything we've talked about so far can be seen as people making tentative steps towards something that's recognisable to a modern gamer, this next one is *the one.*

At Massachusetts Institute of Technology (MIT), they had a PDP-1 (Programmed Data Processor) – $120,000 worth of computer the size of a large car, which was one of the earliest to have a keyboard and monitor. Incredibly, and for reasons that are unclear to me, the university's Tech Model Railroad Club (TMRC) were allowed to dabble on this insanely expensive piece of hardware at night, writing programs that could be printed out onto ticker tape. In 1961, a member of the TMRC, sci-fi fan Steve Russell – aka Slug – began to create a game which would eventually be christened 'Spacewar!'* It may be that Slug was a reference to his lack of urgency, as after creating an early prototype in 1961, it took a lot of nagging from friends and another six months for Steve the Slug to finish the game the following year, with an estimated 200 hours of work invested.

The game featured two rocket ships battling in space, both controlled by players, as there simply wasn't enough computing power to give the second rocket artificial intelligence. You could control the speed and direction of the ships, and fire torpedoes at your enemy, by using the toggle switches on the PDP-1. While Spacewar! was immediately a hit with Russell's friends in the TMRC, they all began to contribute additional features: one gave the game an accurate star map for a backdrop by bolting on another application referred to humorously (but truthfully) as 'expensive planetarium'. Another added a sun with accurate gravity, which could be used by the players to build momentum and catch out their opponents, or pull them towards a fiery death if they weren't careful. A third friend added a hyperspace button, which would immediately teleport you to a new location if you found yourself in a sticky situation. By this point, Spacewar! was so popular that players were getting sore elbows operating the switches on the PDP-1, so the TMRC created remote controllers that you could wire into the computer too. While all these things were undoubtedly improvements over the original, you can't help but wonder if Slug was slightly affronted over their 'help'. 'Oh,

---

* Yes, really. Our video game god is a model train enthusiast called Slug.

sure, *I* created the first video game ever, but *you've* all got suggestions for how it could have been better.' Never has a feedback sandwich been more needed.

Not only that but, rather than being the billionaire god-father of gaming, Steve 'Slug' Russell never made a penny from Spacewar! The hardware simply wasn't commercially viable, and the game remained a fun diversion, but nothing more. TMRC freely shared the game to anyone with a PDP-1 that wanted it. Digital Equipment (the manufacturers of the PDP-1) even started using it to demo the system, and gave it away with purchases of the computer. Programmers at institutions with other computers also started to make their own versions of Spacewar! on whatever computers they had available. One place that had Spacewar! running was the University of Utah, where a young man called Nolan Bushnell was studying engineering. As well as playing Spacewar!, Bushnell began to create his own games, having spent many evenings in the lab learning to program in the FORTRAN programming language (and its simplified version, GOTRAN). Early attempts included 2D and 3D versions of noughts and crosses, and a game referred to as Fox and Geese, where you controlled a fox trying to pick off a stray goose from a gaggle, while they swarmed en masse to smother you; this was notable in that the geese were controlled by a simple piece of AI (Artificial Intelligence) rather than a second player.

During summer holidays, Bushnell worked at Lagoon Amusement Park in Salt Lake City, where there would have been many of the coin-operated amusements we mentioned earlier, and so it was no great leap for him to consider that people would be drawn to play on computer games like Spacewar!, if only they could be produced at a cost that allowed for profit.

While Bushnell was thinking about ways of getting games into public spaces, at Sanders research lab on the other side of the country in New Hampshire, Ralph Baer was thinking about how to get games into people's homes. As head of the Equipment Design Division at Sanders (a defence contractor), Baer had a certain amount of leeway with what to do with his team of over 500 people and, in 1966, he set one of them, Bill Harrison, to work on something a bit different – a device which would allow people to manipulate an image on their television (almost twenty years after the prototype Cathode-Ray Tube Amusement Device had been left to gather dust). Their first attempt involved a lever you pumped furiously to change the colour of a box on the TV from red to blue. You'll be relieved to hear that, at this stage, they were just seeing what they could do because, with all the will in the world, light-pump games aren't a thing.

It wasn't long before they added another member to their team, the more creative and brilliant (but, according to Baer, notoriously lazy) Bill Rusch – available primarily because his boss didn't want him. When Rusch wasn't playing his guitar loudly from their office to the confusion of the rest of the workforce, he would occasionally create new games that used the emerging technology they were developing. After some time, they had several working prototypes: a two-player chase through a maze (as with Spacewar!, both players were controlled by humans due to a lack of power available for computer-controlled characters), a shooting game with a plastic rifle and, eventually, a table tennis game. Most people in the company were confused as to why a military defence contractor was putting pretend ping pong on the telly but, thankfully for All Future Gamers On Planet Earth, Herbert Campman (Sanders' corporate director of research and development) had developed a taste for the shooting game in particular. I suppose guns were at least *vaguely* on brand, and so Campman gave them a bit more time and a small amount of funding to continue work.

Meanwhile, as Baer continued to work on his pet project, Bushnell graduated in 1969 and was hired by the electronics company Ampex as a research-design engineer. He didn't particularly enjoy the work, and amused himself by spending his free time attempting to create that coin-operated version of Spacewar! he'd had in mind, using a new (and, crucially, cheap) Texas Instruments minicomputer. So committed was he to the project, that he turned his two-year-old daughter's bedroom into a workshop and had her sleeping in the living room. I've not been able to confirm this, but I imagine his wife was both delighted and impressed. No doubt she'd have been even more certain she'd married the right guy when it became apparent it was too expensive to be profitable – an affordable version would lack the required processing power meaning gameplay would be too slow.

He wasn't doing this alone, though. He'd agreed to work on the project with two colleagues from Ampex: Larry Bryan and Ted Dabney*. Eventually they came to the conclusion that, rather than trying to make the game run on Texas Instruments' hardware, they'd be better off creating custom hardware that solely did the tasks they needed, using hardware borrowed from Ampex. Thankfully, Ampex allowed employees to take components for free, for personal projects, so this new endeavour was totally fine and above board (unlike when *you* steal reams of paper from work for your home printer, you massive thief). When they needed components their company didn't have, though, they had to get creative. They used a second-hand black and white TV for the system's monitor, and their coin mechanism had the money falling into an empty paint thinner can.

Despite this spit-and-sawdust approach to manufacturing, the final machine worked. It was not without compromises though. As you'll remember, Spacewar! had been a two-player game, but Bushnell's was solo, with the player attempting to attack two simple AI spaceships without getting shot. Nevertheless it was impressive enough to get the attention of Nutting Associates, who Bushnell was introduced to via his dentist. I could give you more information about that, but it's much more fun if you create your own story in your head of how or why that happened. My version involves a tiny computer enthusiast that lives in someone's gums.

Nutting Associates had recently had some success with 'Computer Quiz' – a novelty machine with projected multiple

---

* Some reports say they actually used Dabney's daughter's bedroom as their office but, as was the case with Sega's Periscope, the truth is blurred.

choice quiz options and buttons for the answers, itself an adaptation of a military tool for training soldiers*. Computer Quiz was no niche product; it had strong sales when compared to pinball machines of the time. Bill Nutting, in need of a follow-up hit, hired Bushnell and licensed his game, which was named Computer Space as a nod to Computer Quiz. From his time at Lagoon Amusement Park, Bushnell was aware of the need to 'draw people in' so he placed emphasis on the cabinet within which the game would sit too, ending up with an incredibly futuristic, curvy, fibreglass frame that caught the eye.

When the first one went into a bar called the Dutch Goose[†] in 1971, people weren't sure what to make of it, but eventually it did okay. However, this turned out to give Nutting and Bushnell false hope. The Dutch Goose was very close to Stanford University campus. While the more savvy crowd that frequented this drinking hole were willing to persevere with the game's *pages* of instructions, in more traditional 'blue-collar' bars people simply didn't have the patience or interest required to learn how to play. Unfortunately for Nutting, they'd made 1,500 Computer Space machines. They never sold them all and Bushnell, who partly blamed Nutting's marketing of the game for its lukewarm

---

* How testing soldiers' knowledge of sixties' chart hits improved their warzone skills is beyond me.

† The Dutch for Goose is Gans. I only know this because I googled it in the hopes the translation would lend itself to some lightly humorous wordplay. I assure you, no one's more disappointed than me with the outcome.

reception, decided to set up his own company with long-term collaborator Ted Dabney. Although it hadn't been a roaring success, they were receiving sufficient royalties for Computer Space to make the leap. This new company's name? They chose an astronomical term referring to the alignment of three celestial bodies (for example, the sun, earth and moon): Syzygy. Or at least that would have been the company's name if it hadn't already been taken. So Bushnell took a word from the Japanese game Go instead: Atari.

While Bushnell and Dabney were doing well enough to set up their own company, spare a thought for Bill Pitts and his friend Hugh Tuck who, also in 1971, built their own arcade version of Spacewar!, known as 'Galaxy Game' (so-called because they didn't want to invoke any anti-war sentiment with the title). Programmed on a $14,000 PDP-11 mini-computer and housed in a custom cabinet they built, the game was also placed at Stanford University – Pitts and Tuck had both studied there, and cut their teeth on the computers overnight.

Including Galaxy Game's monitor and other hardware, in total it cost approximately $20,000 – roughly twenty times what it cost to make a slot machine at that time, and the equivalent of over $100,000 in today's money. This was only possible thanks to the continual investment of money by Tuck's wealthy parents. At ten cents a go, Galaxy Game would have required 200,000 games to be played to break even. A second, improved, version of the machine which could support two games at once did remain at Stanford until 1979 as it always drew a crowd, but the development itself was abandoned by mid-1971 as Pitts and Tuck had spent an incredible $65,000, although they claim it did eventually make this back. As anyone who's ever invested $65,000 knows, the primary goal is always to just eventually get $65,000 back eight years later, with no remuneration for the risk, or hours of work, or any accounting for inflation, or any profit whatsoever.

While Galaxy Game was, by all accounts, a far more faithful recreation of the complexities of the original Spacewar! when compared to Bushnell's diluted, simplified Computer Space, crucially Bushnell had chosen to focus on commercial viability, whereas Pitts and Tuck had focused on technical accuracy, to their (literal) cost. Back in Ralph Baer's world, he'd also had a tough couple of years. The big challenge was finding a company that understood and embraced the potential of what he had. As Sanders was a defence contractor, they simply weren't in the business of retailing entertainment products, so a commercial partner was needed. The fact Sanders had shrunk from 11,000 to 4,000 employees in the intervening period also put pressure on monetising this new technology which was being referred to as the 'Brown Box' thanks to the wood-grain stickers applied to the machine's exterior. If the defence contractor you worked for had just let 7,000 employees go, you can imagine how popular this would have made the still-employed Baer and his lazy guitar-playing mate as they Pritt-sticked fake wood to their television colour-pump.

At first, Baer had approached cable TV companies. The hope was that, rather than the current solution of making games not look like a few blobs on a screen by attaching transparent colour overlays to TVs with static electricity, cable companies could actually broadcast full colour, photo-realistic backdrops, on top of which the gameplay would be overlaid. An exciting prospect at the time, and imagine the potential of it today, you could have a darts game play out over footage of Piers Morgan's face. Sadly, this was not to be. When they couldn't find a cable company that was willing to get onboard, their next port of call was TV manufacturers. Magnavox eventually licensed the Brown Box (renamed the 'Magnavox Odyssey') but, in the eighteen months it took to get a production version completed, the retail price had been severely inflated – Baer originally envisioned a $19.95 price point, Magnavox went with $100.

Many key elements were now missing, too. The output was black and white instead of colour. The gun peripheral and associated game 'cartridge' (separate games were on plug-in circuit boards) were a $24.99 additional purchase, rather than included.

The Odyssey was heavily promoted alongside Frank Sinatra's 1973 comeback *Ol' Blue Eyes Is Back*, at fifty-eight years old, he was hardly the youthful icon that would appeal to a younger audience in the era of David Bowie and Elton John. For all its flaws though, the Odyssey was on the verge of being the first – and only – consumer video game product, and an optimistic Magnavox began to preview it at several industry events. At one of these, in Burlingame, California, on 24 May 1972, an attendee that spent some time there on the system's ping pong game was someone we've already met who, the following month, would apply to have his company, Atari, incorporated: Nolan Bushnell.

2

ATARI ASCENDS

One of Atari's first sources of revenue was the pinball company Bally, who got Atari to develop extra-wide pinball machines. I don't know enough about pinball to understand why wider machines would have any bearing on the amount of fun they offer; I'm entirely happy to see my balls travel primarily vertically*. Bally also commissioned Atari (via their arcade game subsidiary, Midway) to create a space-based racing video game, having been impressed with Bushnell's Computer Space. To help with this project, Atari took on Al Alcorn, an engineer from Ampex but, rather than immediately setting Alcorn off on this new commission, Bushnell first set him a training project to get him familiar with developing games. The task was to create a simple version of ping pong: 'one ball, two paddles, and a score'. To avoid disheartening Alcorn, Bushnell claimed this was for a contract with General Electric† – a company, in fact, he'd never even spoken to.

Alcorn tried to develop this game based on Bushnell's

---

* Don't @ me.

† ★★★ Boring company name klaxon. ★★★

notes from creating Computer Space, but they were apparently incomprehensible. Yet, he persevered, and along the way managed to reduce the cost by finding much cheaper components. He also introduced a number of game mechanics that would significantly enhance the game beyond its original simplistic brief. The ball's trajectory angle now changed depending on which bit of the bat it bounced off. The longer it took for someone to score a point, the faster the ball would get. He even added a sound to the system for when it bounced off the walls and paddles*, and amended the controls so the paddles now only moved vertically, not horizontally as well (as they had on the Odyssey), to simplify its gameplay. The cabinet itself for this game, soon to be christened 'Pong', was not so much crafted as thrown together. The inside was a mess of wires, the outside more like a mailbox than the futuristic fibreglass Computer Space cabinet, and the screen was an old black and white TV. After almost three months, Alcorn's prototype was complete, and everyone was surprised at how much fun it was. Bushnell added a few flourishes of his own, including a bread pan for collecting coins†. In contrast to Computer Space's manual, the instructions were reduced to a single line: 'Avoid missing ball for high score.'

Bushnell offered Pong to Midway as an alternative to the racing game they'd requested, in the hopes of getting the cash from their contract sooner, but they declined.

---

* The Magnavox Odyssey, in contrast, had no sound capabilities.
† Lest this has confused you, I am literally talking about a tray to bake bread in.

As Atari already had a side-business in distributing pinball machines*, they were able to install the first Pong prototype that August (1972) in one of their locations, a downbeat little bar called Andy Capp's, in Sunnyvale, California, which was notable only in that it had an unusually large games room – several pinball machines, a jukebox and a Computer Space cabinet. To give you some indication of what sort of environments Atari operated in initially, Steve Bristow (another old contact previously employed by Ampex) was brought in to collect money on the route, and would frequently take his wife along for the ride, carrying a hatchet. She would have taken a gun, but they couldn't get a permit.

The Pong cabinet was stuck on top of a wine barrel in lieu of a table and all was well until, a couple of weeks later, the bar owner called to let them know it had stopped working. When Alcorn came to determine the cause of the problem it quickly became apparent – when he opened the coin box, the money came flowing out. While a bucket full of quarters was a good start, to grow the business Bushnell needed credit. At the time, no bank would lend them the money, as there was still a negative reputation around the industry thanks to its associations with gambling and money laundering. The best Bushnell could get was $50,000 from Wells Fargo, which the company immediately put into manufacturing more Pong cabinets.

As their initial office lacked the space for this, Atari rented

---

* Distributing pinball machines gave Atari a reliable source of income in their early days, as they were able to get them cheap, fix them up, then place them in local bars.

an old roller-skating rink and began to hire workers to assemble the machines. To save money, they hired unskilled labour. However, the savings were short-lived when many of the less-than-desirable recruits took to stealing the TVs and other parts, in order to sell them for drug money. Naturally, Atari politely asked these employees to leave and, in the hopes of preventing further issues, the company introduced other benefits. They'd have 'Friday night beer bursts', and would allow employees to play Pong on-site for free. Also, while marijuana use was not officially sanctioned, the smell of weed often permeated the air. It says something about the general vibe of a company that 'don't steal our products to fund your habit, but it's fine to smoke it in the building' seems to have, broadly speaking, been their policy on drugs.

Despite the initial issues with theft, the Pong cabinets (the first of which were released in November 1972) were hugely profitable for Atari as a result of the cost-cutting approach, with machines being sold for around three times the cost of manufacture. They also took payment before making them, so cash flow was strong. This insistence on payment up-front was possible because word had begun to spread about how profitable Pong was. While many pinball machines would generate $50 a week, Pong could easily do four times that, helped in part by charging twenty-five cents a go, whereas pinball offered three games for the same amount. Video games were more reliable than electro-mechanical and pinball games too, as they had far fewer moving parts that required maintenance or repair.

In the years that followed, Atari would release a number of

different Pong variations in an attempt to meet demand, and to freshen up the gameplay. Personal favourites of mine include Quadrapong – a four-player, four-sided cocktail table version, where each player had several lives, and had to defend their own goal, and Rebound – a two-player version of volley-ball where the ball bounced vertically over the central net. Rebound is not dissimilar in appearance to Tennis for Two in fact, and arguably more like tennis than Pong ever was, due to Pong's reliance on the ball bouncing off the gameplay arena's edges, just like it doesn't in tennis.

It wasn't all Pong machines though. Atari created a number of other games in different styles and genres. The next game after the original Pong was the game Midway had origin-ally commissioned, Asteroid*, which had two rockets racing through an asteroid field from the bottom to the top of the screen. Being paid by Midway for the creation of this didn't stop Bushnell from almost immediately releasing a near direct copy of it himself under the name 'Space Race', which led to a legal tussle that resulted in Atari agreeing to forgo any royalty payments. Which seems a light punishment, really. If a third party provided Cadbury's with Dairy Milk chocolate bars, but then immediately started selling identical chocolate bars to the exact same retailers, I imagine Cadbury's might do slightly more than refuse payment[†]. Shortly after Space Race, Atari released another two-player game, Gotcha, which was a top-down chase through a maze, notable in being the first arcade

---

*   Not to be confused with Atari's 1979 game, Asteroids.

†   This is a very poor analogy and I expect to receive tweets to that effect.

game that had a full-colour monitor option. Previous games had either been black and white or, at best, had colour overlays affixed to the monitor to create the illusion of areas of colour. Sadly, colour isn't the most notable thing about Gotcha. The most notable thing about Gotcha is that instead of joysticks, the cabinet had two 'pink orbs' used to control the characters by squeezing them, and thus gripping their internal controller. This, combined with the promo poster of a woman being grabbed from behind, led to some feeling it was very much *not okay*. Atari fairly quickly released a traditional joystick version after something of a backlash. By this point, they couldn't afford bad publicity as they were no longer operating in the market alone. Many companies were releasing their own, cloned versions of Pong. Firms such as Nutting Associates, Midway, Sega and many others flooded the market and, by the middle of 1974, the majority of Pong machines were non-Atari. While some companies, such as Midway with their Pong clone, Winner, paid licence fees to Atari, many didn't and by the time Atari began to apply for patents in an attempt to squash their rivals, it was too late. Patents take a long time to process, and Pong clones were already everywhere.

As you've probably noticed from the people we've met so far (Dabney, Alcorn, Bristow), Bushnell spent a lot of time dipping back into the staff pool at his former employer, Ampex, and, in 1974, Atari acquired a company called Cyan Engineering, which was founded by former Ampex employees Steve Mayer and Larry Emmons. Cyan Engineering acted as an independent (but wholly-owned) consultancy that was able to, in Bushnell's words, 'build the technical stuff that couldn't be built"*, thus giving Atari an advantage over the competition. The first game presented to Atari by Mayer and Emmons was the first car-racing video game, Gran Trak 10. The track was viewed from above, with remote control-style mechanics so, if you push left on your stick the car turns to its left, if you push right on your stick the car turns right. It's very intuitive – basically: If your car is driving to the left of the screen, you have to press left to go down, if it's going down, you need to press left to go right, if it's going to the right, you need to press left to go up and, if it's going up, left is left. The opposite's true for going right. Right?

Gran Trak 10's cabinet came complete with steering wheel, gear stick and pedals. The novelty of this made it hugely popular with the public and it became Atari's bestselling game in 1974, just the hit Atari needed. At least, it would have been if an accounting error hadn't led to it being sold for $100 less than it cost to make.

Atari were beginning to struggle. Their rapid growth meant they needed to deliver more machines, faster, which in turn meant Atari more frequently sent out rushed machines with faults, and Atari's determination to innovate with non-Pong games, plus the aforementioned proliferation of rivals and Gran Trak 10's accounting mishap, all led to Atari's profits becoming squeezed. Another big factor restricting Atari's growth was distribution. In many cities, there were just a couple of big companies distributing to arcades, drugstores, bowling alleys and so on, and there was an informal rule that

---

* Kent, S.: *The Ultimate History of Video Games* (Three Rivers Press, 2001).

each company in an area would supply different products. For example, one distributor might exclusively provide Bally pinball machines, another only Williams'. Bushnell, frustrated by this, set about finding a way around this, so that Atari could supply their hardware to all distributors, and get their systems into every location.

There had been a big kerfuffle in the industry when several long-term employees of Atari quit and immediately founded a rival company, Kee Games. Kee quickly made a name for itself providing outlets with reliable adaptations of Atari games at a lower price point – titles like Elimination (Atari's Quadrapong), Spike (Atari's Rebound) and Formula K (Atari's Gran Trak 10). While Atari still primarily provided arcade machines to the largest distributor in an area, rival distributors loved being able to get one over on Atari by bypassing them and getting hold of very similar games. The joke was on the distributors though; Bushnell actually got his neighbour, Joe Keenan, to found and front the new company which was, in fact, one hundred per cent owned by Atari. The lengths they went to in order to perpetuate the myth they were rivals within the industry was arguably unnecessarily excessive. On one occasion, Bristow got his wife to chat with a security guard while he snuck into Atari and threw 'stolen' hardware out of a window and loaded it into his car. For any budding management scholars, this 'Kee Games' theory of business can be summarised as follows:

1: Smash your own windows.

2: ?

3: Profits.

Obviously, the guys at Kee Games were a talented bunch and eventually they wanted to do more than just repackage Atari titles and damage their property. Initially they did this by adding features such as the ability to 'spike' the ball in their version of Rebound, but later they began to develop entirely new titles. Bristow's first big independent hit for Kee was a game called 'Tank' (November 1974). The gameplay was simple: two tanks in a single-screen war zone, attempting to shoot each other while navigating obstacles and avoiding mines – arguably, it was a land-based version of Spacewar! with a simplified game mechanic to make it easier for consumers to understand and play.

Atari took the success of Tank as the opportunity to announce that Kee would be 'merging' with Atari, thus bringing both company's teams (and, crucially, their revenues) back under one roof. Joe Keenan then became president of Atari, as he'd demonstrated a flair for that aspect of the business that exceeded Bushnell's. It was good timing as, by now, it wasn't just Atari and Kee that were innovating with their games – over in Japan, the arcade industry was really taking off too.

Nintendo had some success with a light gun game, Wild Gunman, which used film projection to allow players to shoot at video of cowboy actors, a huge novelty at the time. Light guns had actually been something Nintendo had dabbled in for a while. In the early seventies they'd sold the Beam Gun, which was a light gun that came with a lion you could shoot to make it 'roar' and a bottle that could 'explode' when you shot it. Quite what you did after those first ten seconds had passed I have no idea, but it did well. Nintendo subsequently adapted this technology to create shooting ranges in disused bowling alleys (which had a boom and bust in the sixties) – these were known as 'Laser Clay Ranges' which, in turn, were adapted for games like Wild Gunman.

Meanwhile, Tomohiro Nishikado was creating early hits for his employer, Taito. His version of Pong, Basketball, had drawn attention for its use of graphics resembling humans for the players, rather than the traditional bats, and baskets to aim for instead of the empty 'goals' at the edges of Pong's screen. The same year, Nishikado's Speed Race became the first racing game to have a scrolling playfield, rather than just a single screen. Midway licensed both of these and released them in the USA, but it was 1975's Gun Fight – a side-on Wild West shoot-out – that gave them their breakthrough hit. Based on yet another Nishikado game, Western Gun, Midway enhanced it with the help of David Nutting. David was the brother of Bill Nutting, whose company Nutting Associates had released Nolan Bushnell's Computer Space game in 1971, shortly after David had left the company due to a disagreement between the brothers, and formed a rival, Nutting Industries. You could say it was *a lot of trouble over Nutting**.

By 1974, David was developing cutting-edge microprocessor technology for Bally which, in 1975, they licensed to a little-known third party, Mirco Games, as Bally themselves weren't convinced about it. Mirco's pinball table, Spirit of '76, thus became the first to use a microprocessor instead of

---

* mic_drop.gif

electro-mechanical components to register points. While this was initially released to little fanfare, the use of microprocessors in pinball soon became the industry standard due to their lower cost and reduced maintenance requirement. Nutting then spruced up Nishikado's Western Gun for Midway[*] by adding a microprocessor into the mix[†]. 'Gunfight', as the game then became, was the first arcade game to use a microprocessor, and it allowed for sharper graphics and more action – in this instance by adding stagecoaches which passed through the battle to create cover for the players to hide behind. Nutting also used the microprocessor to great effect the following year in the hugely successful Sea Wolf, a video game version of the electro-mechanical Periscope we'd seen from Sega ten years earlier. We won't get into all the technical aspects of why the introduction of this new hardware changed gaming so dramatically, but the key thing to note is that it heralded a shift from the previous circuit boards, which had to be manufactured from scratch for each game, to microprocessors that allowed for multiple games to be written in software which then told the generic hardware how to behave. This in turn led to a shift in the people who make games from electrical engineers to computer programmers. An early employee brought into Atari to take advantage of this new technology was Dave Shepperd, who created one of the first first-person

---

[*] Reminder: Midway is the arcade game manufacturer owned by the pinball manufacturer, Bally.

[†] The Intel 8080 microprocessor, if you're curious.

driving games, Night Driver*, which created a buzz in the arcade thanks to its sit-down cockpit cabinet.

Atari weren't quite ready to ditch the old TTL (transistor-transistor logic) circuits completely though, and the guy who was going to give them their final hurrah with 1976's Breakout was an ex-employee who'd recently returned to the company after an extended pilgrimage to India. Described by his Atari colleagues as filthy, obnoxious, and with a poor understanding of electronics, it's another name you've probably heard before: Apple Computer Inc. founder, Steve Jobs.

Breakout was essentially a vertical, solo version of Pong where you had to use the ball to break through a brick wall, and the main concern was to minimise the number of circuits (aka chips) used in its manufacture in order to reduce its cost. At the time, Atari would ship around 10,000 copies of its most successful games so, when you factor in manufacture, repair and other costs, it was worth approximately $100,000 to Atari each time a single $10 chip was removed from a cabinet's design (another reason the switch to microprocessors was so appealing). Most people weren't interested in this technical challenge but, with the offer of a financial incentive by Atari, scruffy Steve Jobs embraced it. Or at least he appeared to. At this time, Jobs was already beginning to develop the Apple II computer that would be central to the explosion of the

---

* It would be remiss of me not to point out that this game drew *significant* influence from the groundbreaking, but rarely discussed, German 1975 arcade game, Nürburgring (named after the German race track), by Reiner Foerst.

personal-computer industry with Steve Wozniak, who worked for Hewlett Packard. Both Jobs and Wozniak were members of the 'Homebrew Computer Club' – enthusiasts who experimented with building their own hardware. Jobs, it turned out, didn't design anything for Atari's Breakout; he got Wozniak to do it for him. 'Woz' got it down to less than 30 integrated circuits, but it was so minimised, so complex, no one else had the skill to replicate it! Atari eventually got someone else to give it a go, and it released with 100 chips but, as promised, Jobs received the agreed bonus: $750 + $100 per chip removed, ending up with around $5,000. Jobs neglected to mention the $100 per chip bit to Woz though, and just split the $750. Wozniak didn't find out about this until they were at Apple years later. In his own words: 'He [Jobs] believed that it was fine to buy something for $60 and sell it for $6,000 if you could do it.'[*] Anyone who's been to an Apple store will know this philosophy is something he stuck with throughout his career[†].

I know what you're thinking and, yes, now *is* a good time to introduce the Japanese Mafia to the story.

Namco had been working closely with Atari for several years as their exclusive Japanese distributor but, when Namco released Breakout in Japan, they hit a problem. The market was quickly flooded with a large number of counterfeit versions manufactured by a Yakuza clan. As Namco only distributed, not manufactured, the cabinets, Masaya Nakamura

---

[*] Kent, S.: *The Ultimate History of Video Games* (Three Rivers Press, 2001).
[†] Slam! Take that, big business!

reached out to Atari, pleading for supply to be rapidly increased, to combat the knock-offs but, when a hungover Bushnell failed to fully comprehend the situation and increase supply, Namco made the decision to manufacture the machines themselves and flooded the market with what were effectively their own clones. As Bushnell had not communicated the issue to his Atari colleagues, when orders stopped coming in they just assumed Breakout wasn't very popular in Japan. It says something about how well Atari were doing that when the company was struggling in a particular country, it didn't merit sobering up to deal with it, although it also heralds the beginning of a lack of attention to detail that would grow worse with time. Namco continued to distribute Atari's games, but it wasn't long before they began to create their own, to reduce their reliance on their partner. Not that Atari paid much attention as, by this point, they were increasingly looking away from the arcades, and into people's homes.

The success of Pong in the arcades had helped the Magnavox Odyssey during the early seventies, as it offered consumers the chance to enjoy Pong, or at least something not dissimilar, in the home. It's unsurprising therefore that, by 1974, Nolan Bushnell had set one of his engineers, Harold Lee, to work on a home version of Pong. By this point, digital technology had surpassed the old, more expensive analogue tech that the Magnavox had been built on, but a home Pong system was by no means an obvious win. The Odyssey came with twelve games, Pong had just the one which, as you may be aware, is eleven less. Many retailers had been stung by the Magnavox system; while it had been successful, it had not been over-whelmingly so*, and there was an assumption that there simply wasn't a market for Atari's new alternative, which was set to retail at the same price, $100, but with fewer games. The only interest Atari had was from the sports department of Sears, who had success the previous year with ping pong tables. Most people I know tend to either be sporty *or* into games, so I'm not sure why they assumed success with one would suggest strong sales for the other but this didn't really matter as Sears requested exclusivity and Atari declined.

This was to Atari's cost. They failed to make a deal with anyone else and missed 1974's lucrative Christmas period so when, in early 1975, they still had no buyers, they opened up discussions with Sears again and arranged a demonstration. The deal was almost scuppered for a second time when the machine failed to work at the demo. It transpired that the giant antenna broadcasting from the roof of Sears Tower was broadcasting on the same frequency as the Pong prototype. Thankfully, a quick-thinking Alcorn was there as part of Atari's team and a tweak with a screwdriver solved the prob-lem. Sears then asked how many units Bushnell could deliver for the following Christmas. Bushnell said the most they could deliver was 75,000. Sears wanted 150,000. This was

---

* While the Odyssey remained on sale into 1975, Magnavox ceased to release new games for it in 1973.

impossible. Atari simply did not have the resources to achieve this. Bushnell said yes.

The only way to get the money needed to begin production on that scale was to source investment from venture capitalists, and the man who came forward to help was Don Valentine, a now-legendary investor in technology. Some other companies in which Don's company, Sequoia Capital, have been early investors in over the years include Apple, Cisco, YouTube and Google*. Unluckily for Don, by the time he and Atari were ready to do a deal, Atari's fortunes were on the up thanks to their official 'merger' with Kee Games so, at the very last minute, they decided to double the price. You have to admire the bravado of this: They were the ones that needed to borrow money, the 'merger' was essentially non-sense and yet they had the chutzpah to drop this bombshell. They were right to do so, though. Unimpressed, but knowing a good thing when he saw it, Valentine agreed to the new terms.

These new relationships between the hippy-led Atari and the far more corporate Sequoia Capital and Sears led to some adjustments on both sides, early on in the relationship. On one occasion, suited-and-booted Sears executives came to visit Atari to check on production, only to see Bushnell emerging in T-shirt and jeans on top of a box he was riding along their new conveyor belt. That evening, worried about damaging

---

* Also Yahoo, Instagram, WhatsApp, PayPal and many more. Seriously, look him up, Don Valentine's investment history is insane.

their relationship, Bushnell attended the prearranged meal with his whole team dressed in smart suits and ties. The Sears execs arrived in jeans.

Christmas 1975 went far better for all involved. Sears sold all 150,000 Atari machines, under the Sears Tele-Games brand, and it instantly became Sears' most successful product. In 1976, Atari also released their own-brand version, as well as a number of new variations, just as they had in the arcades, with titles like Pong Doubles (allowing for four players at once), Super Pong (a two-player version with four game variations) and Super Pong Ten (a four-player version with ten games). As you can imagine, Magnavox weren't overly delighted with Atari's new-found success in the home market, and so they finally took legal action against them for their appropriation of the Odyssey's tennis game. At first it seemed they got what they wanted, with Atari settling out of court, and paying a licence agreement of $700,000. However, in the grand scheme of things this was a bargain for Atari. Securing the rights to be Magnavox's sole licensee, Atari effectively had a free legal team thrown into the bargain as, from this point, Magnavox aggressively prosecuted any other companies who released rival Pong systems.

And there were many. The market was flooded in 1976 and 1977 with countless imitations thanks to the proliferation of a multi-game chip developed by the company General Instruments – the catchily-titled AY-3-8500* – which had four

---

* ★★★ Boring company *and* product name klaxon. ★★★

Pong variations* and two shooting games onboard, and only cost $5 per unit for anyone that wanted to manufacture their own Pong machine. The first company to get their hands on the chip was the Connecticut Leather Company, thanks to a tip-off from none other than Ralph Baer. Hell hath no fury like a programmer scorned, and Baer had become frustrated at Magnavox's handling of its own series of home Pong systems. Connecticut Leather Company might not *sound* like an obvious name for a hi-tech consumer electronics manufacturer but by this point in time they were more commonly known as Coleco, having diversified into many other markets over the years. While General Instruments wouldn't offer anyone exclusive use of the AY-3-8500, they did handle orders on a first come, first served basis, which meant Coleco were able to snap up all the available initial stock and get their machine, the Telstar, to market first in time for Father's Day 1976 at a price of just $50. Magnavox and many others did eventually get their hands on the chip, once General Instruments had increased production, but this early advantage helped cement Coleco as a key player in the market. The fact Coleco's console had a one hundred per cent leather exterior also gave it a sense of class lacking on rivals' systems†. It has to be said, if your policy is you won't give anyone exclusivity, but your first customer buys all your stock which means they are the only

---

* The fourth variation, 'practice' allowed players to experience the thrill of Pong without the unbearable pressure of an actual game of Pong.
† No, obviously not really.

company with your product for an extended period of time, you're only fooling yourself.

I keep saying there were lots of Pong systems being released but, to paint a bit more of a picture, in 1976 and 1977 Atari released Hockey Pong, Pong Doubles, Super Pong, Super Pong Doubles, Super Pong 10, Ultra Pong and Ultra Pong Doubles. Coleco released the Telstar, Telstar Classic, Telstar Deluxe, Telstar Ranger, Telstar Alpha, Telstar Colormatic, Telstar Regent, Telstar Galaxy, Telstar Gemini and Telstar Arcade*. Magnavox released the Odyssey 100, Odyssey 200, Odyssey 300, Odyssey 400, Odyssey 500, Odyssey 2000, Odyssey 3000 and Odyssey 4000. And that's just three of the companies that were releasing these systems to the US market. In Europe there were dozens of companies building versions of what would become known as the PC-50x line of consoles, again built around the AY-3-8500 and its variants†, while in Japan there was Epoch's Electrotennis (notable in that it transmitted its signal wirelessly), Bandai's TV Jack series, and also the first home system developed by the Odyssey's Japanese distributor, Nintendo. The Nintendo Color TV-game 6 was particularly successful in Japan, thanks to a retail price equivalent to just $36.

November 1976 saw the beginning of the second generation of home video game consoles, with the release of the

---

* Give that one a google – it's got gearstick, gun and steering wheel peripherals all sticking out of it, and it looks *insane*.

† My family had opted for the Adman Grandstand TV-game 2000 before I was born, making Pong the first video game I ever played. A wonderful baptism in gaming, but one which also makes me seem older than I am when asked about my first game. Livid.

Fairchild Video Entertainment System, later known as the Channel F. Like the original Odyssey, the VES reverted to inter-changeable cartridges they dubbed 'video carts', which were similar in design to the then-popular eight-track music cart-ridges, rather than the many systems listed above which had focused on having a finite set of built-in games. The Channel F didn't need the colour overlays the Magnavox Odyssey had relied upon, as this home system was in colour and, notably, was the first home system to make use of microprocessors, which we saw earlier making an impact in the arcades. How-ever, the Channel F struggled to establish itself due to this proliferation of home systems – the market was flooded and people were no longer as excited or impressed as they had once been.

In the midst of all of this, what actually got consumers really excited at Christmas in 1976 was handheld gaming, specifically Mattel Electronics' Auto Race, a result of Marketing Director Michael Katz pushing his team to adapt LED calcula-tor technology into a game. Essentially, Auto Race was a portable version of Taito's 1974 arcade game, Speed Race, but rather than a traditional screen it had a simple series of LEDs (light-emitting diodes) that represented the player's car and oncoming traffic. At just $24.99, this new innovation, which allowed consumers to play a video game (albeit a very basic one) anywhere, was a real breakthrough, and a must-have. Mattel went on to release many more titles with a variation on this use of LEDS, focusing on sports such as American football, hockey and baseball. Significant praise is due to Michael Katz for the branding of these as action-packed sports games given they could equally be described as 'games where you press some buttons to make a red rectangle go past another red rectangle, over and over again'.

You'd be forgiven for thinking that, from everything I've told you, during this period Atari just released variations of home Pong and, in fairness, that did appear to be the case to most people at the time. However, there was a more cynical reason for this. Atari's settlement with Magnavox granted the latter to any technology developed by the former for a twelve-month period up to 1 June 1977. So, on 4 June 1977, just three days after that clause expired, Atari announced work on their latest product: a brand new console. How this can possibly be legally okay is a mystery to me – I find sleepwalking hard enough to get my head round, but this contract seems to have accepted the possibility that Nolan Bushnell woke up the night after the clause expired to discover he'd slept-created-a-new-games-console.

Anyway, Bushnell had recognised the need to continue to innovate and set his team the task of creating Atari's next generation system. They managed to identify a cheaper microprocessor than the one used in the Channel F and the outcome was Atari's Video Computer System (later known as the Atari 2600) that would, like the Channel F, have games on interchangeable cartridges. The console itself had a series of switches that allowed players to change game modes, difficulty levels and other settings. The VCS was a huge undertaking for Atari and, with sales from home systems diminished, and the same being true for arcade revenue, Bushnell took the decision to sell the company to Warner Communications (formerly known as Warner Bros.) in order to raise further funding for the ambitious project. Warner were naturally keen to keep the existing team on, including Bushnell as chairman and Keenan as president. In addition to the $28 million they paid for the company, making its owners instant millionaires, Warner invested $100 million in completing work on Bushnell's vision for the VCS and readying it for launch, including an initial line-up of games based on early Atari hits like Pong, Tank and the Gran Trak series.

The decision was made to make the profit margin low on the system itself, then make a killing on the interchangeable game cartridges instead (manufactured for under $10, but sold for $30), and 400,000 Atari VCSs were manufactured for Christmas of 1977. Unfortunately, many of these failed to ship in time and those that did entered a market where there was still uncertainty as to whether this home gaming thing had been anything more than a fad. So, in early 1978, Atari were left with a huge quantity of stock.

Most of Atari's competitors exited the market around this time and, in fact, Warner brought a consultant in, Ray Kassar, to determine whether they should liquidate Atari. However, he felt the system still had potential and encouraged them to persevere. Bushnell argued that they needed to innovate again, but Warner, not unreasonably, felt it needed to persevere with the VCS, rather than immediately throw their latest product on the scrap heap and write off a massive loss, especially when the only person suggesting they should was the guy who'd convinced them to fund the creation of it in the first place. Increasing tensions between the old guard and the new investors escalated to the point that, in November 1978, Bushnell was dismissed from Atari, and Kassar replaced him as CEO. This only served to exacerbate tensions. Kassar's previous experience was in textiles, but he felt this would not affect his ability to manage Atari. Many of Bushnell's engineers, on the other hand, felt that the creative challenges of designing video games might be a bit different to those faced by people that make flannels.

Clearly, the games industry had changed. By the summer of 1978, video games were big business, with all the structure and restrictions that brings. It was no longer just Atari, a company run by a few hippy programmers with a licence to print money. The home market was flooded. The arcade scene was sluggish. But there was one person in particular who was about to reinvigorate the industry: Tomohiro Nishikado.

3

THE GOLDEN AGE
OF ARCADES

When Tomohiro Nishikado's Space Invaders was released by Midway in the USA, its success was stratospheric*. *Star Wars* dominating cinemas the previous year no doubt fuelled people's desire for science-fiction, but what made Space Invaders stand out in the arcades was the use of a microprocessor. Nishikado, inspired by Nutting's use of the technology on his earlier game, Western Gun, implemented it himself to great effect. The game was heavily influenced by Atari's Breakout, but the microprocessor allowed a far higher level of graphical fidelity – no longer were graphics simple rectangles and squares. Breakout's bat became a spaceship, the ball became bullets, and the stationary wall of bricks became a descending fleet of aliens. Sound was used to great effect too, speeding up as the aliens got ever closer, ratcheting up the intensity. Evocative yet simple, sounds were also present for bullets and the occasional spaceships. Gameplay was simple:

---

* Beginning a chapter with such appalling wordplay is unforgivable and demeans us all.

shoot the aliens and don't get shot, but it was by no means easy; Nishikado himself struggles to complete the first level of his own game!

What really helped it to encourage repeat plays was the introduction of the high score. Most books will tell you it had a high-score table, where you could enter your initials. It didn't. But it did retain the highest score at the top of the screen (without initials), which set a goal to be exceeded. Another myth perpetuated about Space Invaders is that its success in Japan led to a shortage of the 100-yen coin, but this is also nonsense. Business owners with one, or multiple, Space Invaders cabinets* didn't choose to swim around in massive rooms filled with coins like Scrooge McDuck. They tended to take them to the bank to cash them in, at which point the coins re-entered circulation, because THAT'S HOW MONEY WORKS†.

The game's control system wasn't necessarily how you're picturing it. There was a fire button, but instead of a joystick to move left and right, there were two buttons, one for each direction. These details often get overlooked, but they're important; at this stage, even something as seemingly ubiquitous as a joystick wasn't an established solution. Atari's big hit that year, Atari Football (as in American football, that is), used a trackball to control the on-screen players, inspired by

---

* Some retailers in Japan stopped selling things altogether and just filled their outlets with multiple Space Invaders machines.

† Having been so smug about these fact corrections, I look forward to having the many flaws in this book pointed out to me upon its release.

Nishikado's 1973 Soccer game which was the first game to use this control system. I say trackball: in Atari's prototype, they actually used a cue ball from a pool table, as a way of lowering cost. Atari Football created a lot of buzz in arcades as, to make your quarterback and receivers run, you needed to spin the trackball as fast as you could; people would get bruises and blisters from the force of their enthusiasm, which either suggests the gameplay was incredibly compelling, or it tended to attract the worst sort of alpha-male show-offs. That may be unkind, as speed was important for a second reason; you only got ninety seconds of play per twenty-five cents, with the option to continue for additional coins. This meant that, if anyone wanted to play a full American football game on the cabinet (one hour of play) it would cost ten dollars. Atari Football doesn't live on in the public consciousness in the way Space Invaders does but, when it launched, it was arguably just as popular. However, when the football season finished in January, interest quickly waned.

Not that this mattered to Bushnell. As part of his settlement with Atari, he gained a restaurant trial site they had experimented with which would go on, under Bushnell's leadership, to be a hugely successful franchise business, Chuck E. Cheese's*. The business sold pizzas, as they were cheap and easy to make, and people were used to waiting around for them to be made. This was important because Chuck E. Cheese's had an arcade on-site to keep customers busy (the

---

* Joe Keenan also left Atari to join Bushnell at Chuck E. Cheese's.

real reason for the venture). When ordering a pizza, customers would get tokens allowing them to play on the games, but only for a few minutes. They could then buy more tokens, allowing parents to keep their kids occupied while waiting for dinner, for a price. It was a business model not dissimilar to the drug dealer's 'the first one's free' approach to business.

The concept wasn't entirely new. Joel Hochberg (a guy we'll be meeting again later) had recently opened a games room himself to piggyback on the Space Invaders craze, and had worked for a company that had set up a similar dining/amusements location all the way back in 1961, although that had obviously been electro-mechanical games. However, whereas Hochberg targeted adults, Bushnell targeted kids. Bushnell also had those old-style amusements where you could win tickets that could be exchanged for prizes, harking back to the sort of attractions he would have seen during his summer job in Salt Lake City as a young student. To avoid it seeming old-fashioned, Bushnell got the Cyan Engineering guys down in Grass Valley to create animatronic robots for the restaurant, and these would 'perform' a stage act while people were waiting. All of these elements combined to create the sort of family-friendly tone you might associate more with a Disney attraction than the traditional seedy view of arcades, and their associations with gambling and 'the wrong crowd'. As a result, towns that had banned arcades completely found Chuck E. Cheese's restaurants to be an acceptable alternative, allowing Bushnell to access a whole new market under the guise of 'restaurants', in a manner reminiscent of when he had created Kee Games to access additional distribution networks.

Whatever you think of Bushnell, he was an incredible lateral thinker.

The most impressive thing about Bushnell for me though, is that the Chuck E. Cheese's mascot, which went by the same name, was a rat. If you can make a restaurant chain successful when the face of the brand is an animal more associated with transmitting Weil's Disease than pizzas, you're very good at doing a business. To give you some sense of just how successful a Chuck E. Cheese's franchise could be, it would cost $1.5 million to open a branch. Which is a lot of money. But a good site could make that back in just six months.

The terms of Bushnell's departure from Atari included a non-compete clause, so he wasn't allowed to make video games again for some time, but with Chuck E. Cheese's this couldn't have mattered less. Arcades were becoming a licence to print money and Bushnell found himself in a position not only to profit from Atari games, but from all games.

While Bushnell was on the up, the engineers he'd left behind at Atari were feeling rather undervalued. Kassar was heavily focused on the home market, and would often shower more praise on those who converted the company's arcade hits to the VCS than on the games' original creators. They retained a sense of humour about it all, though: when Kassar told *Fortune* magazine the arcade engineers there were 'high-strung prima donnas', they all wore T-shirts to work bearing that slogan.

While they might have felt unappreciated, they continued to take pride in their work. Atari's arcade team developed their own vector graphics generator, inspired by the success of 1977

Cinematronics game, Space Wars, which had used a vector display to give the game far sharper lines than was possible on a conventional screen (albeit only in black and white). Atari's first game using the technology was 1979's Lunar Lander, in which you had to, unsurprisingly, land on the moon. This was made difficult due to limited fuel, and the effect of gravity. It was also made difficult for younger players thanks to the cabinet having a huge lever you pushed away from you to control the lander's boosters. When released, it snapped back into place, leading to a number of younger players losing not only their concentration, but their teeth.

This design flaw was an unusual misstep for Atari, who had several systems in place to assess games while in development. The Stubben Test involved their six-foot-five-inches tall, 275-pound engineer Dave Stubben attempting to smash the machine to pieces with enthusiastic and vigorous play. Sadly, they'd not had the foresight to do a complimentary test that checked to see if smaller gamers might be attacked by the machines.

Despite hitting kids in the face, Lunar Lander did fine, but it was Atari's next vector game that finally toppled Space Invaders from the top of the arcades and led Atari to abandon its no longer necessary sideline in pinball machines altogether: Asteroids. Based on an idea by the VP of the coin-op division, it was engineer Ed Logg, who had recently finished Super Breakout (an updated version of the original), that was tasked with creating the game. In it, the player has to clear the screen of asteroids, which get repeatedly smaller when shot. It would have been difficult to successfully implement Asteroids on a normal screen as it was vital for the gameplay that you could tell which direction your tiny ship was pointing. On a vector monitor you not only got precision gameplay, but it also looked incredibly crisp, bright and futuristic.

Its controls were very similar to those of Spacewar! many years earlier – rotate left and right, thrust, fire, and hyperspace. However, while people hadn't been ready for this level of complexity when Bushnell's arcade version of the game, Computer Space, had launched eight years earlier, people were now better versed in the language of playing arcade games, and took to it more easily.

Just as Space Invaders had done, it rewarded players with extra lives for good performance and had its very own marching soundtrack that effectively replicated the sound of an increasing heart rate as the game intensified. It also had the occasional flying saucer appear to attack the player, to prevent them lasting too long on a single credit. However, with practice the game could be mastered. Theoretically, you could play Asteroids indefinitely. One kid set a record by playing for over thirty-six hours, accruing so many extra lives they could pop for meals and presumably (though this seems to be less frequently mentioned in contemporary reports) poos*. The late seventies was an exciting time in the emergence of gaming as a medium. The affordability and proliferation of microprocessors allowed games to have more complex graphics, vector

---

* I really am so very sorry.

monitors introduced gamers to high-resolution images, and there was a third innovation that really spruced things up: colour! Sure, there'd been the occasional colour monitor along the way but nothing had really broken through in the way our next game did. Even games like Space Invaders only gave the illusion of colour through transparent coloured overlays affixed to the black and white screen.

The first game to really make the most of colour was Galaxian. Not only was it in colour, but individual characters had multiple colours within them. Furthermore, the enemies didn't descend as one block like in Space Invaders, they swooped in multiple formations. Galaxian was released in the USA by Midway, but it wasn't licensed from Taito, it was from Atari's former Japanese distributor, Namco. Taito had done so well with Space Invaders that they had started to release their games themselves. Had Atari been more nurturing of their relationship with Namco, perhaps Galaxian would have been distributed by Atari in the USA, but instead Midway secured the title, helping to cement them as a key rival. In many ways this is like when my friend Paul moved to a posh school and stopped hanging out with me so I became friends with Stephen Sarre instead, because he stayed at my comprehensive. Loyalty is everything, Paul, I hope you realise that now. I hope you realise the massive error you made. YOU WILL NEVER HEAR FROM ME AGAIN, PAUL, WHEREAS ME AND STEPHEN, EVEN TO THIS DAY, OCCASIONALLY 'LIKE' EACH OTHER'S FACEBOOK POSTS. STICK THAT IN YOUR ALL-BOYS SCHOOL IN BEDFORD.

Atari were still doing well on their own terms. Designer Dave Theurer's Missile Command saw another outing for their trackball as a controller, a great choice for the game as it allowed a much-needed higher level of precision than could be offered by a joystick, and a simpler control mechanic than a pair of directional paddles. The trackball was used to direct the cross-hair of your missile launcher, with the aim of protecting your cities from enemy projectiles, because what's more fun than the threat of nuclear holocaust? The game did good business as, at the time, most hits were still focusing on space and war, but a young developer at Namco was about to create a game unlike anything that had come before, and introduce the world to gaming's first mascot.

Toru Iwatani didn't want to make video games. He wanted to make pinball machines. Namco didn't want to make pinball machines. They wanted to make video games. So Iwatani made video games. His first video games for Namco – Gee Bee, Bomb Bee and Cutie Q – were all video game versions of pinball. Fair play. I have no idea how he got away with this three times in a row. Eventually though, he set himself a new challenge: to create a non-violent game. He hoped such a game might appeal to female gamers, gaming having already gained something of a reputation for being a predominantly male pastime, no doubt in part thanks to the less-than-pleasant environments where many arcade machines were found. Feminist? You decide. In the words of Iwatani: 'When I imagined what women enjoy, the image of them eating cakes and desserts came to mind"[*]. Not only did the main character in the game then spend all their time eating, even their appearance was food-inspired, taken from a pizza Iwatani was eating, with a slice removed[†]. If you haven't twigged yet, we're talking about Pac-Man.

Well, sort of. He was originally called 'Puck Man' in Japan, but they chose to rename him in the West to reduce the risk of offensive graffiti amendments. Which sort of makes sense but, if that was such a big risk, how come Nintendo released an arcade version of Duck Hunt?

Whatever he was called, the game was huge, replacing Asteroids just as that had replaced Space Invaders before it. Pac-Man was *everywhere*. Not just in the usual places you'd find arcades but anywhere you could fit one, from hotel lobbies to doctors' surgeries. Arcades didn't have a Pac-Man machine. They had rows of them. There was even a hit song, *Pac-Man Fever*, in the charts. And the merchandise! If you can think of a thing, there was a version of that thing with a Pac-Man on it[‡], including the cover of *Time* magazine. You might assume from all this that Iwatani became the richest man in the history of the universe, but actually he only received a modest bonus, as Japanese firms culturally don't tend to offer additional remuneration for work that is an expected part of the job. So that sucks.

If you're reading this book, you're no doubt already aware

---

[*]   Donovan, T.: *Replay: The History of Video Games* (Yellow Ant, 2010).

[†]   This probably isn't true either, but is widely circulated.

[‡]   No, not that. Shame on you for even thinking it.

of Pac-Man – yellow-circle-man gobbles up dots and ghosts – but what you might not be aware of is the complexity of the seemingly-simple gameplay. Each ghost has behaviours unique to them, the knowledge of which can be used by advanced players to their advantage*. It's also a very realistic game. For example, Pac-Man moves quicker along empty rows, rather than the ones where he eats pellets, which is just like in real life. Imagine running down a street. Now imagine running down a street again, but this time, you're eating a bag of Minstrels. It wouldn't massively affect your speed, but it definitely shaves the edge off. Really ahead of its time.

The game was the first to feature cinematic 'cutscenes' both during the cabinet's 'attract mode' (introducing the characters) and between levels of the game as interludes, rewarding players for their progress, although many questions are left unanswered. We always assume Pac-Man's the hero, but why was he being haunted? *What did he DO?*

Pac-Man's also notable for not being a simulation of something pre-existing like a shoot-out, or sports. Instead, its scenario was fantastical. This did nothing to dent its success though. Quite the opposite. The game was so successful that strategy books were published to give gamers an edge. All this surprised Namco. They really weren't convinced the game would be a hit at first, given how different it was to everything

---

* While the ghosts are known in the West as Blinky, Pinky, Inky and Clyde, the translations of their original names are somewhat more illustrative of their behaviour: Chaser, Ambusher, Fickle and Feigned Ignorance.

else popular at the time. They were far more convinced that their other title that year, Rally-X, would be the breakthrough. Similar in some respects, it instead had a car driving round a maze collecting flags while avoiding other cars.

While all this was happening, Atari continued to tinker with vector graphics and looked to their 1974 hit, Tank, for inspiration for their next big release. Battlezone placed the battle (albeit one versus the machine this time, rather than a second player) in a 3D environment. The game was viewed through a fixed periscope viewer, as had been the case with Sega's Periscope and Midway's Sea Wolf.

Processing power was still severely limited, so the brief for the design of each in-game object, including the tanks, was to minimise the number of lines being required to draw them (lines being the key ingredient in vector games). Nevertheless, the game was a hit, allowing players to feel they were immersed in a real world, in which things would be happening, whether they were looking at that particular portion of the world at that moment in time or not.

Battlezone chose to stick with Tank's dual-stick controls meaning that, rather than a single four-directional stick that would allow you to move forwards, backwards, left and right, as would make *total sense*, it instead had two two-directional sticks. Push forwards or backwards on both, and you'd go forwards or backwards, but push forwards on one and backwards on the other – and you'd rotate either left or right. I'm not entirely sure if real tanks are even steered like this but, if they are, might I humbly suggest that, if you're in the business of building giant metal cars with poor visibility and huge guns sticking out of them, it would actually be in everyone's interests to make driving them as intuitive as possible.

It must have been fairly realistic, as the game soon attracted the attention of a group of retired Army generals, who wanted to create a version of it for training soldiers. While an obvious area of potential for this emerging technology, Ed Rotberg, the game's creator, was very against this. Programmers like him and his colleagues could quite easily have worked in military-related industries, but had often made a conscious choice not to. The financial incentive was simply too high for Atari to resist, though, and soon they were adding rotating turrets, multiple guns and target types, configurable ballistics and more to the game, for this private contractor. Pac-Man might have introduced gentler gameplay, but war was still big business.

That didn't mean there couldn't be fresh takes on the war genre though, and it was leading pinball manufacturer Williams who would offer it the following year, with Eugene Jarvis' Defender. Jarvis felt many games failed to justify their violence, so Defender was so-called as a key feature of the gameplay was to recapture kidnapped astronauts and return them to the planet's surface. He felt defending was more emotive than merely attacking, as you're protecting something rather than just destroying. It was a gamble for Williams. They'd not released a video game since their 1973 Pong clone Paddle Ball, but they could no longer afford to ignore the market. Jarvis wasn't even a games developer originally – he'd developed pinball machines for Atari before moving to Williams, where he continued on pinball for some time. It says something about how embryonic the industry still was that they'd just get the pinball guy to make a video game, when his experience was limited to having worked at another company where other people did that for a job[*].

To date, many of the biggest games had their action play out on a single screen, including flagship titles like Pong, Space Invaders, Asteroids and Pac-Man. Jarvis wanted Defender's screen to scroll, like it had done successfully before in games like Taito's Speed Race. To keep up with the competition, he wanted to use a colour monitor for the game, developing a system that could show up to sixteen colours. In Eugene's words, 'Wow! This was more colors than you'll ever need.' Of course, in years to come, he'd be as shocked at his naivety then as my wife was a short time after she decided we'd get rid of any of our cutlery that didn't match[†].

Defender almost never happened as, on the opening morning of the 1980 Amusement and Music Operators Association trade show, Jarvis was still finishing the game on the showroom floor. When he finally got it working, initial reaction was muted. Gameplay was so fast-paced and intense that, for many, it was too hard, and it was all over far too quickly – first time, you might barely last long enough to press each button once! While people had got used to more complex input systems (like Asteroids, Defender had five buttons offering similar functions, plus a joystick), frankly, the feeling

---

[*] To be fair, his pinball machines were some of the first to use microprocessors, so he had programming experience in that area.

[†] I'm just saying, we're always running out of forks.

was that Williams had a flop on its hands but, crucially, this game came at a time when bragging rights in the arcade were high. People that considered themselves to be accomplished gamers persevered, determined to master it. An unexpected, but welcome, side-effect of all this was that, because games could last such a short amount of time, and people kept coming back to it, for a while it was by far the most profitable arcade cabinet an operator could own. The game fed people's desire to conquer it with not one, but two high-score tables. You could get your initials on the day's best players, but also the cabinet's best players of all-time. I imagine the people on those tables are the same sort of masochists that find Dark Souls fun*.

In all seriousness, you can't underestimate the allure of the arcades. My younger brother once became so engrossed in an arcade game at the Butlin's holiday park in Bognor Regis that, in preference to walking away from the game, he wet himself. He was twenty-six years old†.

So, Namco and Midway were doing great together with Pac-Man, Taito had done well enough with Space Invaders to set up on their own, and Atari continued to release innovative and successful new cabinets on a regular basis. Even Pinball manufacturers like Williams were finding their place in this

---

* Yes, you've guessed correctly – I'm rubbish at Dark Souls.

† Obviously he wasn't. He was thirty. (He wasn't, he was maybe five. But this is too much fun.)

new market, but Nintendo had yet to break through in the US arcades.

Nintendo's game Radarscope (a Space Invaders/Galaxian hybrid) had done reasonably well in Japan, second only to Pac-Man in fact. Envious of his US rivals' successes, the company's president Hiroshi Yamauchi hired his son-in-law, Minoru Arakawa, to set up an American division. Don't mistake this for nepotism though. When Yamauchi took control of Nintendo in 1949, the first thing he did was fire his cousin, and every manager that had been loyal to his grandfather who ran the company before him, to ensure everyone was clear he was now in charge. Arakawa came from a respected Kyoto family, studied at MIT and had already built a successful career in America in property development, so his value was clear.

At first, the new operation in America was provided with only limited funds and so the best it could manage in terms of distribution was to outsource to a small trucking company run by two guys, Ron Judy and Al Stone, who had previously just been reselling arcade machines as a side-business. Nintendo couldn't even afford to pay the pair anything other than expenses but, as a sweetener, offered them a large commission should they manage to secure any sales on their behalf.

They had placed Radarscope cabinets in test locations and it had done well, so Arakawa took the gamble of a big order of 3,000 units. However, popularity waned and by the time the cabinets arrived via boat four months later, they knew they were in trouble. The travel time wasn't helped by the fact that Arakawa had set Nintendo of America up in New York (on the

East Coast) rather than on the West Coast, which, for the geographically challenged among you, is much nearer Japan. Learning from this mistake, it wouldn't be long before they moved the office to Seattle (West Coast), but the damage was done. Radarscope failed to make a mark in the US; of the 3,000 cabinets they shipped to America, at considerable cost, they only managed to sell around 1,000.

By this point in time, arcade machines were increasingly the same at their core – a cabinet, a monitor, and a bunch of integrated chips – if you added new chips to this base, a cabinet could be repurposed for another title. A young artist, Shigeru Miyamoto, who had designed art for Nintendo's Radarscope cabinet, was tasked with coming up with their next game. He was to focus on the creative, while Gunpei Yokoi (Nintendo's head of engineering) would ensure it was technically viable for the unsold Radarscope cabinets to be easily converted. Just like Eugene Jarvis with Defender, Miyamoto was by no means an obvious choice for the job, but Yamauchi didn't have any other engineers and, or programmers available and the US business simply wasn't worth the resource at this time. Yokoi was unconvinced Miyamoto would be up to the task, and the same was true for Arakawa. They would soon be proved wrong, though.

Previously, games tended to be created by a single person, meaning game designers had to have the creative ideas, the ability to create the art *and* the technical skills to program it. The division of labour between Miyamoto and Yokoi allowed the two men to play to their strengths (creative and technical, respectively) and combine their talents to create something greater than either of them would have been capable of individually.

Miyamoto had enjoyed games like Pong and Breakout in the past, but felt they'd benefit from having more of a story, as was the case with movies or books. At the time, Nintendo were developing a relationship with the owners of the cartoon character Popeye for their hugely successful Game & Watch series (more on those in the next chapter) but a final agreement wasn't in place so, instead of Popeye the Sailor Man gobbling up spinach and rescuing Olive Oyl from Bluto, Miyamoto's game featured a carpenter* grabbing hammers to smash his way to a damsel in distress being held captive by a giant Gorilla. Eagle-eyed readers will spot the similarities, because they are the same.

More so than any other game, Donkey Kong had a narrative. Sure, Pac-Man had its cutscenes, but they didn't move a story forwards. Donkey Kong begins with an animation showing him climbing the structure with the kidnapped Pauline. Reaching the top, he jumps up and down to damage Jumpman's route. The game then begins, and we attempt to climb the tower and rescue Pauline but, each time we do, she's whisked away by Donkey Kong until eventually, at the game's end, we remove the structure's rivets, causing Donkey Kong to

---

* Merely known at first as 'Jumpman', for he is a man . . . that jumps, Miyamoto's Jumpman follows the convention for ending character names with '-man', such as Iwatani's 'Puck Man'. Before that, Iwatani also called one of the characters in Cutie-Q 'Walk-Man', because the character walked around. Genius.

tumble to the ground, while we're reunited with her. As a result of all this, the game has a new sort of goal people hadn't seen until this point. While we can still attempt to get a high score, that really becomes a secondary objective. The player is more driven to reach the end of the game, so as to find out how the story ends.

Christening his game 'Stubborn Gorilla', and with a focus on cracking the American market, Miyamoto attempted to translate the title into English, opting for (King) 'Kong' in place of 'Gorilla', and 'Donkey' as an unknowingly poor and confusing synonym for 'Stubborn' – hence Donkey Kong. Donkey was not, as is often assumed, a misspelling of Monkey. If you thought Donkey was a misspelling of Monkey, but you know Kong means Monkey, ask yourself: why would he call the game 'Monkey Monkey'? Surely he'd just call it 'Monkey'?

Having said that, in writing this I've since discovered the scientific/Latin name for the Western Gorilla is 'Gorilla Gorilla', so maybe it was just that Miyamoto's Latin was better than his English. The *Western* Lowland Gorilla's Latin name is 'Gorilla Gorilla Gorilla'. Lazy Romans.

We've got distracted again.

Jumpman's design was no accident. His gloves and overalls allowed players to easily notice his arms' movement, the red cap removed the issue of how to adequately show his hair moving, and the moustache avoided the need to try to animate a mouth. All of these tricks meant that, despite the limited number of pixels used in his creation, he felt 'real' – no stiff hair or frozen arms and face as he moved round the world. He looked and moved more like a real person than any character before him but, back in America, when the distributors Judy and Stone heard the game's title, Donkey Kong, they were crestfallen. It was gibberish (and Gibbon-ish*), and the gameplay was unlike anything else at the time. Their business was already on the verge of going bankrupt after Radarscope's lacklustre performance and this would surely be the final straw.

But after dropping off Donkey Kong in a couple of Seattle bars, it quickly became apparent the game was going to be a hit, and so it proved to be. The game had longevity too. While many machines remained popular for only a few months until the next big thing came along, Donkey Kong (the first platform game as we would now describe the genre) continued to do exceptional business into its second year.

It was estimated video games made twice as much as all Nevada casinos combined, twice as much as movies, and three times as much as baseball, basketball and American football in 1981, a great year for video game companies. Thanks to the generous commission arrangement Nintendo had previously offered them, instead of going bankrupt, Judy and Stone became millionaires. It wasn't just the distributors who were relieved. Nintendo of America were also in dire financial straits, having been on the verge of being kicked out of their office by landlord, Mario Segale, who would later be immortalised by Arakawa in the retrospective naming of their currently

---

* Dear oh dear . . .

nameless carpenter. I imagine at the time he'd have rather just had his rent.

Meanwhile back at Atari, Dave Theurer was digging into his nightmares once again, for a follow-up to the nuclear-war inspired Missile Command. This new game was initially inspired by a brainstorming session suggestion of 'First-Person Space Invaders', but after it was decided that was insufficiently original*, Theurer adapted it by drawing on a memory of a movie that had haunted him since his childhood, where monsters emerged from a hole to attack humans. *Way to over-react, Dave.*

The game required a vector solution for Theurer to be able to realise his vision and, at precisely the right time, there was a new colour vector generator being developed. He switched to that, allowing him to create a game, Tempest, that really drew the eye and stood out from everything else in the arcades. To control the game there was a fire button for shooting, and a single rotational dial. Originally the gun remained fixed while the hole rotated but in testing this quickly made players feel sick, which many considered to be a negative. When it was swapped to rotate the gun around the edge of the hole, the problem disappeared, which was lucky, and also makes no real sense.

The combination of the vector display and the dial allowed the game to be incredibly fast, which proved exciting. However, the game also tended to run hot. So hot, in fact, it kept

---

* As if that had ever stopped anyone else that made video games.

failing or, in some cases, literally melting! This proved unpopular with people that bought it, as their ability to monetise it was negatively impacted by it being *on fire*. The game also had a strange coding glitch where if players hit a specific score (179,480 points, fact fans) it gave them forty free credits, meaning people who knew of this exploit could play for hours on a single quarter. In the days before downloadable patches, this was a huge issue and both these facts meant that Tempest was destined not to become the big hit that many at Atari had expected it to be. More general issues with the reliability of vector monitors led to vector games as a whole beginning to be made less and less and, of course, graphics on traditional games were now getting better and better, with more colours and higher resolution.

The next big success in gaming was to come not from Atari. Nor was it to come from Namco or Midway, despite the fact it was a sequel to their smash hit, Pac-Man. In fact, this new game was created independently by two MIT students, Doug MacRae and Kevin Curran. MacRae had accrued a bit of income from a pinball machine and three Missile Command cabinets he'd purchased and placed in local sites. When Missile Command started to make less money, him and his friend Curran used their know-how to work out a way of bolting self-made 'enhancement kits' onto the circuit boards to modify the game. 'Super Missile Attack' was the name they gave their Missile Command hack and, after proving successful, they began to sell it to others for $295 a go. This was far cheaper to operators than an entirely new arcade cabinet, and a licence to print money for MacRae and Curran, who could produce them from their hastily-founded company, General Computer*, at just $30 per unit.

When they began this venture, Pac-Man was still the most popular game in the arcades, so they set themselves the goal of modifying that title next. This proved much harder, as its code was far less efficient than Missile Command and twice as long, but they persisted and eventually managed to create something that they felt would freshen up any ailing Pac-Man cabinets that needed to solicit new players. However, before they could get anywhere with this new Pac-Man enhancement kit, Atari took them to court for Super Missile Attack. Atari were understandably concerned about the idea of third parties undermining their business, by allowing customers to just modify existing machines without giving them a penny, rather than buying their latest games. The case was eventually settled out of court, with Atari offering Curran and MacRae jobs making new games exclusively for them, as long as they ceased making enhancement kits. Everything seemed resolved, but there was one small but, it turned out, vital clause which would have a profound effect – Curran and MacRae were no longer allowed to make enhancement kits *unless they got permission from the original copyright holder.*

Obviously Atari couldn't conceive why anyone would ever grant such permission so it seemed a non-issue but, when they had dropped the case against Curran and MacRae, they had

---

* ★★★ Boring company name klaxon. ★★★ It really is as if many of these guys were competing to outdo each other in the Blandest Company Name of the Year awards.

done so 'with prejudice', and so were bound by the terms upon which they had settled the action. This meant Curran and MacRae could go to Midway and 'prove' they'd beaten Atari in court. They figured that, if they played it right, it would appear to Midway that they were legally entitled to release their Pac-Man enhancement kit, and so grant them the permission they actually needed to avoid breaching their Atari agreement. What they couldn't have foreseen was that Midway were currently uncertain as to what their next game would be, having been caught by surprise by Pac-Man's phenomenal success and so, rather than give their blessing to the enhancement kit, they reached an agreement with Curran and MacRae to work with them in creating an official Pac-Man sequel, based on their work to date.

At the time, their enhancement kit was called Crazy Otto, and it gave Pac-Man some long legs, and changed the appearance of the ghosts. Midway obviously wanted something to build on the brand of the original game, so the decision was made to lose Otto's legs and create a female counterpart to Pac-Man instead. Originally, this character was going to be called, unsurprisingly, Pac-Woman, but several female employees suggested Miss Pac-Man instead. However, someone then pointed out that in one of the new game's cutscene animations, Pac-Man and Miss Pac-Man received a baby delivered by a stork, so calling this new character Miss would mean the child was born out of wedlock. The character was briefly then renamed Mrs. Pac-Man before finally being permanently christened Ms. Pac-Man, presumably because by that point they'd decided that the vaguer the name, the better, in the hopes of making everyone shut up about the marital status of a fictional yellow circle.

The sequel wasn't just a case of applying some cosmetic changes to the original though. Gameplay was faster, and there were four mazes instead of Pac-Man's one. It also removed patterns for the ghosts as people had learnt ways of avoiding them in the first title, and the bonus objects moved around instead of being stationary. Lastly, the fourth ghost this time was named Sue instead of Clyde, named after MacRae's sister. You might think it's weird to name a ghost, which is dead, after a family member, but in MacRae's defence you only think that because it totally is.

All of the above changes were implemented via the cheaper method of an enhancement kit so – fun* fact klaxon – there was never a Ms. Pac-Man arcade board – every Ms. Pac-Man was an original Pac-Man cabinet with the enhancement kit bolted on top!

Ms. Pac-Man was by no means the only sequel during this period. As developers sought to capitalise on previous games' successes, it made sense to release not only sequels, but also new titles heavily 'influenced' by the big hits and, on some occasions, direct clones. In this chapter we've talked about the most iconic titles of the era, but there's so many more which deserve a quick nod.

Pac-Man and Ms. Pac-Man led to Junior Pac-Man and Baby Pac-Man, the latter being a pinball/video game hybrid which,

---

* The concept of fun is subjective, so you can't prove me wrong. 1–0 to me.

incredibly, led to Curran and MacRae suing Midway, claiming *they* had created the Pac-Man family and should get money from all 'Pac-Children' games, such as Baby Pac-Man, which they'd not had any creative input in at all. Even more incredibly, they won the case.

Pac-Man's success led to many other maze-chase games coming to the market, some almost carbon copies, while others introduced new gameplay mechanics, such as providing the protagonist with weapons as a way of fighting back against whoever was chasing them, titles like Wizard of Wor (Nutting) and Berzerk (Stern), which also had an early example of synthesised speech. Then there's games like Mouse Trap (Exidy), Pengo (Sega), Dig Dug (Namco) and Escher-inspired Q*Bert (Gottlieb) – the only hit video game from the Baffle Ball guys! Those last two may seem more tenuous for those that know them, but the maze-chase remains at the heart of both, even if they vary in their execution. Of course, the maze-chase harks back to far earlier titles like Atari's Gotcha, or even Cat and Mouse on the Magnavox Odyssey, but Pac-Man was the first to really perfect the formula.

Space Invaders inspired Phoenix, a 1980 Taito game with an early example of a boss level. Also that year was Moon Cresta, a Nichibutsu title which gave the illusion of vertical scrolling thanks to its moving starfield in the background. Taito, Sega, Gremlin and others released many versions of this under various names, sometimes with pallet swaps or changes to the graphics. Then the following year saw Galaxian sequel Galaga from Namco, and Gorf from Nutting, both released in the US by Midway. Namco released Xevious in

1982, this time publishing via Atari in the US, who had also released Centipede, the first coin-op game to have a woman with a significant development role – Dona Bailey, who had previously helped Cadillac use microprocessors to introduce cruise control in their cars. Centipede itself was followed up by Millipede.

Defender inspired Scramble (Konami), Vanguard (Tose) and Zaxxon (Sega), and had a sequel in Stargate (aka Defender 2) again created by Eugene Jarvis, who also took inspiration from Gun Fight and Berzerk for 1982's twin-stick shooter Robotron: 2084.

Many of these early arcade cabinets had a quirk where you could get free credits using cigarette lighters. It had to be the cheap little ones that had an electrical spark in them and, basically, if you held them against the metal coin plate and flicked them, the spark would trigger the internal mechanism, and you'd get a random number of free goes.

Or a fire. And, I know what you're thinking, it feels like there should be a joke in there somewhere about the band Arcade Fire but I've had a look, and there isn't.

Moving on . . . Asteroids was quickly followed by Asteroids Deluxe and, later, Space Duel. Atari also integrated elements of Lunar Lander into 1982's colour vector title, Gravitar. Konami got in on the action with Time Pilot, while Cinematronics joined the party with Star Castle. Cinematronics were also the pioneers behind 1983's Dragon's Lair – a LaserDisc game that allowed the player to play, essentially, a cartoon – drawn by former Disney animator Don Bluth, which led to him being courted by Steven Spielberg. The pair eventually worked together on animated films such as *An American Tail* and *The Land Before Time*.

By this point, games also began to have multiple levels with different styles, such as Atari's The Adventures of Major Havoc or, possibly most successfully, 1982's movie adaptation, Tron (Midway) which had levels resembling Breakout, Blockade (more on that one in a moment), a maze-chase à la Pac-Man, and a multi-directional shooter. Donkey Kong developed the platforming genre with Donkey Kong Jr. and Donkey Kong 3, but also inspired the Taito platformer Jungle King and the visually similar Burger Time (Data East). Even Pong lived on in games like Warlords (Atari), and Missile Command had its gameplay flipped on its head by Liberator (Atari again).

Star Fire, a 1979 vector game by Exidy, shamelessly took inspiration from the *Star Wars* movie, and was actually the first game to allow initials to be entered in its high-score table. Atari's official 1983 Star Wars game takes clear influence from this title and demonstrated the power of an official licence in drawing in the punters. Exidy also have their place in gaming history thanks to their 1976 game Death Race, which has the dubious honour of being the first arcade game to gain mass-media coverage questioning the violent nature of games, due to its core gameplay mechanic of using a car to run over what appeared to be humans in order to score points (Exidy half-heartedly claimed they were gremlins).

Atari's Qix, Williams' Joust (which would in turn inspire Nintendo's Mario Bros. and Balloon Fight), Namco's Pole Position and Nichibutsu's Moon Cresta all brought something new to arcades. And we've not even mentioned Konami's 1981 road-crossing sim, Frogger, which must deserve a place here because it's my mum's favourite arcade game. It was released in the USA by Gremlin, who had recently been acquired by Sega and had, two years prior, released Blockade, the forerunner to what every Nokia phone owner in the late 1990s would recognise as the game Snake.

I never really got Snake. The food that you eat in it is apparently meant to be apples, but snakes don't eat apples – they're carnivores. And they don't look like apples – they're squares. Why not say it was slices of ham or Scottish breakfast sausage? That's square. Or, if you're *obsessed* with the idea of it being an apple, there's a really easy fix; just call the game Worm. Worms love apples.

In case it's not immediately apparent from the barrage of titles above, we're now very much at the point in time where it's clearly impossible for this book to cover every game of note. I could literally fulfil my 80,000-word brief many times over by simply listing the titles of every game released between now and 1998. In retrospect, that would have been a far easier book to write. Let's just summarise by saying that, during this period, there were loads of great games involving racing cars, space, shooting stuff, being chased around mazes and hopping along platforms, with the occasional bit of Pong thrown in for old time's sake.

And yet, by the middle of 1982, during all of this, the arcade business began to falter. There was no cataclysmic event. Rather than it being a case of the bubble bursting, the industry simply stopped growing exponentially. The problem was, people had over-reached. Locations that simply couldn't generate sufficient income from games alone failed, and many distributors had offered credit to businesses that then defaulted. Of course, the more cabinets there were out there, the more thinly this spread the number of customers at each location, too, and there were many more systems in people's homes now as well. They didn't *have* to leave home to get their gaming fix. So, distributors and manufacturers ended up unpaid, and with stock they couldn't shift.

Video games were still big business, though. In 1982 *Star Wars* director George Lucas created a new division, Lucasfilm Games, to enter the market, Walt Disney Pictures made the hugely successful video-game-themed motion picture, *Tron* (which itself received the arcade adaptation mentioned above) and, of course, the home market was still moving on apace. So, let's now travel back in time to where we started in this chapter with Space Invaders.

But this time, the aliens are in people's homes.

4

THE ARCADE . . .
IN YOUR HOME!

Despite Bushnell's advice, Atari chose to persevere with the VCS, and they were rewarded for their commitment. Throughout 1978 and 1979, the explosion of classic arcade games kept people interested enough in games that they still wanted to have something similar to play with at home, but it was in 1980 that the VCS really took off. Warner VP Manny Gerard suggested the company approach Taito about getting the rights to release Space Invaders for Atari's console. This would be the first time an arcade hit from a third party was licensed for the home market. While Kassar still didn't really understand video games, he did understand marketing, and his push to promote the game, in the hopes of it being a system-seller, proved correct. Space Invaders became the bestselling game of 1980, and quadrupled the VCS's sales.

Not that Atari weren't still trying to innovate themselves. Around the same time, one of the consumer division programmers, Warren Robinett, set out to create a graphical version of the text-adventure games (no pictures, only written words) that were doing the rounds on PDP computers in educational establishments. You might think that graphics were added to his game, Adventure, to demonstrate how advanced the VCS's hardware was, but really it was as much a case of the solution being better suited to the platform. A VCS game could only handle 4KB of code, and text descriptions would quickly gobble that up. Also, the VCS had a joystick, not a keyboard, for input, so typing instructions into the game with the joystick via an on-screen keyboard would have been incredibly time-consuming.

Now's as good a time as any to explain the difference between bits and bytes. A 'bit' is actually a portmanteau of binary digit (a single 0 or 1), whereas a 'byte' commonly consists of eight 'bits' (for instance 00101010). This offers 256 different possible combinations of noughts and ones for a computer to use as its most basic unit of information. So, bits are the smaller ones, and are represented by a lower case 'b', while bytes are bigger, and are represented by a capital B.

It gets more confusing. A kilobyte (KB) is commonly assumed to mean the nearest multiple of 256 to 1,000, which is 256 x 4 = 1,024 bytes, or 8,192 bits. However, this is now properly referred to as a kibibyte (KiB), while a kilobyte (KB) is 1,000 bytes, because what this needed to make it less confusing was more terminology.

Similar nonsense applies to millions with megabytes (MB), mebibytes (MiB) and megabits (Mb), but the important thing to notice is that the smallest one is the one internet providers always use in their blurb, to fool you into believing their rubbish service is eight times better than it actually is, because who could be bothered to learn all this nonsense? I only know it because I looked it up for this book, and writing it while my kid was sat next to me getting angry about cereal nearly killed me.

Back to Adventure. It wasn't the graphics that helped create buzz for the game, it was the introduction of video games' first 'Easter egg' – a secret hidden within the game's code. Robinett, inspired partly by the rumour of a hidden message on The Beatles' *White Album* which could only be heard by playing the record backwards, wanted to make his secret hard to find. You might be expecting something pretty exciting. Whatever it is you're imagining right now, forget that and think instead of the most rubbish thing you could find hidden in a game. I don't know what you're picturing now, but I'm confident it's still a lot better than what he actually hid, which was a grey dot. A single pixel, placed on a background of the same colour, in a seemingly inaccessible part of the game's maze.

Total rubbish. But, if you somehow managed to find it, and then took it back to another location, it would unlock a secret room in the game which had 'Created by Warren Robinett' written in vertical letters – his 'name in lights', effectively. He never told anyone about it though. The secret room took up five per cent of the storage on the cartridge and he could easily have been fired for such a wasteful endeavour. It was only when, in 1980, a kid wrote to Atari saying they'd discovered it, that anyone else found out about it. When this became more widely known, thanks to coverage in the new *Electronic Games* magazine, it generated a great deal of buzz and added to Atari's reputation.

This 'Easter egg' would never have existed were it not for the fact that, at the time, games were still being created by a single programmer. Unlike today, where big games can have hundreds of people working on them, Robinett created everything for Adventure alone: concept, art, sound, programming, the lot. Obviously, few people would be great at all of these. Robinett, by his own admission wasn't the greatest artist. It's why the dragons in the game look more like overweight ducks that borrowed Oscar Pistorius's prosthetic legs.

Whatever you think of the game, you have to admire the ability of a single person to create something like Adventure. Sadly, just as had been the case with the coin-op division, creativity in the home division became less valued within Atari. While the business grew commercially at an astonishing rate, its programmers – who wished to be seen as creative artists in the same way as musicians, novelists or film-makers – were seen as replaceable and interchangeable by any other kid with programming skills, as if creativity would just be a given in anyone that had learnt how to code. This attitude was no doubt exacerbated by VCS hits like Space Invaders, as it opened the door to programmers simply being required to port third parties' products, rather than to innovate and create internally.

Atari conducted some internal research to analyse which games of theirs had sold the best, with the aim of encouraging their programmers to churn out more games in a similar vein. The results were surprising: just four of the company's thirty designers were responsible for games worth over sixty per cent of Atari's $100 million in sales the previous year, somewhat more than their $30,000 salary with no bonus. Clearly it wasn't the case that just any programmer could create a hit and, rather than inspiring everyone to make more games like the hits, the research instead inspired the four guys capable of making them to quit and found their own company, Activision, to independently create VCS games.

While engineers were leaving Atari, their rivals were glancing over the fence, jealous of the company's success. Mattel, who had done well with their early LED handheld games, launched their own system to compete with the VCS, which they called the Intellivision (a shortening of 'Intelligent Television'*). Released two years later than the VCS in 1979, it benefited from a superior CPU and more memory, allowing it to deliver superior graphics. This might not have been enough on its own, but Mattel wisely chose to carve out a niche with sports games – seeking licences from flagship governing bodies like Major League Baseball (MLB), the National Football League (NFL – American Football) and the National Basketball Association (NBA), and even lesser-known ones like the American Backgammon Players Association (ABPA). This gave their products the feel of being the 'legitimate' digital version of each sport and hobby which is just as well – I can't imagine anything worse than unofficial backgammon.

Another Atari rival, Coleco, also wanted another bite of the cherry after their success with the Telstar systems, and introduced the ColecoVision in 1982, again benefiting from

---

* Fair warning – we're entering the era of rubbish portmanteaus.

advances in technology unavailable to their competitors. Of course, Atari's brand and back catalogue of original games (the VCS had been going for five years at this point) gave them a key advantage, and Mattel had their reputation for sports titles, so Coleco chose to focus on securing licences for home versions of arcade games. By this point, many top-tier titles like Space Invaders had of course already been snapped up by Atari, but there were plenty of mid-tier ones which were sufficiently popular to be recognisable, such as Mr. Do! and Zaxxon.

Luckily for Coleco, they also managed to secure one spectacular title to bring out when the console launched, packaged right in there with the console itself, which almost guaranteed it would be a huge success: Donkey Kong. Nintendo had granted Coleco six months' exclusivity for the game and you might quite rightly be wondering why them instead of Atari but, at the time, Coleco was building a reputation for arcade titles they converted to tabletop versions using similar, primitive, LED technology to that used in Mattel's Auto Race – games like Pac-Man, Frogger and Galaxian had already been released by the company, housed in detailed miniatures of the original arcade cabinets. In fact, Michael Katz, who had led the development of Mattel's Auto Race had since moved over to Coleco to help build this new area of their business, and his influence on the company's direction is clear here. Their ability to release Donkey Kong for their new home system *and* create a tabletop LED version gave them access to more markets than Atari, which appealed to Nintendo. What's more, following the lead of third parties like Activision, Coleco had begun to explore creating versions of their games for the Intellivision and VCS too. So, after having the chance to benefit from Donkey Kong's exclusivity on the ColecoVision to give the hardware a sales boost at launch, they could then go on to release Donkey Kong on their rivals' systems too. They were the complete package. A one-stop shop for making money in the home market.

Not that Nintendo weren't dipping their toe in that market at all, though. Since 1980, they'd been releasing simple, hand-held LCD (Liquid Crystal Display) games themselves. Gunpei Yokoi had been inspired on a commute home one day, when he saw a businessman tinkering with a pocket calculator. Struck by how much more fun it would be to play with a game – though one should never underestimate the joy of mischievously typing 5318008 – Yokoi set to work on repurposing the technology for fun, much in the same way Mattel had in the mid-seventies with their LED games, but his use of LCD displays would allow his games to have far more detailed graphics than the LED handhelds' abstract red rectangles.

Christening his new product Game & Watch*, the first release in April 1980 was Ball, a juggling game, which became a big hit, not least due to its low price of 5,800 yen (approx $23), although that's still nowhere near as cheap as an actual set of juggling balls. Nintendo went on to release dozens of Game & Watches over the next decade, eventually including adaptations of hits of theirs like Donkey Kong and Mario Bros. I was lucky enough to secure a reissued version of Ball via the

---

* Not a watch. Barely a clock.

Club Nintendo Stars Catalogue in 2011 which, if nothing else, tells you I wasted a fortune on the Wii's Virtual Console on retro games I ended up playing once, then never looked at again. But at least I got something back, in the form of a hand-held retro game I ended up playing once, then never looked at again. So that's a win.

Nintendo continued to innovate throughout the eighties with these toys, and many of the innovations seen in the Game & Watch franchise later found their way into other products. Nineteen eighty-two's Oil Panic was the first to have two screens, with gameplay continuing from one through to the other. It also folded in half, clamshell-style, protecting both screens when it wasn't in use, foreshadowing the Game Boy Advance and Nintendo DS by many years. When they released the Donkey Kong Game & Watch that same year (incidentally, the first to be based on an existing game of theirs, rather than an original title) it featured a new directional pad, aka D-Pad, for controls – this is the instantly recognisable 'plus' we've seen on controllers ever since, used for left, right, up and down.

Coleco's tabletop Donkey Kong found its way to Japan as well, where it was released under the Game & Watch Tabletop spin-off brand, further demonstrating Nintendo's complete lack of regard for the meaning of the word 'watch'. Nintendo then grew this sub-brand with its own range, with titles like Mario's Cement Factory and Mario's Bombs Away – the latter of which saw an uncharacteristically violent Mario in a warzone blowing up humans with bombs. I say uncharacteristically. When you boil it down, what actually is Mario? He's a plumber that jumps on turtles, then kicks them at other turtles. I guess it's possible that he's severely allergic to turtles – he dies on contact with them – but, even if that's true, it seems unnecessarily violent. I'm allergic to cats, but I've never stamped on a cat and then kicked it at another cat. I just avoid cats. Worst case: EpiPen.

Anyway . . . back in handheld land, rivals also began to release similar products, such was the success of Game & Watch. Bandai released handheld games that were powered by solar energy, rather than batteries, and gave the 'two screens' their own twist by placing them on top of each other, creating a sort of layered 3D effect to their games. Nelson licensed the game Pac-Man and made an actual watch you could wear on your wrist and play on. Nintendo soon did the same with a number of their most famous franchises. Atari had also dabbled in handhelds with Touch Me, a 1978 adaptation of an unsuccessful 1974 arcade memory game of theirs, where players had to correctly follow a sequence of flashing lights and press the corresponding buttons. You might wonder why Atari bothered to release a handheld version of a failed arcade game but, by this point, the idea had been repackaged far more successfully by Milton Bradley, who had released their hit electronic game, Simon. There's a lovely bit of poetic symmetry here as, in the same way Bushnell saw Baer's Odyssey and created the more successful Pong, Baer saw the arcade version of Bushnell's Touch Me and reappropriated it as the far more successful Simon.

Essentially, as the market for video games exploded, a lot of companies were copying a lot of other companies in the hopes of getting a share of this incredibly lucrative market. However, as before, some companies took offence to this. One of them, Universal, threatened to take Coleco and Nintendo to court unless they provided them with a royalty on Donkey Kong sales, as they felt it was a violation of their copyright for (King) Kong. To be fair, a Gorilla kidnapping a woman and taking her to the top of a building does *seem* familiar and so Coleco conceded, and an arrangement was put in place. Nintendo's legal counsel, Howard Lincoln*, however, advised them to fight and they were right to do so as, it transpired, Universal had themselves argued in court that King Kong was public domain, in order to win a battle with the film's original owners, RKO Pictures. So, Universal threatened legal action, which their own previous legal action proved was nonsense. As a result, not only did Universal lose the fight, Nintendo then sought, and got, damages for lost revenue as compensation for Universal's aggressive threatening of the many companies to which Nintendo had licensed the Donkey Kong character.

Arakawa was so impressed with Lincoln's work for Nintendo that he asked him to come on board full time. Lincoln was reluctant just to come on board as legal counsel, so instead they reached the agreement he would take the role of Senior Vice President, Arakawa's number two. Nintendo subsequently took action against Universal again, as Universal had licensed King Kong to a company, Tiger Electronics, who

---

* Introduced to the company via Judy and Stone, he had been their attorney and had helped negotiate Nintendo's agreement regarding Coleco's use of Donkey Kong.

had created a rip-off version of the Donkey Kong game. So, not only did Universal NOT get licensing revenues on Donkey Kong, Nintendo ended up getting Universal's licensing fees from Tiger's King Kong! Coleco and Atari then also went back for compensation from Universal against royalties they'd previously agreed for the ColecoVision and VCS versions of Donkey Kong.

Although Atari were successful in that particular legal battle, they had been less lucky in an ongoing dispute with Activision. Atari felt that, as the VCS was theirs, they were automatically entitled to exclusive rights to creating its games. In their defence, their business model involved selling the hardware for barely more than cost, in order to build the market for the games, where it made its money. Activision would be benefiting from the market Atari had made, without sharing the cost of its creation. However, the court ruled in Activision's favour, and Activision went on to release their games with their developers' names on the box, finally giving them the recognition they'd craved but been denied at Atari. Activision grew apace, with games like River Raid, Pitfall and Kaboom! becoming huge hits on the VCS and helping Activision to overtake Atari as the fastest-growing company in the history of the USA. It wasn't long before more Atari employees followed Activision's example. One such venture, Imagic (Imagination-Magic), soon did well: Demon Attack, a galaxian-esque title that was their first game, was one of 1982's bestsellers. Imagic also took on ex-Mattel staff, and began to release games for not only the VCS, but the Intellivision too and, later, the ColecoVision. Whereas previously Atari could be confident that, if they released a game for the VCS, it would sell, now that they had competition this was no longer guaranteed – their games had to be good. The indignity of it! Not being able to release poor quality products that were still guaranteed to make huge profits.

Of course, Atari weren't beaten yet. They had a back catalogue of arcade classics like Asteroids, Missile Command and more that they could adapt for the VCS. Atari also got incredibly lucky when it found itself with exclusive rights to Pac-Man on home consoles. This was thanks to a deal made back in 1978 with Atari's Japanese distributor, and creator of Pac-Man, Namco, before they'd had any hit games. Incredibly the deal only required Atari to give Namco fifty cents per $25 cartridge sold. Space Invaders had been a hit, but this had the potential to generate a phenomenal amount of income. The blind luck of this is staggering – the company Atari had paid so little attention to that they didn't give it a second thought when Breakout got ripped off by the Yakuza was now going to gift them a huge windfall. All they had to do was not make a massive mess of the whole thing.

Obviously Atari expected the game to do well, given its domination of the arcades. However, even the most optimistic forecasters should have questioned their production of twelve million Pac-Man cartridges. That's a lot of copies of Pac-Man. If you laid twelve million copies of Pac-Man end-to-end, you could create a path to and from the moon *six* times . . .

I imagine . . . I've not done the maths . . . But it sounds about right.

Anyway, regardless of moon measurements, twelve million

of anything is a lot of copies of a thing. Especially so, when you factor in that, at the time, there had only been ten million VCSs sold. They figured not only would *everyone* buy a copy, but two million more people would buy a VCS just to be able to play Pac-Man at home. Ever so slightly aggressive. Not that Todd Frye, the programmer who made what turned out to be this dreadful version of Pac-Man, cared. He had a deal whereby he got a royalty for every cartridge manufactured. Not sold. Manufactured. Hence the well-known phrase 'A Lucky Frye''.

The game released with an inferior, repetitive map, graphics that were a pale imitation of the original, no 'paku-paku' sound effect as Pac-Man eats the pellets, poor flicker on the ghosts (limitations on how many things the VCS could display at once meant each ghost could only be shown on alternating frames) and no cutscenes. Many people wanted refunds when the game came out, and the release of Pac-Man on the VCS is a key moment in Atari's history. It was a very visible case of Atari releasing a bad game, at a time when rival companies were making games for the VCS of equal or higher quality to theirs, and rival systems with superior hardware to the VCS were available.

And those rival systems kept on coming. One thing neither ColecoVision nor Atari could bring from the arcades to the home was the crispness of Vector games, and this gap was filled in 1982 by the Vectrex, from General Consumer

---

* No, A Lucky Frye isn't actually a thing. But it might be one day. Loads of people don't bother reading footnotes.

Electronics* – not to be confused with General Computer or General Instruments, but only an idiot would make that mistake.

If the Vectrex was anywhere near as innovative as their company's name they'd be sure of a hit. Rather than plugging into televisions like its rivals, to gain the required high-resolution fidelity it came as a tabletop unit that included its own in-built black and white vector monitor. The Vectrex may never have existed at all, if it wasn't for its company's president Ed Krakauer's chance encounter with a supplier who'd had a deal on cardiogram machines fall through. He offered to sell them to Krakauer for less than the cost of manufacture and, at those prices, he could afford to have a game console designed around them, and release it for a competitive $199. This seemed like a good idea until they sold out as, once they did, that was it – it was simply too expensive to make more! At least, that's the yarn often told. Once again it's not true though. It seems people that tell stories about video games in the eighties are mostly compulsive liars. Regardless of its lineage, parents liked the Vectrex as its separate monitor meant the family television was kept free, a big deal when the television was still the only screen in the house, but the system nevertheless struggled to find a place in the market. Other consoles were colour, this was black and white, although they did provide colour overlays to place on the screen, using the same workaround we'd seen with early arcade cabinets and the Magnavox Odyssey.

---

* ★★★ Boring company name klaxon. ★★★

Yet more companies also tried to find a place in this increasingly crowded market: Magnavox with the Odyssey[2], Bally with the Astrocade, and Fairchild with the Channel F 2 (little more than a reworking of the original). Several systems also released add-on voice modules that would allow them to 'speak'. Christmas of 1982 was set to be a real battleground between many competing manufacturers. With all this competition, Atari recognised the need to improve upon its ageing hardware, and threw its hat in the ring with a successor to the VCS, the Atari 5200. It was only at this time that Atari rebranded the VCS as the Atari 2600, to denote its relative status[*]. With many core arcade titles such as Space Invaders, Super Breakout, Defender and more available from its launch in November 1982, you'd struggle to fault its software, but the hardware was still a failure when compared to the Coleco-Vision – the 5200 had inferior graphics, and came at a higher cost. Arguably the worst thing about it though was its controllers. The joysticks didn't self-centre, meaning they just flopped over when you let go[†], thus continuing to send directional requests you didn't want to the console and making games like Pac-Man almost unplayable.

Nineteen eighty-two really wasn't a good year for Atari, but it was about to get even worse. If you think Todd Frye was

---

[*] I imagine this had been eating away at some of you for a very long time. Now you know why I've stuck to calling it the VCS until now, even though only a crazy person wouldn't call it the 2600.

[†] We all know the obvious joke to make here, but let's strive to be better people.

pushing his luck, wait until you meet Steve Ross. The head of Warner Communications (of which Atari was now a subsidiary) had done a deal with Steven Spielberg to make a video game adaptation of the blockbuster movie *E.T.* in the hopes of luring Spielberg into making movies for Warner. The deal promised Spielberg a $25 million royalty from the game, no matter how well it did. Under those terms, the game would have to be incredible to turn a profit. Given this, you would rightly assume that Steve Ross worked closely with the guys at Atari every step of the way to ensure he gave the game every chance of being a hit. But the deal was signed and sealed in late July, before Atari even caught wind of it.

The remit was to get an E.T. game into the shops by Christmas, the time of year when video game sales are traditionally at their highest. While this is true, the *E.T.* movie came out in the summer, so by Christmas it was already going to be a bit behind the times. Furthermore, as Atari's CEO Ray Kassar tried to explain to Steve Ross, it takes at least six months to program a game, get the semiconductors delivered for the cartridges themselves, manufacture it, organise distribution and so on but, by the time Steve Ross pressed go on the project, the guy programming the game had just six *weeks*. For those of you unfamiliar with time, weeks are smaller than months. Your flabber will be gasted when I tell you that, somehow, E.T. the video game turned out to be a big steaming poo. Which is a pity, because they decided to make five million copies.

It wasn't that the guy programming it, Howard Scott Warshaw, wasn't capable of programming something better. His action-shooter, Yar's Revenge (released earlier that year), was the bestselling original game on the VCS. But six weeks simply wasn't enough time and so the game consisted mainly of the colour green, an alien that looked more like a coathanger, and gameplay which was almost exclusively falling in, and getting stuck in, holes. It made Pac-Man on the VCS look good. Which, lest we forget, it wasn't.

The combination of the 5200 and E.T. led Atari to slash its fourth quarter forecast from fifty per cent growth to just ten-to-fifteen per cent. Warner Communications' share price fell by over thirty per cent and Atari was left with several million copies of E.T., both as a result of low sales, and an impressive amount of refunds. So, they did what any sensible person would do – they drove out to the New Mexico desert, dug a massive hole and buried the lot of them*.

To make things worse for Atari, Coleco began to make outlandish bids for licenses to successful arcade games, knowing Atari would then feel the need to outbid them in the hopes of retaining some sort of advantage over the competition, just like those idiots on *Homes Under the Hammer* that bid on development properties way past the point they could ever hope to turn a profit†.

And it wasn't just Atari that was in trouble; the whole industry was on its knees. Atari's high-profile series of errors had dented consumer confidence. The large number of alternative systems had flooded the market. Activision's victory

---

* Yes, really. Check out the documentary *Atari: Game Over*.
† It's only in writing this book I've realised how much daytime TV I watch.

meant that many inferior third parties also entered the market, and so the overall quality of games was in decline. Even advertisers got in on it, leading to titles like American pharmaceutical and consumer goods company Johnson & Johnson's 'Tooth Protectors' game, which was little more than an interactive toothpaste advert, and Purina's 'Chase the Chuck Wagon', promoting dog food. Were it not for the poor quality of these two early games, I'm sure 'toothpaste' and 'dog food' would be up there today along with other genres such as 'platformers' and 'first-person shooters'.

Retail stores were left with many unsold games, so sold them off cheap. They also stopped buying new ones, so games companies' warehouses were left filled with stock. When those companies went bankrupt, liquidators then attempted to shift the merchandise, leading to more games flooding the market, for just $5 instead of the standard $40. Any company that had managed to survive this long would struggle to sell their latest game at full price, regardless of how good it was, given consumers could buy eight alternative (and probably inferior) games instead, to the anti-delight of children everywhere on Christmas and birthdays. And, of course, all of this was happening around the same time we saw the decline of the arcades. To many, it appeared that the whole video game thing had indeed been a fad, albeit one that had managed to get a second wind in the late seventies. To make matters even worse, the USA was in the midst of a recession too, with one in ten adults unemployed. Fuel prices were rising, and America's a country that relies on cars, so this reduced people's disposable income.

Hardware manufacturers began to compete on price as well. Mattel reached a point where they were losing something like $70 per unit on the Intellivision which is, obviously, unsustainable. In 1984, they sold the business off to a senior employee who, I can only assume, must have been an absolute idiot. I guess he might have haggled to get something else thrown in to sweeten the deal – perhaps an ice cream truck with a broken freezer, or exclusive rights to distribute vomit-scented pot pourri. Unsurprisingly, the Intellivision struggled on for several years, before ultimately disappearing from the marketplace as a key player.

Coleco decided to abandon the console market in the hopes of moving into the emerging market of home computers with the Coleco Adam, the feeling being that as hardware costs fell, people might be more inclined to purchase a machine that did more than just play games. However, the Adam's eventual release was plagued with defects in both the hardware and the programming, and it never really took off. The company did manage to find success with a line of dolls known as Cabbage Patch Kids, but ultimately went bankrupt in 1988. To be honest, they did well to extend their business for as long as they did, given they were essentially selling the offspring of a man that fell in love with his allotment to children, without getting taken to court for gross indecency.

Atari began selling versions of games it had the licences for on other systems like the Intellivision and ColecoVision, destroying its own exclusivity in a desperate effort to generate income during this tough time. In July 1983 the company suffered yet more bad press when Ray Kassar resigned as CEO after it emerged he'd sold off shares just prior to the company announcing lower-than-forecast profits, historically not an action considered to be a positive indicator of senior management's confidence in a company's future. Despite attempting to save the business through downsizing, and outsourcing of certain roles overseas to lower costs, eventually Warner were unwilling to continue trying to save the sinking ship. Looking for a buyer for Atari's consumer division, they managed to find one who had been having far more luck in the emerging home computers market than Coleco: Jack Tramiel.

5

THE COMPUTERS ARE COMING

Before Jack Tramiel founded his company, Commodore International, in the mid-fifties, he had lived through a great deal. He survived the concentration camp, Auschwitz, and moved to the USA after World War Two ended, joining the US Army where he learned to repair typewriters. While this might not seem to be a traditional military training, in a time before computers the army ran on typing machines. At one point it was even illegal for civilians to buy typing machines as they were needed for the war effort. Frequently, important military documents would be needed in quintuplicate which, it turns out, is a real word.

When Tramiel left the Army, he used money he'd saved to found his own typewriter repair company, eventually moving to Toronto where he secured a contract to manufacture them. Many typewriter manufacturers disappeared as computers began to become commercially available, but Tramiel was always looking to the future. Initially partnering with Casio, Commodore were soon making their own calculators, and by 1976 had acquired the microprocessor manufacturer, MOS Technology, whose 6502 microprocessor would shortly become a key component in many of the leading brands of computer. As a result, Commodore were able to provide themselves with the chip for significantly less than it would cost for their rivals.

One of the earliest computers to use the 6502 was Wozniak's Apple I, which was handmade (including some parts 'borrowed' from Atari). There were only around 150 produced in total – sold for a mischievous $666.66 – but it was good enough to convince his friend Steve Jobs to found the company, Apple Computer. As soon as the Apple I was finished, Woz set to work on its successor, the aforementioned Apple II. A key challenge he set himself was for it to be able to run a version of Breakout in the programming language, BASIC. He wanted proper sound, colour graphics, and connectivity for TV and game controllers, at a price people could afford. Despite various technical challenges, Woz was successful and upon completion he and Jobs demoed it to Commodore's board (including Tramiel) in the hopes of securing funding, but they declined. Don Valentine (early investor in Atari) also declined but did introduce them to Mike Markkula, a former Intel employee who helped out. This delay in financing had one particularly frustrating disadvantage for Apple. By the time the Apple II launched, Commodore had already released their own solution, the Commodore PET (Personal Electronic Transactor), which included keyboard, monitor and cassette facility for just $599, less than half the price of the Apple II. A third company, Tandy, also entered the market with the TRS-80, which they sold via their Radio Shack stores. TRS-80 might sound like gibberish, but it was actually an abbreviation for 'Tandy/Radio Shack, Z80' (Tandy having opted for the 6502's main rival, Zilog's Z80 microprocessor).

Despite the higher price, Apple still managed to carve out their place in the market thanks to one vital factor – the Apple II was in colour whereas the TRS-80 and PET remained monochrome. Lest we forget, we've whizzed back in time here from the previous chapters, all the way to 1977 in fact, the year all three of these systems were released. That's one year before the black and white Space Invaders arrived in the arcade with its colour overlays stuck on the screen. A colour computer really was cutting edge, and this was the very dawn of the consumer market for home computers, although the high price meant they were still very much of limited appeal.

Unsurprisingly, it wasn't long before Atari got involved. The Atari 400 and 800 both launched in 1979 and were actually very similar to each other. The main difference was that the 800 had a proper typewriter-style keyboard rather than a cheap plastic sheet 'membrane' one – which offers similar reliability and accuracy to when you try to subtly send a text message on a smartphone without looking at the screen, while drunk. And this was a time before autocorrect.

The 800 also had a disk drive, whereas the 400 supported slower-loading cassettes. Both had a cartridge slot, though, and many of Atari's classic games were released on the system, with more advanced versions than those found on the Atari 2600 thanks to the computers' superior graphics capabilities. In fact, the Atari 5200 games console released three years later in 1982 was pretty much a reskinned version of the 400/800, albeit with keyboard, disk drive, etc. removed, and benefiting from the reduced cost of its hardware in the intervening three years. Neither the 400 nor the 800 ever really caught on. The 800 was a computer that failed to compete on spec with the Apple II or Commodore PET, and the 400 was an overpriced console. Furthermore, whereas Apple encouraged third parties to make software for their machine, Atari threatened to sue anyone for doing the same*. Texas Instruments also entered the market in 1979 with the TI-99/4 (and later, a revamped model, the TI-99/4a) but ended up exiting the market after unsuccessfully attempting to compete against Commodore in a price war they were ill-equipped to win.

The high price of computers in the late seventies really was a huge barrier to their acceptance by a wider market. Even if people could afford one, many weren't quite sure what they'd do with it if they did! A common one people would talk about at the time was cataloguing record collections but I can't begin to imagine how computers helped. If you kept your collection in alphabetical order, or maybe categorised by genre, why would you need to fire up your computer before walking over to the shelf your records were on? And if your record collection was stored more haphazardly, how on earth was being able to search for an obscure album track on your computer going to be any help in finding the particular record it was on in the Stig's dump you called your lounge?

Given how utterly useless computers were, and are, for anything other than games†, thankfully there'd been plenty

---

* Remember, the Activision/Atari legal battle didn't end until 1982.

† It's possible I may be slightly biased.

more since 1962's Spacewar! on the PDP-1. Enthusiasts with access to early computers through educational establishments, big business or government departments continued, incredibly, to be allowed to develop their creative ideas and, when computers entered the home, people looked to these pioneering hobbyists for inspiration. Many of the earliest computers had lacked screens, instead relying on printouts for output so, naturally, turn-based games were well suited to them. As a result, there are a number of examples of adaptations of simple games like Tic-Tac-Toe and Hangman, or board games like Draughts and Battleships. Within this context, sport might less obviously be suited to printer-based gaming but the limitations of the systems were seen as creative challenges to overcome. Don Daglow's Baseball (1971) allowed a player to manage their team in a game, reporting each outcome via printout like a radio transcription. Printers weren't fast back then, so this would have been an incredibly slow and tedious process, but in a way that makes it far more like baseball than more recent interpretations.

An iconic game in the USA, The Oregon Trail, was created on an HP 2100 computer that same year, to teach children about nineteenth-century pioneers, although it wasn't until several years later that this early version began to be adapted and enhanced for other, more widely available systems, giving a whole generation of American youths a disproportionate expectation of death from dysentery. Even Lunar Lander, Atari's impressive vector game from 1979, had taken inspiration from this period. 1969's Lunar on the PDP-8 allowed a player to input how much thrust to use based on a report of current speed and remaining fuel, with each gameplay 'round' representing one second of travel time. A graphical version had also surfaced in 1973, having been commissioned by DEC (Digital Equipment Corporation)* to demonstrate the capabilities of their cutting edge DEC GT40 graphics terminals.

That same year, Steve Colley created Maze on an Imlac PDS-1 at a NASA research centre, becoming the first game to use a system's graphics to create a 3D world with a first-person view. The following year, Greg Thompson and Dave Lebling at MIT adapted it (remember, at the time people frequently shared and improved upon each other's code) to allow for up to eight people to compete against each other on multiple systems connected via ARPANET†, giving us the first online 'deathmatch' almost twenty years before Doom would define the genre. Such was its popularity, legend has it that it was soon banned as half of all data on the network whizzing between Stanford and MIT was due to the game. Maze even had computer-controlled players for when eight humans weren't available, and the ability for players to send each other text messages during gameplay. Another early game to incorporate 3D graphics was Bruce Artwick's late-seventies flight simulator which, by 1982, had been licensed to Microsoft, and released as Microsoft Flight Simulator 1.00, some three years

---

* ★★★ Boring company name klaxon. ★★★
† ARPANET was the precursor to the modern internet, created by the Advanced Research Projects Agency (ARPA – hence – ARPA NETwork) for the United States Department of Defense.

before the release of their first version of Windows (at this time, Microsoft were focused on MS-DOS, their text-based operating system*).

An Atari game influenced by another early title was 1979's hit on the VCS, Adventure, which was a visual interpretation of Will Crowther's 1976 PDP-10 game, Colossal Cave Adventure (sometimes referred to as 'ADVENT' as this was its file name when it was passed around between people)†. The game was originally created by Crowther just to amuse his children. A story would unfold and occasionally the player would be prompted to enter simple commands such as 'drink water' or 'throw knives', basic language more reminiscent of the way I speak when hung-over, and drunk, respectively. Despite this simplicity, the original game was huge for its time, taking up 256KB of memory‡. When Scott Adams attempted to adapt it for the TRS-80 as Adventureland he had to make a number of compromises to squeeze it into just 16KB. He succeeded, and Adventureland became the first text-adventure for home computers.

---

* MS-DOS was actually a development of 86-DOS which Microsoft had purchased from a company called Seattle Computer Products (★★★ Boring company name klaxon. ★★★).

† Actually, it was Don Woods' adaptation of Colossal Cave Adventure that was the main influence. Crowther's original version was considered lost until discovered in 2007 in an archive of Woods' Stanford student account.

‡ Remember, at the time Atari VCS games were just 2KB or 4KB, so this should give you some sense of the difference between these institution's massive computers and home systems.

The influence of Colossal Cave Adventure was so great, though, that he was by no means the only person inspired by it. When several friends at MIT adapted it for what would become known as Zork, they actually made it bigger (a massive 1MB), giving the game a fantasy setting and developing a language parser which allowed the computer to interpret more complex sentences – instead of 'open chest' the player could type something like 'go to the chest and open it' and the computer would filter the key words and respond accordingly. It could even manage more complex ideas like 'drop everything *except* the lantern'. While the PDP-10 could manage this huge game, when they finally began to adapt it for release to the consumer market via their new company, Infocom, they had to break it down and split it into three separate games. This did nothing to hamper the trilogy's success though – Zork 1, 2 and 3 were some of the first commercially successful games on home computers, adapted for almost every available machine.

Part of the appeal for players was that the text-only style forced people to imagine the visuals, like reading a book, allowing their minds to conjure up images far in advance of what any computer of the time could have managed. This literary flavour to some games, along with the more considered, turn-based gameplay of many titles (both a result of creative solutions to technical limitations) led to computer games gaining a reputation for appealing more to a person's intellectual side, when contrasted with the immediacy of video games. This was to some extent further enhanced by computers also being used for word processing, digital address books, pointlessly filing record collections and so on, rather than consoles which were seen primarily as toys.

Many others would continue to build on the foundations of Colossal Cave Adventure too. Roberta and Ken Williams met just after graduating from high school, and were married before they turned twenty. Ken got a job as a programmer and from time to time would bring a computer terminal home, and would show Roberta (who was at home looking after their two children) games like Colossal Cave Adventure, with its printer output. As if it wasn't weird enough that companies and institutions were letting people use their expensive computers to make games, they were now seemingly letting employees take them home to play games too. Imagine trying to walk out of your office today with the company printer, explaining to security that 'it's okay, I'm going to play games on it'. Somehow, Ken got away with it, and Roberta enjoyed playing the game, but felt she could create something better. Her first attempt was to adapt the Agatha Christie novel *And Then There Were None*, a current bestseller, as a game, which she mapped out on paper. She convinced Ken to code the game, which they subsequently dubbed 'Mystery House', on their new Apple II computer, and Ken even created an algorithm to allow it to include colour images to complement each scene, a rare improvement over the mostly text-only titles of the time.

In 1980, there wasn't really an established method yet for distributing games, so entrepreneurs like the Williamses would simply copy it themselves, photocopy some instructions, and then distribute them in sandwich bags to anyone who'd stock them (places such as Radio Shack in the US) which led to an amusing incident on one occasion, where they accidentally left their sandwiches at a shop, and almost ate their game*.

Charging $24.95 for Mystery House, they initially assumed it'd just be a fun hobby but within three months they'd made over $50,000. Wasting no time, they moved to a new home near Sierra National Forest in California, and renamed their company Sierra Online.

They followed up the game with several more, and were soon doing so well they were offering other programmers free accommodation in exchange for a thirty per cent royalty for publishing their games, and employed Ken's old boss, Don Sutherland, to look after the management side of things. One sign-up during this period would be Al Lowe, who would go on to create the notorious Leisure Suit Larry games. Another was Richard Garriott, with Sierra publishing the sequel to his smash-hit game, Ultima.

Garriott was carving out a name for himself as one of the earliest innovators in the emerging genre of role-playing games (RPGs). Beginning in 1979, his forerunner to the Ultima series, Akalabeth: World of Doom, was an early home title to offer a first-person view. Words like 'Doom' and 'Akalabeth' might make it all sound very cool and edgy, but that's somewhat undermined by the fact the illustration on the game's instructions was drawn by his mum.

---

* No, of course they didn't, but if every other book about video games can perpetuate myths, I figure I'm allowed to invent a couple of new ones.

Prior to Akalabeth, Garriott had been creating text adventures based on the hugely successful fantasy tabletop game Dungeons & Dragons on his school's PDP-11, not in any official capacity, purely for fun. He may never have got the far more ambitious Akalabeth game working if his father hadn't bet him half the cost of an Apple II that he wouldn't manage it. When he did complete the game, he had no idea selling it was even an option, but when his boss at a computer store said it was better than what they were selling, Garriott went into business. In a similar way to the rapid success of Sierra, Garriott made $150,000 in a very short amount of time, so decided he'd probably stick with it. He stuck with his education too, though, and his follow-up, Ultima, was created in spare time with a friend, Ken Arnold, during his freshman year at the University of Texas. It would have been called 'Ultimatum', but they found out a board game company was already using that name, so they shortened it.

He managed to make even more money than with Akalabeth, but had frustrations with the publisher he'd signed up with, California Pacific Computer*, so the sequel, Ultima 2, ended up being published by Sierra. By that point though, he was making so much money he set up his own publishing company, Origin Systems, which would publish the series, and many other games, thereafter. These games really were hugely popular†. Ultima 3: Exodus, released in 1983, continued Garriott's successful run, but there was some backlash

---

* ★★★ Boring company name klaxon. ★★★

† Another series that began around the same time, Wizardry from Sir-

about the game's moral ambiguity so, from Ultima 4 onwards, the series began to implement a reward system to encourage good behaviour, although the player wouldn't necessarily realise they'd fallen foul of it at first. Short change the blind shopkeeper and you'll get away with it, but when you go back later she'll refuse to share information with you as punishment for being a dirty little thief.

Sierra might have lost the Ultima franchise, but they soon had another hit of their own with 1984's King's Quest, the first adventure game to have animated graphics and a protagonist worthy of the game's epic-sounding title: Graham. The game did well enough to pay off the debts the company had begun to accrue during the early-eighties 'crash' in the games market, and went on to become a hugely successful series for the company.

It wasn't just the US that saw success in this area. Over in Australia, Beam Software created a text adventure adaptation of the Tolkien novel, *The Hobbit*, which went on to sell over a million copies. It was one of the earliest games to receive an updated version to address bugs which unintentionally, but brilliantly, included an additional bug that made the game unwinnable. In Japan, Henk Rogers (who had moved there in the mid-seventies to work in his father's gem business) almost single-handedly kick-started the Japanese love of RPGs. The NEC PC-8001 computer represented forty-five per cent of the market in Japan and, as a huge Dungeons & Dragons fan aware

---

Tech, is frequently cited as a huge influence on many that followed and enjoyed similar success.

of the success of games like Ultima, he set to creating his own adventure, The Black Onyx. Upon release in the winter of 1983, though, despite advertising, he barely sold any copies. Traditional dice/pen/paper role-playing games had never caught on in Japan so people just didn't know what to make of Rogers' game. Confident in its quality, he took it upon himself to visit games journalists and educate them in the gameplay. Once they understood it, they began to rave about it in their magazines, and eventually The Black Onyx was selling at a rate of 10,000 copies per month. Despite this, it remains virtually unknown in the West to this day.

But we're getting ahead of ourselves. Back in the late seventies, games like Colossal Cave Adventure and Maze had set Roy Trubshaw, a student at the University of Essex in England, to considering the possibility of a virtual world that multiple people could inhabit together. His friend Richard Bartle encouraged him to make the text-based world he was attempting to create more game-like and when Trubshaw got busy with his degree, Bartle set to completing it. He added puzzles to the world, and added levels to show players' progress too, but made them terms like 'warrior' and 'necromancer' rather than just a numerical progression like Level 1, Level 2, Level 3 and so on. Released in 1980 as 'MUD', which stood for Multi-User Dungeon, the title was a nod to an early FORTRAN port of Zork they'd enjoyed, known by its filename DUNGEN (dungeon). The game may not have spread to the extent it did, had it not been for British Telecom testing something in 1983 called EPSS – the Experimental Packet Switching System. This allowed some universities (including the University of Essex) to connect to ARPANET, which meant Bartle and Trubshaw could connect to other sites like Xerox PARC, Stanford University, MIT and others across the globe, and allow computer users in those locations to access MUD. Around the same time, the University of Essex also let users outside their campus log in to its computer systems during off-peak times, which further grew MUD's reach.

As MUD spread, many programmers began to create their own versions, with their own original virtual worlds – or unoriginal in the case of the free-to-play MUD, Rock, which was based on the kids TV show *Fraggle Rock*. The biggest of them all though was AberMUD, based at Aberystwyth University. While it wasn't considered the best version, crucially it ran under the Unix operating system, which was what most US universities were using. Within six months of release, there were a thousand copies running in America. These games became generically known as MUDs but, given that people could play them at home over dial-up modems, they really missed a trick by not calling them baud games.[*]

While all that was going on, William Hawkins III (nicknamed 'Trip' by his grandmother as he was the third William in the family), was founding Electronic Arts. Hawkins is a very dif-

---

[*] Baud (pronounced 'board') rate is a way of measuring transmission speeds of early modems and this is great wordplay that is, sadly, comedically unsatisfying in its delivery, no matter how many hours I spend reworking this paragraph.

ferent character to many of the people we've met so far. He wasn't an engineer spending his nights programming and playing games in the University's lab, although he was at Stanford. He was an MBA graduate, and before his time at Stanford he'd also studied at Harvard, but his expertise was in marketing. As such, he viewed the emerging business of video games in a very different way to most. He'd actually spent time working at Apple, where he'd helped with their strategy for introducing the Apple II to the business market. When Apple went public, Hawkins became an overnight millionaire. He'd also met Don Valentine during his time there, who provided him with an office when he left Apple to begin building Electronic Arts.

The company took an approach not dissimilar to Hollywood movie studios – have development, production, publishing and distribution all under one roof and, like Activision, Electronic Arts emphasised the importance of its games' designers, hence a name which celebrates the artistry involved in creating them. Bringing his marketing nous to things, Hawkins was conscious of how much packaging plays a part in successful product sales, and he decided his games would have the equivalent of music's album covers, so their games came in custom boxes with attractive artwork and the game's creators' names displayed prominently, rather than the clear plastic bags with photocopied instructions that were the norm in the computer game market until this point. Yes, all it took to stand out in the market at this point and look professional was to put your product in a box. And not just any box – a massive box. These things could have easily stored thirty or forty floppy disks instead of the one or two commonly found inside and are the main cause of global warming*.

EA made the decision to create their games for multiple platforms from the very beginning: Apple, Atari, Commodore and more, and did well as a result. Early successes included Hard Hat Mack, which was reminiscent of Donkey Kong, and Pinball Construction Set, which was helped in its success by computers' ability to allow people to save their creations (console cartridges weren't able to do this yet)[†]. The game was also notable for its early implementation of 'point and click' controls. We might take this for granted, but it was the first time many people had seen and interacted with a Graphical User Interface (GUI). However, it was by no means an original idea. In 1979, during Hawkins' time at Apple, he and Steve Jobs had visited Xerox, where they saw a system called the Xerox Alto. The system had a mouse you used to move a cursor, windows you could move and reshape on screen, icons you could click on to run programs, a word processor with the ability to cut and paste, and more. The system had actually been created all the way back in 1973, but somewhat unbelievably the company had made no real effort to commercialise it. Steve Jobs left, his head spinning, and set to work immediately on the follow-up to the Apple II, which would introduce GUIs to

---

* Pretty sure it's actually cow farts, but I've not checked.

† Being able to create your own gameplay was emerging as an exciting novelty. Another game, the platformer Lode Runner, from the prolific US publisher Broderbund, offered gamers a level editor.

the market: 1983's Apple Lisa. Unfortunately, that cost $9,995 so it didn't do great – even by Apple standards, the price point was pushing it – but the next year, the Apple Macintosh was released for $1,995* and it played a huge part in making computers, which until that point had seemed alienating to many, feel far more intuitive†. Microsoft's first version of Windows was released the following year, bringing GUIs to PCs, but it was not until Windows 3.1 in 1990 that they really established the PC as a rival in this regard.

Electronic Arts, having chosen to enter the games industry in early 1982 when industry growth seemed almost inevitable, were somewhat caught off guard when, by the following year, the industry was entering what Hawkins himself described as the 'dark ages of interactive entertainment'. Any aspirations to enter the crumbling console market seemed unwise now and, as the computer game market grew, there were already growing concerns about piracy, due to the easier duplication of cassettes and floppy disks. Certainly, if you grew up around this time, you almost certainly had a music system with a twin cassette deck that, as far as I can tell, was used exclusively for music and video game piracy. None of us spent the eighties trying to become the new Jazzy Jeff by simultaneously playing two *Now That's What I Call Music* tapes.

The computer game market was increasingly fragmented

---

* Still a huge price tag, but within reach of businesses.
† ICOM Solutions' 1985 Macintosh game Déjà Vu was one of the first titles to make use of this new interface to help establish the 'point and click adventure' genre.

with growing numbers of rival computers of differing capabilities, and it was by no means an easy time for aspiring game publishers. Nevertheless, Hawkins persevered, and sought to differentiate Electronic Arts' games from the competition. Through a friend of a friend, he was able to reach out to Julius Irving, a basketball star of the time, to enquire about using his name, and likeness, for a video game based on the sport. This was the first time celebrity endorsement was used in the games industry, rather than a more general licensing of a sport as a whole, or a successful movie. Hawkins reached out to another player via their agent, Dr. J and Larry Bird Go One on One came to be. While it did well, it hasn't stood the test of time in the same way some of EA's later sports licences would, but it was good enough for them to continue to pursue the idea. In 1984, Hawkins began a relationship with John Madden to create an American football game, but Madden's demand for realism meant it would be years before their first collaboration would reach the market. Not all of this was unreasonable. One early version of the game presented to Madden neglected to include a full roster of players, and omitted the linemen – the big guys that try to stop the defending team from getting to the quarterback. While this was done to help the game run smoothly (the Apple II on which it was being developed couldn't handle a full line-up of players on each team), Madden was understandably indignant, given that when he was a player, he'd been a lineman.

While Stanford MBAs making lucrative deals with sports celebrities is all very glamorous, across the Atlantic in the UK there was a far more grass-roots revolution taking place, thanks in no small part to a man who wanted to put the power and potential of computers into the hands of as many people as possible: Clive Sinclair, known affectionately by his fans as 'Uncle Clive'. I appreciate that these days the idea of a public figure being referred to as 'uncle' seems a bit weird, but these were different times, and it's not Clive's fault everyone else turned out to be dreadful. He introduced the Sinclair ZX80 to the UK in 1980, available in kit form for a mere £79.95 (or pre-made for an additional £20). By far the cheapest computer to date, it could still compete with computers that cost several times as much. It was followed up the following year by the ZX81, which was even cheaper, and even more powerful. The ZX81 was a huge success, inspiring many people to make and sell their own games and, just as in America, this began as a bedroom industry, with programmers copying their own games onto disks and cassettes. The primary method of distributing them initially was through the postal system, as there were very few retailers in the UK that sold computer games. One of the earliest hits in the UK was Kevin Toms' Football Manager on the ZX81, a text-only game that allowed the player to manage their own association football team. So addictive was the game, and the many similar titles that continue to this day, that the game has been cited in numerous divorce cases. On one occasion, a soldier out in Afghanistan was late leaving his base because he was stuck playing an FA Cup Semi Final. That's bad enough, obviously; soldiers are meant to obey orders. But it's much worse than that because the base was under heavy mortar attack while he was playing. I know we're all meant to keep calm and carry on else the terrorists win, but I don't think that applies to soldiers.

Commodore enjoyed success in the USA similar to Sinclair in the UK when they launched the VIC-20 in 1981, where at $300 it was far cheaper than rivals like Apple/Tandy/Atari. Tramiel even went as far as employing none other than Captain Kirk, William Shatner, to advertise it on US television. Back in the UK, the VIC-20 struggled to compete due to the incredibly low price of Sinclair's offerings, but the BBC* Micro, which was launched around the same time, managed to do slightly better, by targeting a different audience. Created by Acorn Computers† (founded by former Sinclair employee Chris Curry – the UK computer scene was similarly incestuous to its US counterpart), the BBC's computer tended to be more for educational use, having been released as part of a campaign to increase computer literacy in young people. Quite why the organisation responsible for *Swap Shop* and the *Shipping Forecast* took it upon themselves to teach everyone computers, I've no idea, but if you were at school in the UK during this time, it's very likely you had access to one.

The BBC Micro had those massive CD-sized floppy disks that were actually floppy, rather than the 3.5" ones that had hard cases. While the system may have been intended to

---

* In case you're unaware, this is the same BBC known as the British Broadcasting Corporation, the UK's public service broadcaster.

† Acorn Computers would go on to release a budget version of the BBC Micro known as the Acorn Electron, which for a brief time did well in the UK, certainly better than the lesser-spotted Oric-1 or Dragon 32/64.

educate, it's impossible to speak of the BBC Micro without immediately acknowledging Elite, the game from David Braben and Ian Bell. Initially more of an arcade game in style, the addition early on in its development of space stations to dock onto led the pair to consider what one might do in such a place. The potential for upgrades to your ship occurred to Braben and Bell, but upgrades would require money. This led to the idea of trade, but also bounties for the space battles from which the game had originally spawned. Visiting planets could be for the purpose of mining valuable resources.

The game's simple wireframe visuals were reminiscent of vector monitors and it is notable for its scope: eight entire galaxies, each with 256 planets, were available to the player on a single floppy disk thanks to an algorithm allowing the game's universe to be procedurally generated. The BBC Micro game that's etched into my memory alongside all my worst nightmares though is Podd, a game in which children could instruct an on-screen character to weep, splutter or, most worryingly of all, burst. No doubt a clear line could be drawn between today's sociopathic lack of empathy between strangers on social media and the state-funded training our children received in the early eighties in coercing someone to explode.

Nineteen eighty-two would have seen the release of the ZX82, had Sinclair not changed its name late on in development to the ZX Spectrum to emphasise the latest machine's colour output (the ZX80 and ZX81 were monochrome). As with all of Sinclair's machines, the remit was to make it as cheap as possible, and accordingly the keyboard's buttons were the smallest size they could be. Each button on the

Spectrum had a BASIC command, the longest of which was 'RETURN' on the Y key. This in turn determined the Spectrum's width, and the available space meant the space bar was instead just another button, in the bottom right corner. Sinclair seemed to have an obsession with shrinking technology wherever possible, his most notable failure being the Sinclair C5 electric vehicle, which had more in common aesthetically with a slip-on shoe than a car.

Again, while the Spectrum dominated the UK in 1982, Commodore's next effort, the Commodore 64 (C64), did the same in the USA. Sinclair had beaten Commodore to the market in Europe, but in America he simply couldn't compete with the C64's marketing. Commodore's success under Tramiel was truly exceptional. In 1977, 100 shares in the company would have cost you less than $200. By 1983, those shares were worth over $70,000. Nineteen eighty-three was the year Commodore overtook Apple in sales, becoming the first company to report revenue in excess of $1 billion. As the console market declined, and the price of computers like the Spectrum and Commodore 64 began to seem within the reach of consumers, the games market began to really take off. And, while computers might still not have been cheap, many of the games were retailing at much lower prices.

The first big hit for the Spectrum, Manic Miner, retailed for just £5.95. Created by Matthew Smith, inspired by the US platform game Miner 2049er which had launched on the Atari 400/800, Smith added surreal touches that were characteristic of much of the UK's output during this period. The game was so successful it allowed Smith to create his own company, Software Projects, through which he released the equally successful sequel, Jet Set Willy. Given how well Manic Miner had done, you might not be surprised its follow-up did so well, but you might be more surprised when you discover the game was impossible to complete due to a series of bugs. In a time before one could simply download an update, this was problematic, though not unsolvable, as they eventually released a set of POKEs (essentially, things users could type into their computer to correct the errors in the game) to combat the issue. Jet Set Willy also had an ingenious approach to copy protection, providing a card with 180 colour codes with each game, at a time when colour photocopying was still basically witchcraft. These days we could just take a photo on our smartphone; back then you had to engage the skills of your local wizard.

There were many great games during this period. There were stranger ones like Hitchhiker's Guide to the Galaxy*, which included your very own packet of 'pocket fluff' with every purchase, and Deus Ex Machina (as much an experience as a game), which provided a separate forty-six-minute audio-cassette with a soundtrack featuring celebrities as diverse as Frankie Howerd, Jon Pertwee and Ian Dury. Then there were more straightforward titles like Boulderdash and Skool Daze although, as a game that included the potential to catch mumps, it wasn't entirely pedestrian and, of course, there were many more RPGs such as Michael Cranford's The Bard's

---

* Based on the book of the same name by Douglas Adams and actually co-designed by Adams himself.

Tale. One company that had a particular knack for turning out hits during this time was Ultimate Play The Game, founded by Chris and Tim Stamper. Their very first game, JetPac, sold an unprecedented 300,000 copies and the pair went on to create many more hits such as Atic Atac*, Knight Lore, Underwurlde and JetPac's sequel Lunar Jetman.

Another person we simply must mention is Jeff Minter, who founded his own company Llamasoft to release games such as Attack of the Mutant Camels, Metagalactic Llamas Battle at the Edge of Time, Sheep in Space and many other even-toed-ungulate-based titles. The low cost of entry in the home computer gaming scene facilitated a spirit of creativity embodied by people like Minter that simply could not be afforded in the far more costly business of creating games for the arcade or consoles. Wonderfully, anyone with a cheap computer, an animal fetish, and the determination to program a game then sit and make copies onto discs or cassettes, could attempt to build a career. Of course, the downside of this is that there were many poor-quality games that were sometimes hard for consumers to filter through in order to find the gems.

The Commodore 64 was, and is, the highest-selling single computer model of all time. Given how well they were doing, you'd think that everything was rosy back at HQ. However, Tramiel was constantly at loggerheads with the company's

---

* Cited as an inspiration for UK children's TV hit, *Knightmare*.

main investor and chairman, Irving Gould. Though the company had been founded by Tramiel, Gould had a huge say in all matters and, when Tramiel announced plans to bring his three sons in to help run the 'family' business, Gould refused. Tramiel threatened to quit if he didn't get his way, but Gould still refused and so Tramiel quit his company in January 1984. Before you feel too sorry for them though, the company was turning over $100 million per year by this point, so they'd probably manage to scrape by somehow.

We're now back to where we began this chapter, but with a lot more context. Tramiel was determined to destroy Commodore, and with Atari's consumer division for sale (the home computers and consoles bit), he could purchase an existing business that would allow him to hit the ground running with factories, warehouses and so on. This new entity owned by Tramiel became known as Atari Corporation*, whereas the bit Warner retained (the coin-op side of the business) became known as Atari Games. Tramiel and his sons, who he brought in to work for Atari Corporation, wasted no time in taking a hatchet to anything they saw as waste. They were ruthless. The company went through even more downsizing, and any equipment that seemed unnecessary was sold off, although employees, sensing the writing was on the wall, helped themselves to a fair amount of it before it could be sold. He also withdrew most of Atari's existing product line of computers (by this point there were a number of models on the market), and set the company to work on the next

---

* Warner actually held on to 25 per cent of the company.

generation of hardware, with the help of many Commodore engineers he'd convinced to migrate over with him.

There's someone else I'd like you to meet now: Atari's Jay Miner. Having played a key part in the development of the chips in the Atari 2600/5200 consoles and the Atari 400/800 computers, he'd begun work on a next-generation computer based on the Motorola 68000 microprocessor, but in the early eighties, prior to Tramiel's acquisition, Atari decided to halt work on it. So, instead, Miner jumped ship and eventually found himself working for a new hardware company that would become known as Amiga Corporation. The business struggled during the 1983 crash but, thankfully, the new chips he'd been working on were sufficiently impressive with regard to their graphics and sound capabilities that when he approached his old employers Atari with his work, the company offered a loan of $500,000 to allow Amiga to continue development of them, in return for a year of exclusivity on the finished products.

Amiga had also had dealings with Tramiel in the past, and had found his goals to be incompatible with their own, by which I mean, they really didn't like him. Few did. In a 1998 interview with *Fortune* magazine, he said: 'Business is war. I don't believe in compromising, I believe in winning.'* Not the easiest person to collaborate with, then. So, when Tramiel took over Atari, Amiga were keen to extricate themselves from their relationship. They reapproached the now Tramiel-less Commodore, and made a deal in which Commodore bought

---

* *Fortune* magazine.

Amiga outright, and agreed to pay off Atari, to put an end to the previous Atari–Amiga exclusivity deal. Amiga were offered the $500,000 they had previously paid, but Tramiel wanted more, and obtained an injunction against Commodore making anything with what he termed 'Atari technology'. While the matter was being settled, Atari were able to get their new computer, the Atari ST, to market in the summer of 1985, ahead of what would become its main rival, Commodore's Amiga 1000. While the Atari ST wouldn't be built using Amiga hardware, some remarked that the level of access Atari had had to Amiga's technology during its development would have certainly been more than helpful . . .

All clear? I hope so. If it isn't, you're going to be livid when I tell you it's even more complicated because companies were going to change hands in the UK the following year too, and I'm going to tell you about that as well.

The follow-up to the ZX Spectrum, the Sinclair QL, had been far less successful and Sinclair ended up selling their entire product range, and the 'Sinclair' brand name, to Amstrad in early 1986. Amstrad (an abbreviation of Alan Michael Sugar Trading*, was a late entry to the 8-bit home computer market, arriving with the Amstrad CPC 464 in 1984. As we've heard several times before, this late entry to the market meant they were able to offer comparable, or better hardware, for a much lower price, and the thing that really helped the CPC was it came with its own monitor, so it didn't have to hijack the family TV. At just £199 with a green

---

*   ★★★ Boring company name klaxon. ★★★

screen monitor, or £299 for a colour one, it included a tape deck within its keyboard unit, a power supply inside the monitor, and only required a single plug to power the whole thing, significantly reducing clutter. For comparison, the monitor-less Commodore 64 was £195.95 and the Spectrum was £175.

Although the Amstrad CPC 464 was the first computer I had as a child, I assure you I'm in no way biased when I tell you that it's the best computer ever, and should have been far more successful than it was*. When we first got the news that my TV show *Go 8-Bit* had been commissioned, I didn't rush out to buy champagne or hit the nightclubs. Instead, I immediately went on eBay to buy an Amstrad CPC 464, then drove to Great Yarmouth with my dad to collect it. No biggie, I'm just a cool guy, and that's what cool guys do.

This was by no means an impulse buy – I had long wanted to revisit the system that had begun my passion over thirty years earlier. You might imagine that a fully reconditioned system like the one I purchased would set me back a lot of money, but it actually cost £80 – an amount which manages to be disappointing in two ways by simultaneously not being large enough to be impressive, and also not being small enough to seem like a bargain.

One game I particularly remember that came bundled in originally was Animal Vegetable Mineral. The cassette had a list of animals, vegetables, and things-that-aren't-animals-or-vegetables on it. It then tried to guess what you were thinking

---

* Fact.

of and, if it couldn't work it out, which it usually couldn't, you told it. No great mystery really but, as a small child, all I knew was that the computer seemed to be talking to me, and knew if I was thinking about a cat. And that was terrifying.

Amstrad even had their own game publishing label, Amsoft, and a mascot, Roland, named after Roland Perry, the company's technical consultant. If you're familiar with Roland and have ever wondered why he looks different in each game it's because, rather than spending time or money creating Roland games, they just bought up the rights to random games and slapped the name Roland on them. In a way, Roland was the one-man Sugababes of his time*.

We've covered quite a lot of ground in this chapter, and it's understandable to see how, by the mid-eighties, many in the West were certain that the days of dedicated hardware that could only play games was over. Computers were more versatile, and gamers could get a lot more for their money. There had been computers in Japan too, of course, although different ones to those found in the West, partly due to the need for higher-resolution displays to accommodate the more complex Japanese text. NEC's PC-88/98 series was the market leader, but they also found competition from Sharp's X1, Fujitsu's FM-7 and Microsoft Japan's MSX (an early attempt to unify hardware standards, which found favour with games

---

* This is such a strange comparison you have to question my judgement in including it.

developers as a result*), among others. However, on the horizon was a Japanese console that would show people that reports of the home video game industry's death had been greatly exaggerated.

---

* Companies like Konami and Hudson Soft would make games for the platform. Konami's famous Metal Gear series, for example, began on the MSX's successor, the MSX2, and Hudson Soft's Bomberman was on pretty much every computer model in Japan.

6

NINTENDO DOMINATE

In May 1983, Nintendo launched the Famicom (short for Family Computer*) in Japan but, despite the name, it was a video game console, not a computer†. Unlike previous consoles, which had come with joysticks, dials or paddles to control the games, the Famicom's controller opted for the Game & Watch's D-pad. It also had two action buttons, whereas many earlier systems had just had the one. This might not seem that impressive given the number of buttons on a modern controller but, back then, this literally doubled your options.

Despite the success Nintendo would go on to have, the Famicom's launch was inauspicious, to say the least. Design flaws in the original model were significant enough to lead Yamauchi to recall the entire first batch, doing little to enhance the company's reputation. However, within two

---

* ★★★ Boring console name klaxon. ★★★ Yes, I'm sticking with this . . .
† In 1984, Nintendo did release a cartridge, Famicom BASIC, which allowed users to create and save computer programs, thanks to an attachable keyboard and cassette deck (released around the same time).

months, 500,000 were still sold – no doubt helped by the fact that the system launched with near perfect versions of Donkey Kong and Donkey Kong Jr. – and Nintendo soon looked to the American market, hoping to replicate their success.

Retailers there, however, having recently been stung by the market crash, weren't inclined to touch anything that smelt even vaguely like video games and, while Donkey Kong had been huge, most people weren't familiar with the name of the company that made it. Game & Watch had floundered in the USA too, and they had no real distribution network to speak of, so Nintendo of America's Howard Lincoln reached out to Ray Kassar who at the time was still with Atari Corporation, and offered them the licence to sell the Famicom, under the Atari brand, everywhere except Japan. Unbeknown to Nintendo, Atari were already hard at work on the follow-up to the Atari 5200, the Atari 7800. This opportunity gave them the chance to hedge their bets. Atari could gain the worldwide licence to the Famicom, but would be under no obligation to actually sell the thing. If the 7800 turned out well, they could push that, if the Famicom looked the better bet, they could switch their focus to that. They couldn't lose, the sneaky little rascals! Terms were agreed and a contract was drawn up.

The deal would never come to pass, though. At the 1983 Summer Consumer Electronics Show in Chicago, Atari saw Donkey Kong running on the Coleco Adam computer, and they were distinctly unimpressed. Atari had previously negotiated home computer rights for Donkey Kong from Nintendo, allowing them to release it on the Atari 800. Seeing Donkey Kong as such a prominent part of a rival computer's promotional activity led Atari to believe Nintendo were trying to pull a fast one on them, which soured relations. Technically, Coleco hadn't actually done anything wrong. 'Home computer rights' in this instance meant games distributed on floppy disk or cassette. The Coleco Adam computer also had a cartridge slot, and so the cartridge version of Donkey Kong running on the Adam at CES fell within Coleco's rights. But Nintendo knew how quickly Coleco had relented in the Universal/King Kong legal battle and so Yamauchi was brought in to terrify them into ceasing use of the game on the Adam, in the hopes of salvaging the Atari/Famicom negotiations.

Some claim Atari never intended to launch the Famicom in the first place, and that the whole thing was a way for Atari to get an inside look at Nintendo's hardware which it might be able to use for its own products, in much the same way as we saw with regards to the Atari–Amiga–Commodore incident. Regardless, Kassar was fired the following month, and negotiations stalled. This was a setback for Nintendo, and the Famicom remained in Japan only throughout 1983 and 1984. During this time, Nintendo sold over three million units and so Yamauchi revisited the idea, this time with the aim of getting Nintendo's American office to handle the launch themselves.

In January 1985, at the Consumer Electronics Show (CES) in Las Vegas, Nintendo introduced the Famicom to the US market, as the renamed 'Advanced Video System'. Doing everything they could to make it not look like a video game console, which was still a big no-no there, it was demonstrated as a full home computer, complete with a keyboard, cassette deck and

BASIC cartridge. Short of giving it one of those little spinny sand-timers so you could use it to cook eggs too, there's very little more they could have done to distract people from the truth of what it was. The response was still very muted though so, for the summer CES in Chicago, they lost the computer peripherals and rebranded it as the 'Nintendo Entertainment System' (NES)*. Included within the package this time would be two new add-ons. The first, the Zapper, was a light gun similar to those consumers had seen in previous years, and allowed Nintendo to create home versions of their popular arcade light gun games like Hogan's Alley, Wild Gunman and Duck Hunt. In Japan, the gun was designed to look realistic but, in America, it was made to look far more like a toy because, frankly, they can't be trusted.

The second add-on was somewhat stranger. R.O.B. (the Robotic Operating Buddy) was a two-foot-tall plastic robot created by Gunpei Yokoi's team that 'watched' your television and responded to the on-screen action within compatible games in what was dubbed the 'Robot series'. This turned out to be somewhat optimistic terminology when the 'series' was canned after just two games. R.O.B. gobbled up batteries, the interactivity he offered could easily be replicated by just pressing the A and B buttons on a second controller and the games were, frankly, rubbish.

Nintendo began to get more interest from retailers, but still left without any commitments to buy. Arakawa was unconvinced that the Americans were ever going to go for it, but

* Always 'Entertainment System', never 'Video Game System'.

Yamauchi persisted, and it was agreed they would do a trial launch in the toughest market in the US: Christmas in New York. As Frank Sinatra once nearly sang, if they could sell a games console there, they could probably sell it in reasonable quantities in many other cities.

To convince reluctant retailers, Nintendo not only offered all stock on sale or return, they also delivered the stock right to the shop floor and set up the displays. All any shop would have to do is provide a space, Nintendo would do the rest. No doubt the company's employees were delighted when they were told their jobs would be expanded to include working extra hours carrying boxes up stairs for no money at Christmas.

Nintendo also spent a small fortune on TV advertising in the area and, while they only managed to sell around half of the 100,000 consoles they'd had shipped from Japan, the NES had been successful enough for many retailers to continue stocking it into 1986. They then began to run similar trials in other regions, but they simply didn't have the resources to distribute fully on a national level, so they reached an agreement with the company Worlds of Wonder, who were riding the wave of success of the bestselling toy of 1985, their talking bear, Teddy Ruxpin*. Founded by several ex-Atari staff members after the company's decline, many of Worlds of Wonder's sales team also migrated over from there, making them well

---

* If you'd have told me when this book was commissioned that it would end up with me talking about the guys that distribute Teddy Ruxpin, I'd have punched you in the face. I still might. I've got a lot of built-up anger.

placed to sell the benefits of video game consoles to retailers*. Their job was made somewhat easier thanks to the arrival of the most advanced video game the world had ever seen: Super Mario Bros.

Given the game's legacy, it may surprise you to discover that no one seems to be able to conclusively say whether the game reached American shores in time for the Christmas 1985 launch. In truth, the reality is probably that it both did, and didn't. It would be several years until video games began to have official launch dates. Rather, games were completed and began to be distributed, and shops would pop them on the shelves when their allocation arrived, as, and when, they got round to putting them out; there wasn't the same fanfare around games' releases then. This whole process might dribble out over several months, so chances are that some stores had Super Mario Bros. before Christmas, if any made it across the ocean from Japan, whereas others didn't have it on the shelves until the following year.

Irrespective of when it was released, Super Mario Bros. is inarguably a landmark in video games. Rather than being a single-screen platformer, as had been the case with the Donkey Kong games and the original Mario Bros., as well as titles like the Atari 2600's Pitfall from Activision, Super Mario

* When Worlds of Wonder went bankrupt in 1987 after overestimating the continued demand for expensive, speaking, robot bears, Nintendo recruited their sales team and thus ended up employing precisely the people they'd been trying to access when they originally reached out to Atari to help them distribute the NES in the US.

Bros.'s platforming action was 'side-scrolling', allowing Mario to dash through longer levels populated with an impressive variety of colourful scenery and creatures. The game's very first level is a masterclass in design, subtly introducing the player to all the main gameplay elements through action, removing the need for any pauses in the fun through text explanations. We take many of the mechanics in Mario for granted now but, back then, no one had ever jumped up to punch a '?' block, and children were actively encouraged *not* to pick up and eat mushrooms they found sliding around on the floor. Super Mario Bros. rewarded curious players. Smashing blocks might provide the player with strength, invincibility or the ability to shoot, and explorers could find hidden worlds in the sewers or the skies, or even skip entire worlds altogether in a rush for the finish. We can't mention the game without praising Koji Kondo's soundtrack* too, as it remains recognisable to this day by even the most casual gamer.

Super Mario Bros. holds the distinction of being the first time I saw a game instantly load from a cartridge instead of from a cassette over the course of several weeks. It was as mind-blowing to me then as those little taps posh people have now that give you instant boiled water so you don't need a kettle. If you're reading this in the future, you may take those for granted although, based on how this year (2018) has gone it's more likely that you're all boiling your

---

* Koji Kondo would go on to compose the music for many of Nintendo's biggest games.

own urine to cook rats in and found this book in the ruins of a Waterstones.

Incredibly, given how much of Nintendo's future success would hinge on their loveable plumber, the first Super Mario Bros. game was not, in fact, exclusive to the system. It, and many other Famicom games, were ported to Japanese home computers like the Sharp X1 and NEC PC-88 by Hudson Soft. The computer version of the first Super Mario game is worth seeking out by aficionados thanks to differences in level design, power-ups and enemies. Of course, you won't bother, that'd be far too much effort, but it's the sort of thing one's meant to say in these sorts of situations.

As we've drifted back on to the subject of Japanese home computers, now's probably as good a time as any to mention another company dipping their toe in those waters, a company we've met several times before, and will be spending a lot of time with in the coming chapters: Sega. In 1983 they had released the SC-3000 and the SG-1000. Two variations of the same product, the 'SC' (Sega Computer) had a built-in keyboard, allowing the user to program on it*, while the 'SG' (Sega Game) was a bare-bones video game console. Over the next two years, Sega would introduce incremental improvements to the hardware, such as the SG-1000 Mark II, then the Sega

---

* No doubt the SG-1000/SC-3000 had some influence on Nintendo's approach with the Famicom's later release of keyboard, cassette deck, etc.

Mark III. This last model is of note as it was rebranded and released in the USA in 1986, as the 'Sega Master System'.

Since we last met Sega, they've been through a number of changes. The company was purchased by an American conglomerate, Gulf & Western, in the late sixties, but David Rosen stayed on as president. When the market crashed in the early eighties, Rosen put in a rescue bid for Sega, along with several investors, including one Hayao Nakayama. Nakayama's company had been successfully building an empire and, rather than try to compete, Rosen had acquired Nakayama's business in the late seventies and kept him on. While this is often explained as Rosen admiring Nakayama's entrepreneurial spirit, a more pragmatic explanation might be that he just decided it's better to have him 'inside the tent'.[*]

Upon acquiring Sega, Nakayama became the first president of Sega of Japan, and Rosen the first president of Sega of America. Sega of America secured an early coup for the launch of the Master System, poaching Nintendo's VP of sales, Bruce Lowry, in the hopes he'd be able to give Sega a similar level of early success to that which was beginning to be enjoyed by the NES. As had been the case for Nintendo, Sega didn't have the necessary retail distribution network to get the product out there themselves, so they formed a partnership with the toy car manufacturer, Tonka.

Christmas of 1986 was a big year for console gaming in the USA, with Nintendo's NES, Sega's Master System and Atari's

---

[*] I'm determined to keep this book family-friendly. Grown-ups, you know the analogy.

7800 all going head to head. We've not talked much about the 7800 until now, and we're not going to, because it was technically inferior and never really made an impact. It's not really that surprising the 7800 was so far behind the competition when you learn it had actually been ready since 1984, but couldn't be released as the new Atari Corporation under Tramiel was locked in a dispute with the console's third-party designers, General Computer Corporation* over whether they should pay them for all the work they'd done†. With hindsight, I imagine Atari wished they'd just accepted Nintendo's offer of Atari becoming the US distributor of the NES.

Sega had to make do with whatever games they could make themselves in the early days of the Master System, as Nintendo pretty much had the rest of the market sewn up. Nintendo's dominance made it easy for them to convince third parties to sign exclusivity deals with them, to help increase the amount of games available only on their system: companies like Taito, Konami, Capcom, Bandai, Namco and Hudson. What's more, Tonka's team didn't have the previous experience with video games that Worlds of Wonder's team did, and so Sega struggled to establish themselves in the US market.

Games-wise, the Master System leant heavily on Sega's portfolio of popular arcade titles, such as Hang On, Space Harrier, Out Run and Wonder Boy‡. Given that the arcade

---

* ★★★ Boring company name klaxon. ★★★
† Unsurprisingly, the answer was, eventually, yes.
‡ And more. Enduro Racer, Alien Syndrome, Fantasy Zone, After Burner ... they really did have a great back catalogue to draw on.

cabinets of the first two had given you actual motorbikes and cars to sit on/in, it was hard for the home versions to have quite the same 'wow' factor*, not to mention that arcade games tend to, by design, be relatively shallow, repetitive and short in length. Nevertheless, the games at least offered potential buyers some brand recognition.

Arcade ports aside, the original game arguably most associated with Sega's Master System is Alex Kidd in Miracle World, a platform game created with the intention of rivalling Super Mario Bros. It didn't manage that, but it remains lodged in many people's minds thanks to the game being built in to many iterations of the hardware itself. If you turned the system on without a game cartridge inserted, Alex Kidd was there, looking like an angry baby in a wig, waiting for you to play rock-paper-scissors.

Alex Kidd wasn't always built in to the Master System though. In the very earliest model, there was a hidden maze game called 'Snail' built in, which you triggered by holding both buttons on controller one when you turned it on. Even the staunchest Alex Kidd critic would have to admit it was an improvement on this absolute stinker, which gave you sixty seconds per level in which to navigate a snail through a series of mazes. The 'graphics' consisted of a blue background, lighter-blue lines for walls, the letter 'S' to mark the start, the word 'GOAL' to mark the goal, and a rubbish picture of a snail.

---

* During this transitional period for the arcades, it was these sorts of experiences which people couldn't get at home that helped keep the scene alive.

Relative to that, rock-paper-scissors looked like the video game equivalent of James Joyce's *Ulysses*.

Nintendo's exclusivity clause meant that arcade hits like Ghosts 'n Goblins, Contra and Blades of Steel, as well as original home franchises like Castlevania* and Mega Man, were only playable in the home on the NES†. Mega Man was notable for allowing you to complete the levels in any order, though if you did them in a 'correct' order the game was easier, as you acquired new skills from each defeated boss. In Mega Man 2, for example, you want to kill Bubble Man before you kill Heat Man, because Heat Man takes the most damage from Bubble Man's bubbles. Why anyone would have ever worked that out themselves, I've no idea. The first game even had an Ice Man, which would make a more natural rival, but they binned him for the sequel. Or invent a Water Man. Bubbles aren't a weapon, they're a treat.

Nintendo imposed many restrictions besides exclusivity on game publishers. They could release only five games per year. Nintendo had the right to refuse the release of any games they felt weren't good enough, and there was a zero-tolerance policy of defects. Assuming the game was given Nintendo's 'Seal of Quality', companies were obliged to purchase at least 10,000 copies of each game from Nintendo, who manufac-

---

* Outdoing King's Quest in the rubbish-protagonist-names stakes with its hero, Simon Belmont.

† At least, that was the case for the video game console market – home computers were still viewed as a separate entity, so some of these titles would appear on other, non-console, platforms.

tured all cartridges. They even included copy protection to prevent unauthorised games from working on the NES and, to top it all off, developers were charged a licence fee for each copy of the game too. If it had occurred to them, no doubt they'd have asked for a free pint and a pack of pork scratchings every thirty minutes as well. With all of these rules, you might quite reasonably wonder why any company was willing to sign up to their terms but consider the case of Hudson's, Roadrunner. Prior to Roadrunner's release on Famicom, their most successful game had sold 10,000 copies. Roadrunner sold a million (literally a hundred times as many copies, maths fans) which, despite Nintendo taking a hefty slice of the cash, instantly quadrupled their profits. Namco's Xevious sold so many copies on Nintendo's platform they built an entirely new building with the proceeds. And it wasn't a little shed like the one I bought for the garden when *Go 8 Bit* was recommissioned, it was a proper big one with a lift in it and everything.

Of course, Nintendo undoubtedly benefited the most from their arrangement with publishers, but it wasn't *entirely* out of greed. In the early eighties, unauthorised third parties flooding the market with inferior-quality games had led to the games industry's collapse. Nintendo's procedures and Seal of Quality reassured consumers that all games had been through a rigorous evaluation process before being allowed to be sold, and the hope was that this focus on quality would prevent the market nosediving once again.

You may have noticed that all the companies making NES games that I've mentioned so far are Japanese. American and

European companies were tending to focus on the unrestricted home computer market, but this was beginning to change. One company, Rare, had been formed by the guys behind Ultimate Play The Game. They'd managed to reverse engineer Nintendo's hardware and, as a result, managed to do things that no one else had. Upon showing their work to Nintendo, the company realised the value of this team and gave them a licence to make games for the NES. Setting up an American division headed up by Joel Hochberg[*], the Stamper brothers released a large number of games for the system; many arcade conversions of titles like Marble Madness and Narc, but original titles too, such as R.C. Pro-Am and the punishingly difficult Teenage Mutant Ninja Turtles-alike, Battletoads.

Previously, Nintendo hadn't issued licences to anyone outside Japan but in 1987 they began to cast the net wider. Another early adopter was the company Acclaim. It may seem surprising that Nintendo would grant one of its first international licences to a company that, at the time, had yet to produce a single game, but Acclaim was no ordinary company. Acclaim was founded by three guys from Activision. It was so called to ensure it came before Activision alphabetically, as well as before another rival, Accolade, which was also formed by ex-Activision employees. Activision had followed the same philosophy itself when its founders left Atari. Quite why these

---

[*] It was Hochberg who had encouraged the brothers to reverse engineer the NES, when Nintendo were reluctant to provide details to non-Japanese developers.

otherwise intelligent people had assumed success was contingent on the alphabet remains unclear and, if they were so certain that made any difference, why not opt for Aardvark or the good old-fashioned taxi approach to company names with AAA Games Co*?

Acclaim didn't intend to make games; instead, they would identify popular titles from abroad or from the home computer market, and publish them for the NES in the USA. Early successes included Tiger Heli and 3D World Runner, though later they would begin to purchase the rights to successful TV shows and movies like *Rambo*, *Airwolf* and *WWF Wrestlemania*, and engage third parties (including Rare) to make games around these IPs for them.

Electronic Arts also found success on the NES, although in a less direct way than Rare or Acclaim. Hawkins felt the computer market was the future and abhorred the restrictive licensing agreements of Nintendo. However, when Konami requested to license one of EA's games, Skate or Die, for the NES in 1988, it offered them a zero-risk way to explore the market. While EA only got a fraction of what Konami made, which in turn was only a fraction of the total amount of money the game had made thanks to Nintendo creaming off their substantial share, the money EA made from Skate or Die was still higher than for any other game of theirs to date. Clearly this new market could no longer be ignored.

■

---

* ★★★ Boring company name klaxon. ★★★ (Though this one's my own fault.)

It was the previous year, 1987, when Nintendo really established itself in America, with three games in particular continuing to build their own reputation for quality video games*. Metroid, the science-fiction action game produced by Gunpei Yokoi, helped reassure people that Nintendo could make games that felt more mature than some of their cuter fare. I'm not sure what the embargo is for spoilers these days so, if you've not played it, look away now – at the end of the game after destroying the 'Mother Brain'†, the main character, Samus, removes their helmet to reveal they're a woman, an important milestone in gaming at the time. Clearly whoever wrote the English-language manual hadn't got that far though, as they referred to Samus as 'he' throughout.

From attempts at feminism to the opposite of that, the second big game for Nintendo that year was Mike Tyson's Punch-Out!!, an adaptation of their 1983 arcade game, the similarly excessively-punctuated Punch-Out!!, adding more rivals including Mike Tyson who was the newly crowned heavyweight champion of the world. Taking the lead from EA's licensing of sports personalities, it was a bold move as the deal was actually done prior to him winning anything. It wasn't long before Tyson's personal life began to attract more attention than his professional career though, and

---

* Not that it had ever really been in doubt thanks to early titles for the system like 1984's Excitebike (designed by Miyamoto), 1985's Ice Climber (developed by long-time Nintendo producer Kenji Miki) and 1986's Kid Icarus (produced by Yokoi).

† Yamauchi's office at Nintendo of Japan was often referred to internally as 'The realm of the Mother Brain'.

eventually Nintendo quietly rereleased the game simply as 'Punch-Out!!', replacing Tyson with a new character, the contrastingly inoffensive 'Mr Dream'.

Neither of these games can be said to have the legacy of 1987's third big Nintendo hit though. Shigeru Miyamoto, having honed his craft over the years with games like Donkey Kong and Super Mario Bros., released his most ambitious title to date, the action-adventure game, The Legend of Zelda.

Set in the fantasy land of Hyrule, the player takes control of the Peter-Pan-inspired elf, Link, in their quest to rescue the princess Zelda from the evil Ganon. Rescuing a woman being held captive by a baddie might not seem new for anyone who knows the first thing about the plots of Donkey Kong or Super Mario Bros. but, while the conceit might be the same, the delivery was very different. Rather than a linear game played from bottom to top as in Donkey Kong, or left to right as in Super Mario Bros., The Legend of Zelda, with its top-down view, allowed the player to wander in any direction and explore a whole world.

I have a love-hate relationship with the Zelda series, though not necessarily for the reason you might expect. Firstly, on our spin-off show *Go 8 Bit DLC*, the show's producer and 'friend' Rohan Acharya, refused to let me do a retake after I mistakenly referred to Link as Zelda, an action which guaranteed my Twitter notifications were 18-rated for several weeks. Secondly, I can't hear the name Ganon (the game's antagonist) without thinking of the time I appeared on Paul Gannon's show, *Digitiser*, where he managed to call me both Chris McNeil and Steve O'Neill within the space of ten minutes, a slight made all the more impressive given he clearly had all the ingredients he needed to create my actual name, but steadfastly refused to use it. I hope he drowns in a quarry*.

Anyway, Zelda was inspired by Miyamoto's childhood, when he had explored the local countryside in the village he grew up in, Sonobe. The game had actually been released in Japan the previous year, but it took time to translate the game's text, and there were concerns as to whether it would appeal to the western market. It certainly didn't have the immediacy of a game like Super Mario Bros. or Duck Hunt, although of course gamers in America had enjoyed titles like Atari's Adventure, and the many text-adventures emerging on home computers.

Another issue was that the game had originally been released in Japan as the launch title for a new hardware add-on, the Famicom Disk System. This new platform used writable disks for the games, allowing you to save your progress – essential for a game of this scale. The Famicom Disk System didn't really take off in the way Nintendo had hoped, so it was never released in the USA, thus beginning a long legacy of rubbish/aborted console add-ons for Nintendo and their peers.

This presented a problem for Nintendo, who had a great game by their golden boy, Shigeru Miyamoto, but no way of releasing it in America because cartridges didn't have the ability to save. The solution was to add a battery into the cartridge,

---

* Obviously I'm joking. I wish Pete Gammon nothing but the best of luck in all future endeavours.

specifically to allow the player's progress to be stored*. That wasn't the only problem, though. Disks at the time could store far more data than cartridges (essential to store the masses of text synonymous with these games), so to get the game to work on NES required Nintendo to create their largest ROM cartridge to date, adding to cost.

Still, these challenges were overcome and, upon being released, it became a huge hit, the first NES cartridge to sell over a million copies. In fact, Zelda became more successful in the USA than it had been at home, due to both the original and its sequel, Zelda 2: The Adventure of Link, being exclusively released in Japan on the poorly received Famicom Disk System.†

While Zelda may not have seen the recognition it deserved at home, there were other titles that were doing the business there that had yet to make their way across the Pacific. Dragon Quest, from Yuji Horii, is a hugely successful RPG series which began on the Famicom in Japan, made by the company Enix‡ and influenced by franchises like Ultima, Wizardry and, of course, The Black Onyx. In introducing the first instalment of the game to the more casual audience associated with

* Not all games were afforded this luxury. The notoriously difficult NES game Castlevania was so partially because it was originally a Famicom Disk System title. On the FDS, you could save your progress. On the NES, there was no battery, so you couldn't.
† StarTropics (1990) scratches a similar itch to both of these if you fancy another 8-bit adventure.
‡ Enix takes its name from the first programmable computer, ENIAC, and the phoenix, a mythical bird.

the Famicom, there was a need to help educate players on concepts such as acquiring skills and becoming stronger. Mario, by contrast, is the same from start to finish within Super Mario Bros., there's no 'levelling up' over time, only temporary buffs of invincibility or strength.

Horii brought in some real heavyweights to help with the game. Koichi Sugiyama, a celebrated composer for TV shows, was drafted in to create the soundtrack and Akira Toriyama, a hugely successful manga artist, was engaged for the game's illustrations. While the game was slow to take off upon its release in 1986, articles about it written by Horii in the same magazine that Toriyama was known for (*Shonen Jump*) helped build awareness, and eventually it sold over two million copies. These articles also had the benefit of raising Horii's profile in Japan, in contrast to Miyamoto, who remained virtually anonymous. Nineteen eighty-seven's sequel sold out immediately and 1988's Dragon Quest 3 caused so many students to skip school to grab it on release day that Japanese parliament decreed future Dragon Quest games must be released on Sundays or national holidays!

An equally successful franchise began around the same time, created by Hironobu Sakaguchi, at Square Co Ltd. In 1987 he was getting ready to leave the company but, before he left, he had one more game to make, so chose to call this game Final Fantasy. Again inspired by Wizardry, but also the growing success of Dragon Quest, Sakaguchi was keen to create something far less cute in its style than Horii's hit. The game was heavily influenced by filmic devices, for instance it seemingly begins mid-story, with a princess being rescued before the game's title screen is even shown; there could be little clearer way of setting out to differentiate Final Fantasy from the increasingly clichéd goal of saving a maiden. Final Fantasy was about far more than that: 'Princess Rescue' is merely the prologue. With a clear influence also from Tolkien – elves, dwarves and dragons all appear – Final Fantasy was successful enough on its Famicom release in late 1987 for Sakaguchi to stick around at Square, making a mockery of the game's prefix. At the time of writing there have been over fifty different 'final' sequels and spin-offs.

Of course, with Nintendo benefiting from these two franchises*, it would have been foolish for Sega not to get in on the act, and it did so with the internally-developed Phantasy Star for the Master System, an undoubted promotion from programmer Yuki Naka's previous tasks of arcade conversions. While Phantasy Star might have been the last of these RPGs to get to market in Japan, it was the first to arrive in the USA, in 1988. Hot on the heels of Nintendo's The Legend of Zelda, it was recognised as an exceptional game, and fuelled interest in, and appetite for, this emerging sub-genre of Japanese RPGs. The Legend of Zelda isn't considered an RPG, focusing as it does primarily on exploration and problem-solving, rather than the deeper combat we might expect from the genre, but it certainly occupied a similar enough space in people's minds to build momentum for this new, more considered, longer form of gameplay. To help players, The Legend of Zelda

---

* And a third, Mother, which never made the journey West, though its sequel Earthbound found some fans on the SNES in the mid-nineties.

included comprehensive instructions, a map of the world, and a freephone hotline number for if you got really stuck. Initially staffed by four people, it rapidly went up to over two hundred as customers began asking questions about other Nintendo games too. Eventually, the freephone number was too costly to maintain, but throughout its life the service remained free, with up to 100,000 callers a week paying just the phone network's call price. For anyone under twenty, I'm basically talking about a Google for video games via telephones that were connected by a wire to a wall in your house. The past is weirder than you can ever imagine.

Demand for this service, and an early newsletter, 'Nintendo Fun Club News', even led to Nintendo creating its own magazine in 1988, *Nintendo Power*, which at its peak had a circulation of around five million copies in the USA. A mixture of reviews, previews, and those tips so many people wanted, it also included a two-page list of people's submitted high scores. One person who began to feature on these pages was Apple Computer's Steve Wozniak who appeared so frequently that they stopped printing his name, until he began making his submissions as Kainzow Evets (Steve Wozniak in reverse)*. Another regular name in *Nintendo Power* was Howard Phillips. Originally Nintendo's warehouse manager, he had a knack for play-testing and evaluating their new games, spotting which would be big hits. When the magazine was created, Phillips was tasked with writing game reviews, but they soon realised

---

* My friend Lana tried the same trick but sadly her pseudonym remained unpublished.

this was effectively a dream job for the readers (getting paid to play games) and chose to celebrate that, even going so far as to create a comic strip, 'Howard & Nester', where Phillips would give game advice to the fictional young kid, Nester. Nintendo's 'Game Master', as he became known, was so popular that for a time he was more recognised in surveys in the USA than Madonna, Pee-Wee Herman or The Incredible Hulk.

It was actually *Nintendo Power* that helped Dragon Quest to gain wider recognition in the USA, albeit as 'Dragon Warrior' because there was already a pen-and-paper RPG in the USA called 'Dragon Quest'. Enix didn't have a US base, so Nintendo licensed the first game in the series for sale there, but they vastly overestimated how successful it would be. Left with a pile of stock, they ended up giving away the $50 game with $20 subscriptions to *Nintendo Power* magazine. This was such a bargain that many more people subscribed as a result, helping the magazine to rapidly grow, and gave Enix the confidence (and cash) to release subsequent titles in America on their own. With Enix doing their own thing, *Nintendo Power* looked to replicate Dragon Warrior's success with Final Fantasy, helping build interest by distributing a strategy guide for free to all subscribers. This was successful, but did lead to a confusing quirk associated with the series. Final Fantasy was released in Japan in 1987, with subsequent sequels in 1988, 1990 and Final Fantasy IV released on the Super Famicom (the successor to the Famicom) in 1991. The first instalment of Final Fantasy wasn't released in the US until 1990 though so, when the US market was ready for a sequel the following year, they released Final Fantasy IV as Final Fantasy II for the Super Nintendo

Entertainment System (as the Super Famicom was known in the US). The naming confusion continued when the West skipped Final Fantasy V and released Final Fantasy VI as Final Fantasy III and, in fact, the version of Final Fantasy IV released in the West hadn't even been the proper game. Instead, it was an easier, simplified version known as 'Final Fantasy IV Easy Type', as they didn't think Western gamers were ready for the level of complexity in the original. Charming.

The same year *Nintendo Power* magazine launched (1988), Nintendo released sequels to their two biggest franchises. Zelda 2: The Adventure of Link chose to focus more on combat than exploration and was very different in appearance to the original, but it wasn't as big a change as that seen for Mario's sequel. This was partly because Super Mario Bros. 2 wasn't actually a proper sequel. Japan had a sequel to Super Mario Bros. on the Famicom Disk System which was visually identical to the original but with harder levels, but Nintendo were concerned this would be too hard for American gamers (they really didn't think much of Western gamers' skills, did they?), so they instead reskinned another game from Japan called 'Doki Doki Panic', replacing its playable characters with Mario, Luigi, Princess and the sentient mushroom*, Toad.

Despite being very different to the original, it was still a huge hit. This may well be due to the fact that Mario's creator, Shigeru Miyamoto, was the producer, so it's not as random a choice as it might seem at first. In fact, Miyamoto was far more

---

* Video games really are second only to religion in terms of nonsense we've come to take for granted over the years.

actively involved in the creation of Doki Doki Panic than he was with the Japanese Super Mario Bros. 2*. Koji Kondo provided the music too, so arguably the USA Mario sequel is more of a Mario game anyway† . . .

By the end of 1988, Nintendo commanded around ninety per cent of the US market. They were so successful that they couldn't make enough consoles to meet demand. But this suited them as, having learnt from the lessons of previous generations, they knew it was far better to have the market begging for more product than to overestimate demand and be left with warehouses full of unsellable stock, while retailers slashed prices to shift whatever they still had in their stores. Nintendo's partners were also unable to meet market demand with their games, but this wasn't by choice. 1988 saw a microchip shortage, which forced Nintendo to ration the amount of cartridges each game publisher could create.

For some, the extent to which they were at the mercy of Nintendo was now simply too much, and they began to take matters into their own hands. One company in particular, Tengen, really had a hell of a time as a result. Tengen might not be a name we've heard until now, but we're actually already familiar with the companies behind it. Strap in, this is about to get complicated.

---

* The Japanese Super Mario Bros. 2 was left mostly to the game's director, Takashi Tezuka. Tezuka had been assistant director on the original.

† Yeah, I'm probably pushing my luck there, but you take my point? Right? I mean, you sort of have to. This conversation is very much one way.

You'll remember that, in 1984, Atari split into Atari Corporation (the home division) and Atari Games (the coin-op division which retained ownership of their iconic arcade games). As a result of this, Atari Games were no longer able to use the name 'Atari' when releasing their arcade games on home systems, so they needed a new brand for that market. While Atari Games wasn't the force it once was, they continued to release popular arcade games during the mid-eighties, titles like Paperboy, Marble Madness, Gauntlet, Super Sprint and the movie tie-in, Indiana Jones and the Temple of Doom and, of course, they also had their impressive back catalogue. In 1987, the name Tengen was picked for their new publishing label as, like Atari, it was another term from the game Go, this time referring to the centre point of the board.

In 1985, Warner Communications had sold sixty per cent of Atari Games to Masaya Nakamura's company, Namco. This didn't work out though and, in 1987, Namco sold their interest in Atari Games; some of it went back to Warner, but another chunk went to one of Namco's senior employees, Hideyuki Nakajima. Nakajima had a long history with Atari, actually predating Namco's involvement with them, having been hired by Bushnell to manage Atari's original Japanese operations when they first opened in 1973. When that didn't take off in the way Atari had hoped, it was sold to Namco, and Nakajima was kept on to run things. In 1978, Nakajima had even been responsible for opening a US subsidiary, Namco America.

Confused? You should be. Let's recap.

Atari split into Atari Corporation and Atari Games. Atari Games owned Atari's arcade games, but couldn't sell those games under the name Atari on home systems because Atari Corporation owned those rights. Tengen was formed so Atari Games could sell Atari games, though not for Atari Corporation's Atari 7800, but for Nintendo's NES.

Nakajima had managed Atari Japan, but when Atari Japan was sold to Nakamura's Namco in Japan, Nakajima was kept on. Nakajima later formed Namco America, which invested in Atari Games but, when Nakajima and Nakamura disagreed over Atari Games' future, Nakamura got rid of Nakajima and Atari Games, and Nakajima acquired a stake in Atari Games. Neither Nakajima or Nakamura should be confused with Nakayama, Sega's Japanese president.

Alles klar!

Nakajima approached Nintendo about Tengen becoming a licensee, expecting to receive preferential terms (no exclusivity, more than five games per year) both because of Namco's early support for Nintendo, and because of Atari Games' impressive back catalogue of arcade classics. He was soon disabused of this notion, when Nintendo steadfastly refused to offer Tengen anything but the standard contract, which they reluctantly accepted, but not without beginning to consider ways they might be able to work around Nintendo. When the 1988 microchip shortage led to them receiving a mere ten per cent of the stock they'd requested, they decided enough was enough and endeavoured to take matters into their own hands.

They approached Sharp, who manufactured the chips for Nintendo, who initially said they'd be able to supply them direct, until they discovered they were to be used in unofficial NES cartridges, at which point their availability quickly changed. Many believe that, while there may have been a microchip shortage that year, Nintendo greatly exaggerated it in order to prevent its increasing number of third-party game developers overloading the market with too many games. Given their supplier had literally said they'd got some, that doesn't seem an entirely unreasonable assumption.

Tengen managed to find an alternative chip provider, but they wouldn't have been able to do anything about this, had they not managed to find a way to bypass the NES's security protection which prevented unauthorised games from being played on the system. A court would later rule that it was legal for companies to develop solutions to overcome security protections, but this was not without restrictions and, unfortunately for Tengen, they chose to do so in a very-not-legal manner.

A transcript of the computer code for Nintendo's security system, known as '10NES', was securely held at the US Copyright Office for reference. There was no way of anyone else getting access to this, with one exception. If two companies were involved in litigation relating to that code, they were allowed to take a copy for reference in the case. So, Tengen lied to the copyright office and told them they were in dispute, and managed to secure a copy of the code. With that, Tengen were able to create unlicensed NES cartridges without Nintendo's involvement.

Incredibly, it was then Tengen that took Nintendo to court. With links to retailers as a result of their licensing deal with Nintendo, an alternative supplier of microchips, and the ability to bypass the NES's security measures, Tengen no longer needed Nintendo and they charged Nintendo with 'monopolistic and exclusionary business practices', seemingly forgetting they'd literally just committed an offence against the defendant. Had Tengen not been so bullish, perhaps they would have got away with their unlicensed cartridges, but the outcome of this court case was that Nintendo were able to prove Tengen had illegally obtained the 10NES code, and Tengen were ordered to take all games manufactured in this way off the shelves, and destroy all remaining stock.

It's an incredible thing to have done, analogous to asking someone to pay for your dry cleaning after you soiled yourself in the trousers you stole from their house, because they under-cooked the chicken they served while you were there for dinner, and wouldn't let you eat the crisps you'd brought along instead. Sure, you shouldn't have found yourself in a position where you felt coerced into eating raw chicken, but they were never your trousers to poo in.

A costly mistake for Tengen indeed, but this was by no means their only problem. Alongside all this, they became embroiled in another spectacular spat with Nintendo. In the inevitable movie version of this book, you can now imagine the screen going all wibbly wobbly and, when it calms down, we find ourselves in Russia.

Tetris was created by a programmer at the Moscow Academy of Science's Computer Centre, Alexey Pajitnov, in his free time. The game was based on pentominoes; a puzzle involving plastic shapes comprised of five* squares that had to be laid out

---

* Penta = five.

in such a way that they could fit back in their box. For his game, Pajitnov reduced it to four squares, making a more manageable seven possible shapes rather than twelve. Tetris* originally just had pieces continuing to fall in to the play area and the goal was to fit as many in as possible until the playing area filled up, but this limited the game's length. Pajitnov considered having a longer, scrolling play field, but that wasn't easy to do on the computer he had available, and seemed unnecessarily complicated. Realising that once a player had filled a row of the play area it effectively became useless, he decided to make the squares on that row disappear, creating more space to continue playing and, also, the essence of what would be the final game.

The first version was created on an Electronika 60 – a Russian clone of a PDP-11 computer. This computer only allowed for alphanumeric characters, so he had a friend create a graphical version on PC. As with all these early computer games it began to be circulated, and one place it appeared was the Institute of Computer Science in Budapest, where it caught the eye of Robert Stein. Stein had grown up in Hungary but fled in 1956 after the failed uprising against communism, and claimed asylum in the UK where he formed his software company, Andromeda. Stein was always on the lookout for games from this region that he could sell to Western publishers and so he reached out to the Moscow Academy of Science in the hopes of negotiating the rights to Tetris.

Unfortunately, Pajitnov did not actually have the author-

---

* Tetra = four.

ity to make a deal. Soviet law prohibited people forming businesses and there were no copyright or intellectual property laws; everything was effectively owned by the state. Not that this would have mattered much in his home country – there was no real market for computer/video games in the USSR at this point as it was a rare exception for someone to have a computer in their home. Pajitnov attempted to reply to Stein, but his English wasn't very good and, somewhere along the way, Stein got the wrong end of the stick. Rather than seeing Pajitnov's response as an expression of enthusiasm, and a desire to explore ways an agreement might be reached, Stein thought a deal was done, and began to sell on the various rights.

Home and coin-op rights quickly went to the British company Mirrorsoft which had originally been formed, oddly, as a video game division of Mirror Group newspapers, and was subsequently acquired by the infamous publishing magnate, Robert Maxwell. Maxwell also had stakes in an American company, Spectrum Holobyte, and this led to both companies beginning to release versions of the game on various home computers in their respective territories.

In 1988, Henk Rogers (creator of The Black Onyx) saw one of Spectrum Holobyte's versions at the Consumer Electronics Show (CES) and was enraptured by it, immediately acquiring the Japanese rights that, of course, they didn't actually have to sell him in the first place. Since we last met Rogers, he had bonded with Nintendo's Yamauchi over their shared love of the game Go, even releasing a version of it for the Famicom, and intended to do the same with Tetris.

At a meeting with Nintendo of America's Arakawa, he was shown a prototype of their forthcoming handheld, the Game Boy. Developed by Gunpei Yokoi and his team, they had successfully created an affordable black and white handheld gaming device, which could last for up to ten hours on just four AA batteries. Yokoi had also created a new Mario game for the system, Super Mario Land, unusual in that it was the first title not to have any involvement from Miyamoto, though of course it was heavily influenced by the previous games.

It might have been worth running it by Miyamoto though. The fireballs in it, rather than skipping along the floor and killing enemies like they do in *every other Mario game ever*, bounced once then flew uselessly off into the sky, making me the angriest eleven-year-old you ever did see. To this day, I cannot understand how they could manage to create the Game Boy and Super Mario Land – a huge technical achievement – and not manage to make a digital ball bounce. It's literally what Pong was.*

Anyway, rubbish balls aside, Super Mario Land was an impressive achievement, but Rogers encouraged Nintendo to include Tetris as the system's pack-in game instead. In Rogers' words: 'If you want little boys to buy your machine then pack in Mario, but if you want *everybody* to play your game, pack in

---

* I know it might seem like a minor thing, but I love Mario, and it's horrible when custodians of games get things wrong. While Sonic the Hedgehog is obviously rubbish, I could still have empathy for long-time fans who were disappointed when Sonic 4 was finally released and the physics were all wrong.

Tetris.'* Arakawa tasked Rogers with securing the handheld rights, offering to sub-license them from him if he was successful, so he went back to Spectrum Holobyte to do just this. Unbeknown to Rogers, things had become even more complicated by this point. The British-based Mirrorsoft had sold international rights to Tengen in the USA without Spectrum Holobyte's knowledge, despite the USA being Spectrum Holobyte's home territory. This might not have been a problem were it not for the fact that Tengen then sold on the Japanese coin-op rights to Sega, which conflicted with the Spectrum Holobyte/Henk Rogers agreement. This example is just one of many that led to a complex web of rights issues that it took years to untangle.

I should probably say, if you're familiar with the saga that is Tetris, this might be a slightly different version of events to what you've heard previously. There's lots of different accounts, all slightly contradictory, and I've read the lot and attempted to try to find the underlying truth of what went on. No doubt there's bits here that are slightly off, but what's important is that, essentially, a whole bunch of people just started selling Tetris rights without ever seeming to check with anyone else before they did it and, by this point, it was more of a mess than that time I ate half a kilo of sugar-free jelly beans†.

Unsurprisingly, Rogers was unable to get clarity from Spectrum Holobyte on what was going on so, with the clock

---

* Donovan, T.: *Replay: The History of Video Games* (Yellow Ant, 2010).
† It felt like an egg hatched and a thousand spiders with legs made from tiny needles were running around inside me. A great day.

ticking on the launch of the Game Boy, Rogers chose to cut out the increasingly large number of middle men and reached out to the Soviets directly, this time to the state-owned organisation ELORG*, which had been charged with handling the licensing of Tetris and had begun to formalise things with Stein. On 21 February 1989, Rogers met with them and secured global handheld rights. Intending to impress the Soviets, he also showed them the Famicom version of Tetris he had released through his company, Bullet-Proof Software. Rather than being impressed, ELORG were shocked. They believed the agreement they had managed to finalise with Stein† so far only covered computer rights, not consoles. It seems that, somewhere in translation, the definition of 'home computer' had been misinterpreted. Rogers apologised profusely, and returned the next day with a significant royalty cheque as a gesture of good faith and requested the global console rights that, as far as the Soviets were concerned, were still for sale.

That same day, Howard Stein was also in town to meet ELORG, in the hopes of formally securing coin-op rights – somewhat urgent given Sega had already released their Japanese arcade version. ELORG granted Stein coin-op rights but, in the amended contract, Stein failed to notice that elsewhere the definition of home computers had been clarified to mean those with keyboards – Rogers had successfully taken the console rights out from underneath him. Probably. With

---

* ELORG stands for Elektronorgtechnica. Hope that clears things up.

† Who had, in turn, sold the rights to Spectrum Holobyte, which they had then sold on to Rogers.

all the translation issues, there's every chance Rogers had actually just bought a toaster.

The outcome of all this chaos was that Tengen, who released their NES version of Tetris in May 1989, were forced to remove it from sale the very next month, after Nintendo proved the global console rights were theirs. In a way this was a shame; many felt the Tengen version had actually been a better adaptation, in no small part due to its inclusion of a competitive two-player mode absent from Nintendo's version. Not that this bothered Nintendo. The Game Boy version, as Henk Rogers predicted, made the new handheld the must-have device of 1989*. By the end of its life, over forty million copies of Tetris on the Game Boy had been sold, many of which were packed in with the hardware. Its simple graphics suited the screen, the bite-sized gameplay was perfect for gaming on the go and it didn't hurt that the inspired choice of folk song *Korobeiniki* for its soundtrack was so catchy.

I'll be honest, while I love Tetris, I've always felt Dr. Mario, which launched on both the NES and Game Boy a year later, was the superior game, although it did feel like an odd career move for a plumber. The only time a plumber's ever given me pills was in a field in the nineties and, if anything, despite an initial spike in my mood, they ultimately made my headache much, much worse.

As a result of all the confusion and contractual kerfuffle, Robert Stein ended up with very little to show for introducing

---

* The Game Boy version did include a two-player version, playable by connecting two handhelds via the 'link cable'.

Tetris to Western gamers. This was also the case with Pajitnov initially, as the Soviet approach to ownership meant the rewards were the state's, not his. However, in 1991 his reputation was such that he was able to emigrate to the USA and in 1996, when the rights ELORG had sold reverted to Pajitnov*, Henk Rogers helped him to form the Tetris Company, which would control (and financially benefit from) all subsequent licensing agreements. So, while it would take some time, eventually the man who gave us the bestselling game of all time would reap the rewards.

While others tried to introduce systems to rival the Game Boy, nothing came close. The Atari Lynx (from Atari Corporation, *not* Atari Games, but let's not get into that again) was also released in 1989. The development of the hardware by a couple of programmers who'd previously worked under Jay Miner at Amiga, RJ Mical and Dave Needle, had initially been funded by the video game developer and publisher Epyx in the mid-eighties†. During this period, Epyx grew in success under the stewardship of president Michael Katz, with popular titles like Summer Games, Winter Games and Impossible Mission.

We've met Katz several times in passing along the way, but

---

* Things had changed a lot in Russia by then with regards to private ownership.

† One of their earliest games, 1979's Temple of Apshei, had been a huge hit, comparable in gameplay and success to Wizardry and Ultima.

it's worth reminding ourselves of his pedigree. Heavily involved in the marketing of Mattel's early Auto Race and Football LED handhelds, which in turn led to the Intellivision, he then moved to Coleco to market the ColecoVision before arriving at Epyx. After two years there he then moved over to Atari Corporation and, when Epyx found itself in financial difficulties, Atari Corporation acquired the handheld which, on paper at least, had several benefits over the Game Boy. It had a colour screen, larger than the Game Boy's monochrome one, it had a backlight so you could play in the dark, and it allowed up to eight people to play together, hence the name Lynx (links). On the downside, it cost twice as much as the Game Boy, it was fifty per cent heavier and it required six AA batteries instead of four, which barely lasted half as long. Also, it simply didn't have the games. Tetris and Super Mario Land were huge hits, but the best the Lynx could manage were two Epyx games: California Games and Chip's Challenge. Even if they'd had the best game ever, Atari simply didn't have deep enough pockets by this point to advertise anywhere near the amount that Nintendo could, and the system never really made an impact.

In his book, *Phoenix*, Leonard Herman suggests that, in fact, Atari Corporation had exploited Epyx's financial situation. At first, their deal was that Atari would manufacture and distribute the hardware, while Epyx would take care of software. Atari would pay for games produced but there was an unfortunately worded clause where Epyx had sixty days from delivery to correct any bugs Atari found. Atari consistently waited until near the end of the sixty days to submit their list of bugs, meaning Epyx were unable to fix them within the remaining few days. Atari then held back payment, and eventually Epyx were at the point of bankruptcy. At this point, Atari offered to pay Epyx, but only if they handed over full rights to the Lynx hardware to Atari. Given that, it's somewhat satisfying that Atari's Lynx turned out to be a stinker*.

Sega's Game Gear did slightly better when it launched the following year. Essentially, from a technical standpoint, a portable Master System with a screen†, it again benefited from Sega's recognisable back catalogue, and had the sense to pack in its own Tetris-alike title, Columns. Additional mileage was gained by the introduction of a plug-in TV tuner, although the true portability of this was somewhat questionable given the speed with which it would drain the system's already poor battery life. The workaround was to have the system plugged into the wall if you intended to use the TV tuner for any length of time, at which point it magically became a small, rubbish, normal telly.

Sega still hadn't really made much of an impact in Japan by this point. Arguably the Barcode Battler – a handheld device

---

* Accusations of an aggressive approach to business were also levelled at Atari Corporation's Tramiel during his time at Commodore and it's why, when the Epyx–Atari deal was originally sealed, the Lynx's creators (who had experience of Tramiel from their time at Amiga) chose to exit the business. Epyx filed for bankruptcy protection in 1989, and managed to soldier on for four more years making games exclusively for the Lynx before finally folding completely.

† You could even buy an adaptor that allowed you to insert the much larger Master System cartridges into the device.

that allowed you to scan products and allow the resulting generated 'characters' to fight – was doing a better job of capturing people's imaginations. I remember on one occasion at the end of term a classmate brought one of these into school and tried to convince us that, actually, it was better than the Game Boy because by being able to scan anything it effectively had an infinite number of games. In retrospect, this was almost certainly the angle his cash-strapped parents had sold him in on as they tried to provide him with handheld gaming on a budget, but I struggle to imagine the bullying the kid suffered after trying to convince a room of teenagers that scanning a tin of beans was better than Mario was worth the saving.

Really, there was never a serious battle in the handheld market. While the Game Gear did eventually manage to carve out its own corner of the market in the West thanks to portable adaptations of the latest titles being released on their home consoles, the undisputed champion, wherever you were in the world, was Nintendo's Game Boy. Dominant with its handheld, and the NES unbeatable in the console market, Nintendo seemed un-topple-able*. But that was about to change.

---

* Not a word. Should totally have just gone with 'unstoppable'.

7

HEDGEHOG VERSUS PLUMBER

In October 1988, Sega were ready to release the Mega Drive in Japan. With twice the processing power of the NES, it promised to bring the power of the arcades into the home and to some extent it did, albeit indirectly. Early titles like Space Harrier 2, Super Thunder Blade and The Revenge of Shinobi, while sequels to arcade titles, only existed in these home versions (they'd never been arcade games) in the same way that Disney began to release straight-to-video sequels to successful movies. Super Thunder Blade is very much the *Cinderella 2: Dreams Come True*[*] of the Mega Drive. Thankfully, some proper arcade conversions were on their way: iconic titles like Golden Axe, Altered Beast, Alien Storm, Super Monaco GP, Strider and Super Hang On would soon follow, as would Phantasy Star 2[†].

---

[*] At the time of writing, the proud holder of an eleven per cent approval rating on review aggregation site Rotten Tomatoes. Favourite quote? 'A screaming black vortex of total, irredeemable awfulness.'

[†] If you're after a more Zelda-esque title on the Master System, seek out 1991's Golden Axe spin-off, Golden Axe Warrior instead. It is surprisingly not-rubbish, though also surprisingly Zelda-rip-off-y.

Many of Sega's arcade adaptations were helped in speed of conversion, and appearance, by the fact that the Mega Drive hardware was very similar to Sega's System 16 arcade hardware they were using around the same time.

A kid at my school, Morgan, was one of the first to have a Mega Drive. He was one of the cool kids – it'll blow your mind to discover I wasn't. Morgan was also into skateboarding so I pretended to like skateboarding too, to get closer to him, even going as far as to ask for a skateboard for Christmas. After school one day, I casually appeared with my new toy at the underpass where everyone hung out, in the hopes of befriending Morgan over our shared love of rolling around on wood, with the ultimate aim of getting a go on Shinobi back at his house. I won't bore you with the details but, suffice to say, I learned a valuable lesson that day: it's actually quite hard to fake skateboarding.

Even with a strong early line-up of games, the Mega Drive struggled in Japan. The PC Engine*, a collaborative effort between Hudson Soft and NEC, had already entered the market there a year earlier, and was doing well thanks to NEC's dominance in the computer market which gave them deep pockets when it came to marketing, and strong third-party

---

* The PC Engine was known as the TurboGrafx-16 in the USA, but it failed to establish itself there due to late entry to the market, a lack of software (Bonk's Adventure, featuring a pre-historic baby with a massive head, is probably the best known game for the platform in the West) and lower brand recognition than Nintendo and Sega.

support. This included Sega themselves, who provided them with titles like Space Harrier and Fantasy Zone; a somewhat strange choice, releasing your own games on your rival's system before yours came out. As a result, the PC Engine ended up outselling both the Mega Drive and the NES for a time in Japan. Cheekily, the PC Engine was often referred to as '16-bit' (as opposed to the NES and Master System's '8-bit' CPUs) but in fact the PC Engine only had a 16-bit chip for graphics; its main processor was still 8-bit. As any man will tell you, if you exaggerate the size of a thing by a factor of two, you will eventually be found out, and so it was here. The Mega Drive, on the other hand, was a true 16-bit console.

Sega set its sights once again on the American market but, having struggled to get the Master System to break through over there with Tonka in charge of distribution, they reached out to Atari Corporation, just as Nintendo had done when launching the NES. Again, this would come to nothing, meaning Atari turned down both the NES *and* the Mega Drive. The negotiations weren't completely pointless, however. During the process, Sega of America's David Rosen was sufficiently impressed by Atari's Michael Katz to poach him from Tramiel to become Sega's new American president for the launch of the Mega Drive, which was rebranded the 'Genesis' there as the name 'Mega Drive' was already being used by a computer hardware manufacturer making high-end storage devices. Sega of Japan's Hayao Nakayama was less convinced of Katz's abilities, and only conceded to take him on after the creation of a chief operating officer role in America for Shinobu Toyoda, to help support Katz (or, in truth, to keep an eye on him for Nakayama)*. Launching the Genesis in 1989 in America, Sega attempted to differentiate itself from Nintendo, targeting teenagers. They'd played on the NES as a kid, but now they were older and deserved something cooler. Nintendo was the past, Sega was the future – as their early slogan put it, 'Genesis does what Nintendon't.'

While Nintendo were still very dominant, Sega did manage to secure a third-party partner early on which would help define their brand. Electronic Arts had been impressed by the revenue potential of the NES, but simply couldn't stomach dealing with Nintendo directly due to their heavily one-sided terms, and the fact that the NES hardware was inferior to the latest computers. The Genesis, on the other hand, shared the same 16-bit Motorola 68000 processor found in computers EA had made games for, like the Atari ST, Apple Macintosh and Commodore Amiga. They were familiar with the hardware, conversion of existing games would be relatively straightforward, and Sega would no doubt be more open to a less restrictive agreement regarding licensing, approval, manufacture and so on. Ridiculously, Sega initially tried to impose something similarly unreasonable to Nintendo, but Hawkins simply refused. EA had already pre-emptively reverse-engineered the Genesis (in a legal manner, unlike Tengen with the NES), so he would be releasing games for the Genesis with, or without, their blessing. If you're in need of an analogy, Sega

---

* In the years that followed, some at Sega of America would question where Toyoda's loyalties really lay.

is Theresa May in the Brexit negotiations, albeit with EA, not the EU and, just like Brexit, EA/EU got the terms they wanted and Sega/Theresa acquiesced*.

An early collaboration between the two parties was the game Joe Montana† Football. Initially, Sega had engaged Activision (now operating under the name Mediagenic) to create the game for them, but they were dealing with various internal struggles and by the autumn it became apparent the game simply wasn't ready. EA agreed to use the underlying code from their John Madden Football series to create a title different enough to be passed off as a unique game, with a primary focus on action.

The breakthrough football game on the Genesis was undoubtedly John Madden, though. With its balance of action and simulation, it became the benchmark for how sports games were represented on consoles for years to come. From 1992 the game would become a hotly anticipated annual release, a relief to EA given it had spent a small fortune in the 1980s developing a game that could meet Madden's exacting standards – the EA–Madden deal was signed in 1984, but the first game didn't come out until 1988.

Buoyed up by this new deal with EA, Sega doubled-down on its philosophy of celebrity endorsements as a way to differentiate themselves from Nintendo. Michael Jackson's Moonwalker was a game released at the height of Jackson's

---

* At the time of writing (January 2019) the outcome of Brexit still hangs in the balance, so this might age *very* badly.
† At the time, Montana was the NFL's Most Valuable Player.

fame and, with computerised versions of many of his hits in the game's soundtrack, Sega placed great emphasis on how Jackson had been involved in the game's creation. Disney got involved too, with another 1990 game, Castle of Illusion Starring Mickey Mouse, bringing the much-loved rodent to the Genesis. Sega might not have had a Mario or Zelda, but when you had Joe Montana, Michael Jackson and Mickey Mouse*, did it really matter? The growing success of EA with Sega had other game developers glancing over, longingly. While Nintendo had relaxed some of its more aggressive terms, they were still seen as overly prescriptive. NES games were not allowed to feature any sex, nudity, gratuitous violence or graphic deaths, drug use, criticism of religion, racism, smoking or drinking of alcohol. While some of these may seem more reasonable than others, sometimes it was felt the letter of the law was being followed instead of the spirit. When the LucasArts game Maniac Mansion was ported to the NES, for example, Nintendo insisted the nude Greek statues were replaced, and some 'mature' language be changed. However, Nintendo's approval process was by no means perfect. They failed to spot an Easter egg in the same game which made it possible for you to microwave, and blow up, a hamster. Any

---

* Personally, I've no idea why Mickey Mouse is as popular as he is. He's the most insipid, humourless cartoon character there is and, it's only as I'm writing this that I'm realising how unhealthy it is for a grown man to seemingly have so much pent-up rage for a fictional mouse, and I shall attempt to address what that's *really* about with my therapist in the very near future.

sense of 'getting one past Nintendo' was short-lived however because, as soon as Nintendo found out, they forced the publisher to amend the game before allowing its second run of cartridges to be produced.

One of the first companies to publicly speak out against Nintendo's business practices was Namco, in 1989. It may seem like no big thing now, but when Tengen had begun legal action against Nintendo, it soon became apparent that many retailers had been strongly 'encouraged' to cease stocking their unofficial cartridges. Upsetting Nintendo could severely restrict your ability to get your product to market. Retailers didn't take too kindly to this treatment either, so the potential for the Genesis to shake things up held an appeal for them as well. Nintendo did begin to relax certain terms around this time, allowing companies the right to make their own cartridges and sell their games on other platforms. Depending on who you ask, this was either a noble decision by Nintendo as they were doing so well they didn't need to impose such terms any more, or a response to the increasing amount of litigation flying their way which might have eventually led to the same outcome but at a much higher cost. Regardless, it was a big hit for Nintendo who now only had lots of ways they could cream cash off the top, rather than lots and lots*. Nintendo could still claim royalties on games sold on their platforms and provide the 'lockout chip' for game cartridges. Also, they were still market leaders so, even if companies like Namco weren't fans

---

* Sarcasm, as is often said, is the highest form of wit.

of their approach, it was still worth acquiescing to Nintendo's terms to reap the substantial financial benefits of selling NES games.

Some companies even went so far as to purchase additional licences so that they could release ten NES games per year rather than five. The first two companies to do this were Acclaim, whose new label, LJN, published games like WWF Wrestlemania Challenge*, and Konami, who's new Ultra label saw early success with Metal Gear and Teenage Mutant Ninja Turtles or, as we knew them in the UK, the Teenage Mutant *Hero* Turtles. The BBC, upon broadcasting the original cartoon series, decided the word ninja was too violent for a children's programme. They also removed Michaelangelo's nunchucks (at the time they were banned from *all* films in the UK) but were fine with keeping the other turtles' daggers and sword. This might seem strange to foreigners but, in Britain, we have a strong tradition of children imitating reptiles when attacking other children. However, we only allow them to attack each other with sharp, pointy weapons, not wavy sticks on chains, due to a decree by the Queen.

Nintendo weren't reliant on third parties for game releases, of course. In February 1990 they released the hotly-anticipated Super Mario Bros. 3, with a level of promotion that is phenomenal even by today's standards. There was even a movie, *The Wizard*, released in time for Christmas 1989, that was little more than a feature-length advert for Nintendo.

---

* Which, incidentally, was developed by Rare.

The finale of the film saw children compete on the as-yet unreleased Nintendo game, giving cinema-goers their first look at it. Mattel's infamous Power Glove also featured in the movie, a ridiculous NES controller that converted arm and hand movements to action in-game and was precisely as successful as R.O.B. had been thanks to its total of two rubbish games, both of which could again be played without the expensive peripheral.

Prior to the movie's release, a new animated TV show, *Super Mario Bros. Super Show*, also began to air and, given all of this, you might wonder how the game could possibly live up to the hype. Yet it did. An improvement over the previous games in virtually every regard, it ended up selling over seventeen million copies, and grossed more than Steven Spielberg's blockbuster movie *E.T.* had. Less than ten years earlier, Atari paid a huge sum of money to make a video game about E.T. Now, not only were games making more than movies, the games *were* the movies too.

Meanwhile, back at Sega of Japan, Nakayama was unsatisfied with Katz's progress at Sega of America. Really, he'd never stood a chance once the goal had been set for him to sell a million units in his first twelve months. Arguably this was unreasonable, and in fact many of his actions, such as the repositioning of Sega as a more mature alternative to Nintendo, and the relationship with EA, would be foundations for the company's future success. Still, the decision was made to have him replaced by Tom Kalinske, who had also worked at Mattel during their earlier experiments with handheld gaming in the mid-seventies. However, he was far more well known for his work with their dolls. Under Kalinske's steward-ship, Barbie went from one doll per season to multiple products with different themes and price points, targeting different ages. The huge resulting boost in Mattel's income then pushed them on to replicate this success for boys, which he did with a range of He-Man toys and the subsequent cartoon which existed in no small part to create even more demand for the line of play figures.

Clearly, Kalinske knew how to build a brand. He'd been frustrated at Mattel when, after working closely on the hand-helds, he was sidelined during the development of the Intellivision. So, he agreed to come on board at Sega of America, but only if he would genuinely be given control and the ability to try (and fail) without having to justify his choices. Japan's Nakayama agreed to this, but he couldn't have anticipated the extent of Kalinske's proposed reforms. Kalinske's approach to hardware was in line with the old business maxim of 'give away the razors to sell the blades'. He intended to reduce the price of the Genesis as much as possible, to help it compete against Nintendo. He doubled-down on their aggressive approach to marketing, directly attacking Nintendo, and implemented a game development strategy focused on creating games with the American market in mind, rather than simply adapting existing Sega of Japan titles. Lastly, he insisted that Sega's latest game, their big hope for replicating the success Nintendo had found with Mario, would not be sold, but would be given away for free with the console.

So, not only did he want to destroy Sega's profit margin

on hardware, he also wanted to completely remove the potential for them to derive any income at all from their best game to date*. The Japanese board were appalled. Had he proposed giving away the whole thing inside boxes of Coco Pops it would have scarcely seemed more suicidal. Nakayama, though, agreed to Kalinske's strategy. This is why he'd brought Kalinske in. He'd better be right, though.

Luckily for Kalinske, he was.

Sonic the Hedgehog was a conscious attempt by Sega to try to find a mascot that could go head to head with Mario, given Alex Kidd clearly wasn't up to the challenge. His 1989 Genesis debut, Alex Kidd in the Enchanted Castle, was an absolute stinker and the nail in his 16-bit coffin. Wonder Boy was another regular face published by Sega in the arcades and on Master System (where he was doing well with his Action-RPG sequels) that was considered for the mascot role. Some of you may recognise the original Wonder Boy game as Adventure Island. If you've ever been confused about the distinction between the two, allow me to enlighten you.

Wonder Boy began as a 1986 arcade game developed by Escape and published by Sega. Escape owned the game design, but Sega owned the Wonder Boy trademark. Sega released Wonder Boy for the Master System, but Escape managed to

---

* More than this, Kalinske even allowed people who'd recently purchased the previous console package, which had Altered Beast included, to write in and claim a free copy of the new game as well!

license a version to Hudson Soft without breaching their agreement with Sega, by swapping the main character's graphics, and renaming it Adventure Island. Hudson Soft owned the rights to the new character and title, and the subsequent sequels in the Adventure Island series have nothing to do with Wonder Boy. However, just to confuse things further, Hudson Soft then licensed the rights to the Wonder Boy sequels Monster Land, Monster Lair, Dragon's Trap and Monster World, and released them on the PC Engine, again removing the Wonder Boy likeness, but NOT making those ones anything to do with their Adventure Island franchise. That might seem insane but, to Hudson Soft's credit, their own Adventure Island sequels retained the platforming style associated with the original Wonder Boy, rather than the different Action-RPG style of Wonder Boy's sequels so, in a way, the Adventure Island sequels feel more like follow-ups to the original Wonder Boy than Wonder Boy's sequels do.

I can't imagine that paragraph has helped anyone.

The Sega Master System game Psycho Fox (1989) was another tentative attempt at creating a new mascot and, while he didn't return, he did signal the way forward, having switched from people to animals. So, Sega ran a competition allowing designers to submit their proposals, and the winner was Masato Oshima – a man who, by his own admission, when creating Sonic went to all the trouble of sticking the head of Felix the Cat on the body of Mickey Mouse and colouring him in blue to match Sega's logo. Legend.

In early versions, the character became known as Mr

Needlemouse before being renamed Sonic, because he's fast. The creativity on display during the process really was second to none.

Thankfully, the game's programmer, Yuji Naka, was willing to give the game more consideration than Oshima. Naka had begun at Sega as a junior programmer and was involved in many of the titles we've already heard about. Arcade conversions for the Master System and Genesis, as well as the original games Alex Kidd in Miracle World and Phantasy Star, all exist thanks to his tireless work. If Sega had an equivalent of Miyamoto, Naka was it.

Naka's instinct was to make Sonic simpler than Mario, so there was only a single button, for jumping. There was no need for a second button for running as Sonic would *always* be fast. Level design was relentless – a heady blend of pinball and roller coasters which left the player feeling just on the edge of control. The game's music was written by Masato Nakamura (same surname as the Namco president, just to keep you on your toes, but let's not get into that again), who had huge success as part of the J-Pop band Dreams Come True.* While a hedgehog might seem to be a somewhat random choice of animal, there is some logic to it. At one point in the character's evolution, Sonic was going to be a rabbit, but a rabbit would have had to stop to kill enemies, whereas a hedgehog could roll straight through them and defeat them with his

---

* If you're in the West you may not have heard of them, but they've sold over 50 million records so that's very much your fault, not theirs.

spikes. I'd argue that, given it's a game, which is *pretend*, they could have just given the rabbit a gun or a suit made of knives, but then that's my answer for everything.

Vitally for Sega's emerging brand, the hedgehog had attitude; if you left him standing still for too long he'd glare at you and tap his foot. Upon his release in America in the summer of 1991, the game was instantly hailed as a classic and, for the first time, it seemed Nintendo might have some real competition on their hands – Sonic was undoubtedly a system-seller*.

Luckily for Nintendo, they had something new of their own to respond with. The previous autumn, the Famicom's successor – the Super Famicom – was released in Japan and immediately sold out. Not a huge surprise, given that there had been 1.5 million pre-orders but Nintendo only had 300,000 ready by the launch date. Once Nintendo got round to making more, it soon became the bestselling 16-bit console in Japan, despite being the last to market. Of course, Nintendo launched the system with a new Mario game, Super Mario World, which introduced the world to Mario's dinosaur friend, Yoshi. I say friend: you'd be forgiven for assuming Yoshi wanted to help Mario, hence him gobbling up enemies but, if you watch the game's animation, you'll see that Mario is actually punching the dinosaur in the back of the head,

---

* Sonic wasn't a pack-in game in Japan as they were still unsure if America were making the right decisions. The game still sold okay in Japan, but it didn't create buzz to the same extent.

which causes his tongue to fly out in shock*. Why does Mario hate animals so much?

Other early games for the system included F-Zero, a futuristic racing game, and Pilotwings, an amateur flight simulator – two games very different in tone, but both making very similar use of the console's 'Mode 7' graphics, which allowed programmers to rotate and scale backgrounds to create the illusion of 3D environments. The console's controller gained attention too, thanks to its ergonomic design and the inclusion of a huge-for-the-time six input buttons, including two on the shoulders of the gamepad.

Another console was also introduced around this time, the Neo Geo, which actually came in two forms. The Neo Geo Multi Video System (MVS) appeared in arcades at the beginning of the year, and allowed arcade cabinets to hold up to six interchangeable game cartridges simultaneously. A version was developed for hotel rooms which proved so popular that consumers were buying them for home use and so, later that year, the Neo Geo Advanced Entertainment System (AES) was released. The games were identical on both platforms, but the MVS had different connections so arcade owners couldn't purchase the cheaper home cartridges – home versions cost $199 while identical arcade versions could be up to $1,200. Of

---

* Yes, really. This has since been confirmed by the game's character designer, Shigefumi Hino.

course, even though the home versions were much cheaper, $199 per game is prohibitive for all but the most dedicated gamers and so the Neo Geo was never really more than a niche concern. Fighting franchises like Samurai Shodown, Fatal Fury, Art of Fighting and King of Fighters, as well as titles like the run and gun series Metal Slug mean the system is still held in high regard today.

In America, the Super Nintendo Entertainment System (as the Super Famicom was known in the US; SNES for short) launched two months after Sonic the Hedgehog, but at a higher price. Costing more, and with a far smaller back catalogue of games than the Genesis, it didn't immediately dominate in the way it had back home. Also, for those who'd quite recently enjoyed Super Mario Bros. 3 on their NES, Super Mario World was just more of the same (albeit with better graphics than before). Sonic was new, cool and fast. By contrast, Mario seemed old, fat and slow. The SNES was still a success, but by the end of 1991 Sega had a slightly larger install base as a result of having been around longer.

As with most video game hardware and software of the time, the UK had to wait longer to go 16-bit. The SNES launched in the UK in 1992, where it was the first console I ever had, so it has a special place in my heart to this day. It was my brother's first console too, by which I don't mean we shared it, we had one each. Isn't that terrible? My parents were by no means well-off. Why couldn't we just share? I even had a second controller for mine – he could totally have played with me. I'd like to take this opportunity to apologise to my parents, although I did at least eventually turn video games into a career of sorts. My brother Paul, on the other hand, should be ashamed of himself.

While Sega were doing well, they couldn't afford to take their foot off the gas. Nintendo would surely be fighting to return to the top, and Sonic needed a sequel. Unfortunately, Yuji Naka had quit.

Naka had become frustrated at Sega of Japan. Game development was changing. In the 8-bit era and before, a single person could create an entire game alone. As the hardware became more powerful there was more potential, but this required more work to exploit it, and that necessitated larger teams of people working together, but Sega of Japan seemed reluctant to embrace this. Rather than recognising Naka's achievement, he instead was given a hard time for having needed four designers/programmers to make Sonic instead of three, and for taking fourteen months to complete the game instead of the usual ten. As we heard in the tale of Pac-Man, Japanese employees were also not really compensated financially if their game was a hit. So, Naka was out. Thankfully, Shinobu Toyoda, Sega of America's COO, managed to convince Naka to move to America with his team, and work on the sequel there, for Sega of America, not Sega of Japan, where he would be far more appreciated.

Mark Cerny, an Atari veteran who had designed games such as Marble Madness, had earlier joined Sega and founded the Sega Technical Institute in San Francisco as a centre where a core team could develop further system exclusives to challenge Nintendo. Naka and his team were welcomed there, and work soon began on the follow-up to Sonic.

A key addition to the sequel was a new character, a friend to accompany Sonic on his adventure, but the name caused more than a little conflict. The designers named their character – a fox – Miles Prower – a play on 'Miles per hour'. They thought this was great, but the American execs thought it was rubbish and favoured the name 'Tails', because the fox had two tails, which allowed him to propel himself along like a furry helicopter. As a compromise, it was agreed the character's name was Miles Prower, but everyone called him Tails, which might have been acceptable had Sega not then kept referring to him everywhere as Miles 'Tails' Prower, thus taking a massive Tails-shaped dump right in the centre of the now non-functional original pun name. Why so much effort was expended on Tails I've no idea; you can't even control him in the main game. At least you could punch Yoshi in the head.

Whatever they called this pointless fox, the game was shaping up to be everything Sega needed it to be: bigger, faster, and it even added a multiplayer mode. Proper multiplayer too. One you could play on the sofa with your mates, rather than the modern approach which often restricts multiplayer to online play, and forces you to waste ages on loading screens and in pre-game lobbies. I didn't eat vegetables until I was in my twenties, I should be dead already – I simply don't have the time to waste.

Sega of America wanted to continue their assault on the

public consciousness and decided that the game would be released on Tuesday 24 November 1992, or – as it would henceforth be known – 'Sonic 2sday'. This was a bigger deal than you might realise. Prior to this, games in the West still didn't really have release dates. It's a much larger area to distribute to than Japan. As a result, new games tended to drift out to retailers over a number of weeks. Orchestrating the coordinated delivery of the game across the USA would be no mean feat. But it was more than that – Sega of America intended to release Sonic 2 on the same day across the *entire planet*. Despite being impossible, they achieved their goal with one exception. The Sega of Japan team, beginning to resent the extent to which Kalinske and Sega of America were being placed on a pedestal by Sega of Japan's Nakayama as an example of how things could be done better, chose to release the game the preceding Saturday in Japan. While this wasn't a huge issue in the grand scheme of things – the game was a hit, which was what really mattered – it was a sign of a growing animosity between the two divisions of Sega which would risk jeopardising the success of both parties. Based on their behaviour, you can safely assume that the Sega of Japan execs were the sorts of envy-filled children who demanded they also got a present on their sibling's birthday, though I appreciate that's a bit rich coming from someone who grew up in a 'Two SNES' home.

The battle for market share in the early nineties drove both Sega and Nintendo to constantly produce exceptional games. Sega created new properties like Ecco the Dolphin, which took inspiration from the unlikely source of a book called *The*

Founding, that told the story from the point of view of a hump-back whale, and 'ToeJam & Earl' which was actually one of the other submissions in the mascot competition that yielded Sonic the Hedgehog. While they didn't win that battle, they were deemed worthy of further development and the first game was well received for its unusual play-style*, which owed much to the 1980 computer game Rogue. That game had led the way through the innovation of procedurally generated levels which encouraged repeat play, as each time the game world would be different.† I never played ToeJam & Earl, and never really understood what it was, so I went back and looked at it on YouTube . . . and I still have absolutely no idea. As far as I can gather, an overweight slug walks really slowly round an empty green blob for ages.

Nintendo, understandably, tended to lean more on its previous hits, releasing the third Zelda game, A Link to the Past, to much acclaim, and creating a whole new sub-genre of racing game with Super Mario Kart. The latter wasn't a Mario game at all, initially. It was simply a two-player racing game being developed with Miyamoto's involvement after the surprise popularity of F-Zero. Despite being a racing game, F-Zero was single-player only. The problem was quite simple – the SNES couldn't handle a two-player version of F-Zero. When

---

* Its highly anticipated sequel, Panic on Funkotron, disappointed, by switching to a more generic platforming style.

† Rogue is the progenitor of the 'Roguelike' subgenre of RPGs which also includes features such as permadeath, where your character, if killed, is lost forever.

consoles offer two-player modes, the hardware is effectively having to run two instances of the game simultaneously. To make a two-player racing game work on the SNES, a lot of modifications had to be made. Firstly, the courses needed to be simpler, as split-screen meant drivers had less visibility of what was approaching. Secondly, there had to be a justification for how much slower the game was running, and Go Kart racing fit the bill. The various power-ups (banana skins, red and green shells to fire at each other, etc.) were added to offer some additional excitement, to help distract from the low-octane gameplay not normally associated with racing.

I have a love/hate relationship with the Kart games. They're really fun but I've never been comfortable with the rubberbanding, where the game basically cheats if you're doing too well compared to the competition. I understand it's intended to make the races closer and therefore more exciting, which makes sense given what we now know about the technical issues they were attempting to overcome in its development but, if I've done good driving, I don't want the game to hand itself a weapon that can kill me on the final bend. It's like playing blackjack in a casino where the dealer can pick their own cards if you've somehow got more cash than you started with.

While much of the talk during this time was around Nintendo versus Sega and Mario versus Sonic, it wasn't either company, or either mascot, that would determine who would end up on top in the console battle of 1992. Instead, the game that would be most important that year was a sequel to a rarely-mentioned fighting game from the eighties. The original Street Fighter arcade cabinet offered people the opportunity to use their strength to gain an advantage, by using pressure sensitive buttons that registered how hard you hit them. This sounds like a good idea until you realise it just meant everyone hit the machines so hard that they broke them or, in some cases, their own hands.

The game's sequel, Street Fighter 2, was originally going to be a side-scrolling beat-'em-up. Taking inspiration from Double Dragon*, but benefiting from Capcom's new hardware, the game gave side-scrolling beat-'em-ups a graphical upgrade that made it really stand out in the arcade. When it was pointed out that this new game didn't look or play anything like Street Fighter, they changed the name to Final Fight†. The backstory stated that crime had decreased since Haggar became mayor, but something seems fishy there as the game involves him walking through the city punching every single person he sees until they disintegrate. I can't believe the statistics for assault hadn't had at least a bit of a spike as a result. The game also features several female characters, but Capcom claimed they were transgender to avoid people feeling guilty for hitting a woman. Aside from the obvious fact that hitting transgender people isn't even slightly okay, this

---

* Double Dragon's influence was huge. It heralded a golden age of side-scrolling beat-'em-ups, including Sega's celebrated Streets of Rage series on the Genesis.

† The game was successful enough to warrant a sequel, thus giving the series a similarly nonsensical title to the Final Fantasy series. If you ever want to make a game yourself, try calling it Final-something; you're almost certain to do well enough to make a follow-up.

piece of information was never referenced in the game itself. It's not like there was a whole level that was just Poison and Roxy coming out to their parents.

Gaping plot-holes aside, the game's impressive new art style, with huge characters dominating the screen, appealed to Yoshiki Okamoto (the game's producer) and he set to work on a new game more in keeping with the original Street Fighter. With the large character sprites being put front and centre, each fighter was given detailed consideration to create the game's rich and varied cast, ranging from stretchy yoga instructors to green electric mutants. Each had their own fighting style and special moves, and the game was delicately balanced so that, while each character had their own strengths and weaknesses, it was possible to win using any of them, if a player knew how to make the most of the tools available to them. The game's six buttons allowed players to make choices between speed versus potential damage inflicted, and advanced players could even string multiple moves together into devastating combos.

The extent to which Street Fighter 2 reinvigorated interest in arcade gaming in 1991 cannot be overstated; it's said that the game has generated more revenue than the movie *Jurassic Park*. Just like the old days, Street Fighter 2 cabinets could be seen popping up in pretty much any location that had room for one. The fact that players could choose from eight different characters only served to increase its revenue – people wanted to try them all. Arcades hadn't vanished in the interim, of course, and now's as good a time as any to take a quick look at some of the many games that found success between the decline of arcades in the early eighties and the resurgence of them with Street Fighter 2, which we haven't had the opportunity to mention so far.

Bally/Midway* gave us the James Bond-influenced Spy Hunter and bartending sim Tapper in 1983, which came complete with its own drink holders and an actual Budweiser beer tap as a joystick. This was fine when the game was being sold to bars but, when it proved to be a hit, they had to reskin it for arcades as Root Beer Tapper, to avoid accusations of advertising beer to children.

Sega countered Atari's Star Wars with their own sci-fi licensed vector game, Star Trek. Konami gave us classics like Track & Field, and after Technos gave us Double Dragon, Taito responded with other great side-scrolling beat-'em-ups based on successful TV animations like The Simpsons and Teenage Mutant Ninja/Hero Turtles, both of which allowed four players at once, just like 1985's Gauntlet from Atari.

Taito's 1986 Arkanoid paid homage to (i.e. ripped off) Atari's Breakout from ten years earlier, Namco gave Pac-Man a graphical overhaul with Pac-Mania, Ghosts 'n Goblins got a straight up sequel in Ghouls 'n Ghosts, and Eugene Jarvis harked back to his own twin-stick shooter Robotron with Smash TV, set in the distant dystopian future of 1999.

Shoot-'em-ups thrived in various forms in the arcades throughout the eighties and nineties: Gradius, Commando, 1942, Ikari Warriors, R-Type, Raiden, and Operation Wolf

---

* Midway was purchased by Bally in 1969.

which gave us an actual gun, with recoil*. That was nothing compared to Sega's 1990 G-LOC: Air Battle, whose cockpit cabinet was so advanced it could literally spin you upside down.

Konami's Twinbee helped birth the adorable 'cute-'em-up' sub-genre of shooter, and cuteness was rife in other titles like Bubble Bobble and its sequel Rainbow Islands, as well as the platformer Bombjack (cute, despite your primary objective being bomb defusal). In contrast, the platforming genre began to offer more mature variations, such as action title Rolling Thunder. Rampage had its own unique style, with monsters destroying buildings, while Buggy Boy and Chase HQ were happy to be good, old-fashioned racers.

The point of all this of course is to remind us that, while the arcades might not have been the focal point of gaming in the way they'd been ten years earlier, they'd by no means gone away. In fact, home conversions of these games, and many more mentioned elsewhere in this book, formed a huge part of console and computer game collections. So, given Street Fighter 2's success, whichever console got its hands on it would have a huge advantage in the home. Thanks to their long-standing relationship with Capcom, Nintendo's SNES was the lucky winner in 1992, and its six-button controller was a natural fit.

An exceptional conversion was created, made possible by the use of a huge 16-megabit cartridge – twice the size of the

---

* Released just four years after beer had been deemed too adult for kids in Tapper, it was seemingly now fine to let them play with guns.

huge world-exploration game, The Legend of Zelda: A Link to the Past, which in itself was twice the size of what had previously been a standard cartridge size. As a result, the Street Fighter 2 SNES cartridge cost more, but this did nothing to dissuade fans from purchasing it in their millions*. Sega would get the 'Champion Edition' a year later, which allowed players to choose from the game's four boss characters as well, but this would be matched and trumped by the SNES's update, Street Fighter 2 Turbo, which not only unlocked the bosses but also allowed players to increase the speed of the game for an additional challenge. You can see how at this point the battle for dominance in the video game market was so closely contested that it was now not even about games, but individual features.

Despite securing Street Fighter 2, Nintendo weren't bulletproof. Resentment towards them had been bubbling up since the late eighties when their revenue alone accounted for ten per cent of the trade deficit between America and Japan. When the baseball team the Seattle Mariners was saved from relocation in 1992, thanks to Nintendo of Japan's Yamauchi stepping in personally with the required funds alongside a consortium of local companies, rather than being thanked he was attacked in the media as the gesture (intended as giving something back to the city in which they had grown) was seen

---

* Thinking back to my time playing this game on my SNES, I always remember myself controlling the player on the left-hand side of the screen. It's just occurred to me that, as a kid, I *always* played on the left-hand side, because I always played games alone against a computer-controlled second player. So that's depressing.

as another example of a foreign investor buying up a piece of America. I can't begin to imagine how Yamauchi felt about that. One year, my wife clearly spent less on my Christmas presents than I did on hers and it stuck with me enough to remember it immediately when this came up, but that was probably a couple of hundred quid at most. Yamauchi's sixty per cent share of the Mariners cost $60 million, and he lived in Japan. He didn't even get to go to the games.

All these problems were a million miles away from the guys making computer games, though. Remember them? They'd been really busy while all this was going on in video game land, making many significant advances and, if the major players in the console industry didn't soon start to take more notice of what was emerging in the computing scene, they would do so at their peril.

8

DON'T FORGET THE
COMPUTERS!

While the console games industry grew exponentially, back on computer the graphic adventure genre that Sierra had pioneered continued to grow too, in both popularity and complexity. One company that particularly excelled in this genre was LucasArts. The business was created when Atari gave George Lucas $1 million, on the basis that they had first refusal on whatever came out of it. No doubt they'd have preferred a Star Wars game, or something involving Indiana Jones, but instead he created a new game development studio tasked with creating original titles. When you give the guy that made *Star Wars* a mountain of cash, you're not hoping for a futuristic sports game called 'Ballblazer', but that's precisely what Atari got. At least it wasn't The Phantom Menace.

After experiments in other genres, LucasArts soon became synonymous with what are commonly known as 'point-and-click' adventures, which dispensed with the need to type commands such as 'open door' in the game and instead provided the player with a small set of commands displayed on the screen, which could be combined with clicking on the graphical scene. Want to walk to the door? Click on the word 'open', then the door.* Their breakthrough hit in this genre was Maniac Mansion, which we mentioned briefly in the previous chapter†. Its creator, Ron Gilbert, took inspiration from Sierra games like King's Quest and Leisure Suit Larry but, more than just the game, what Maniac Mansion (and Ron) gave LucasArts was the underlying engine created for the game, SCUMM‡. This would form the backbone of future hits for the company such as Zak McKracken and the Alien Mind-benders, Maniac Mansion sequel Day of the Tentacle, two Indiana Jones games (one based on *The Last Crusade*, the other an original adventure called The Fate of Atlantis), Sam & Max Hit the Road and, most famously, The Secret of Monkey Island.

Humour permeates all these games successfully in a way it rarely has before or since. Monkey Island's 'insult' sword-fight is perhaps the best-known example, but there are many more. The jokes even operate between games; for example, in Maniac Mansion there is a chainsaw object, but you can't use it as it has no fuel. In Zak McKracken, you can find chainsaw fuel but, if you pick it up they reply 'I don't need it, it's for a different game'. As LucasArts (and others) created more of these games, the techniques used began to evolve and become more cine-

---

* When it's there in black and white, the difference between the two ways of playing the game doesn't seem that great really, does it? But the point is you no longer had to guess what words the computer knew, they were right there in front of you.
† The one with the exploding hamster. Which was also the title of the episode of *Friends* that got the most complaints.
‡ Script Creation Utility for Maniac Mansion.

matic, with things like close-ups and panning shots being introduced, as advances in hardware gave them scope to do so. Of course, LucasArts, having its background in film, was a key proponent of this, but computer games weren't only focused on cinematic storytelling. Computers were still very much a hotbed of experimentation in gameplay styles.

One developer, Will Wright, had been fascinated years earlier by a piece of software called Life, created by John Conway, on the PDP-7, which asked the user to randomly colour in a small grid of 'cells'. Upon pressing 'Go' it would employ simple rules based on neighbouring cells to determine whether each cell lived or died. As the computer iteratively made its calculations, hypnotic patterns and animations would emerge, from the simplest of initial inputs*. The influence of this might not have seemed obvious in Wright's first game, Raid on Bungeling Bay, a top-down helicopter shoot-'em-up that made him a pile of cash when his Commodore 64 original was licensed for the NES in Japan. Conway's Life-sim was in there though. Wright, when creating the game, had invented a level-editing tool to make it easier to build the game's levels, and he found himself continuing to tinker with this after Bungeling Bay was released, enhancing it and adding more complexity. It was surprisingly fun just adding new elements to the world, such as traffic†, and seeing how it

---

*   A description of this simply can't do it justice. Seek out a video of this title in action; it's staggering for its time.

†   Possibly the first and last time the words 'fun' and 'traffic' would be used in the same sentence.

behaved. When he met Jay Forrester, an MIT professor who had used early computers to simulate 'system dynamics' for complex entities like cities, all of this came together in a game Wright christened 'Micropolis' which, thanks to the advances in GUIs, allowed the user to build their very own city with the click of a mouse button.

However, his publisher, Broderbund, was unimpressed. There was no way of winning the game, it was simply a case of 'just start building and see what happens', a philosophy seemingly also employed by the cowboys that recently redid my friend's kitchen*. Many other publishers were also unconvinced Will Wright was on to something but, when he met an aspiring games publisher by the name of Jeff Braun at a party in 1987, he showed him the game and Braun immediately 'got' it. Together they formed a company called Maxis and the game was reworked for the growing market of Macintosh, Atari ST and Amiga computers. Released in 1989, the game was rechristened 'SimCity', and heralded the beginning of an addictive new genre. While hindsight might negatively affect how we view Broderbund's resistance, at the time the idea of a game that didn't have a clear goal seemed as pointless as a dance floor in a graveyard. Anyway, Broderbund did eventually agree to distribute SimCity once it was completed, thanks in part to one of the company's producers, Don Daglow (the guy behind 1971's Baseball), having developed

---

* I originally named-and-shamed them in this footnote, but my friend asked me not to, so I've removed the details. If you ever meet me, just ask though, and I'll be more than happy to get you up to speed.

something not dissimilar for the Intellivision, 1982's Utopia – an embryonic turn-based strategy game which saw two human players competing to successfully build neighbouring rival islands.

Around the same time SimCity was being developed, a guy called Peter Molyneux was also beginning to dip his toe back in the games industry after an extended break. His first game, which he'd released himself in the early eighties, had sold only two copies, causing his business to collapse. Somewhat ironic given its title: Entrepreneur. He then spent several years making a living selling business software but, in 1989, impressed by the potential of the Amiga, he founded the company Bullfrog with his business partner Les Edgar, in the hope of more success in the games market second time around. An early game of theirs, the vertically-scrolling shooter Fusion, was picked up for publishing by Electronic Arts' new European division* and, despite selling poorly, the advance they'd received still gave Bullfrog enough to start work on their next game, Populous. This began life as nothing more than an isometric pictograph by Bullfrog programmer, Glenn Corpes. Molyneux loved it, and thought it might be fun to put people on top of it, allowing them to walk around on the 'mountains'. His lack of experience as a programmer meant his skills were limited though, and his little people kept getting stuck at walls. Unable to fix it, he instead gave the player the ability to raise and lower the land. This solution borne out of necessity

---

* EA distributed many other companies' games, including big ones like LucasArts.

became a central gameplay mechanic; you could change the shape of the land, like a god (hence people now commonly referring to games like this as 'God Games') and your task became guiding your people to build their community up to the point that they could defeat the enemy population. It's a rare example of the cliché 'It's not a bug, it's a feature' actually having some merit.

The game was like nothing else, and – as had been the case with Micropolis – publishers weren't sure about it. However, EA again took a punt. Thankfully, by the time Populous was released, SimCity had been on sale for several months and was beginning to get traction, in no small part thanks to a review in *Time* magazine, so Populous benefited from the growth in curiousity about this new type of gameplay. Populous was given a worldwide release, and it made Molyneux a millionaire. It also inspired others to develop the genre, such as 1993's The Settlers which incorporated many elements found in SimCity too, and the 1990 SNES game Actraiser, which had an unusual blend of city-building and platforming elements.

Taking a step back, computer games had, broadly speaking, gone off on two very different tangents. On one side, we had games like those from LucasArts and Sierra becoming more and more linear, and cinematic, with storytelling at their heart and, on the other side, there were these more open-ended experiences like Populous and SimCity, where the player created their own sense of narrative. Someone else who undoubtedly favoured the latter was co-founder of the US publisher Microprose, Sid Meier. His game Pirates! (1987), inspired by Dani Bunten Berry's Seven Cities of Gold', had begun to explore this area of gaming† but, after seeing SimCity and Populous, he was inspired to commit to the idea more fully, firstly with 1990's Railroad Tycoon, but more fully in 1991's Civilization, a defining game in the genre, allowing players to nurture a civilisation through the entirety of human history, across the entire planet. Ambitious barely begins to describe it. Notably, Civilization was a turn-based strategy game, allowing players to consider their choices at their own pace before allowing the rival, computer-controlled, civilisations to respond in kind, much in the same way as board games are played. Indeed, one inspiration for the game was a 1980 board game called . . . Civilization.

One thing that surprised players was that the famously peaceful Gandhi tended to love nuclear war. This was a humorous but unintentional side effect of the way the game continually modified each leader. Gandhi begins the game with an aggression value of 1/255, the lowest possible score. However, when a civilisation discovers democracy, this gets reduced by two. Rather than end up as minus one, the way the game handled this data meant it wrapped round to the highest possible score, 255. So, the moment Gandhi finds

---

* An ambitious 1984 Atari 400/800 game which was based on the Spanish Conquistadors in the Americas.

† Bunten Berry was considered by many to be ahead of her time. Her 1983 strategy game, M.U.L.E. (Multiple Use Labor Element – as if that makes things any clearer), was an influential early multiplayer game, thanks to its blend of both competitive and co-operative play on a single machine.

himself in control of a democracy, he becomes determined to destroy the planet. I'll leave you to insert your own heavy-handed Donald Trump analogy here.

In contrast to slower-paced, turn-based games like Civilisation, real-time strategy games also grew in prominence at this time. Titles like Herzog Zwei, Dune 2 and Mega-Lo-Mania all brought immediacy to this style of game, in fact the term 'real-time strategy game' was coined in Dune 2's marketing. The companies behind these three games were from Japan, America and the UK respectively, demonstrating the speed with which this genre took hold on the global stage.

We've spent a lot of time with the US and Japan so far in this book, so it seems only fair to give my home country a bit of credit for all that was going on around this time, particularly given what a hotbed of creativity the UK was with regards to computer games, thanks to the absence of those pesky licensing agreements found in the console market. Consoles were simply introduced later in Europe too and, by the time the NES and Master System were making inroads, many consumers had already upgraded from their 8-bit machines to 16-bit computers like the Amiga 500 and the Atari ST, which offered far superior hardware. Basically, games looked much better, which we thought was better, because it was. If your only experience of games from this period is console or arcade, you've really missed out, and we truly pity you, with all the patronising smugness traditionally associated with our nation abroad.

My family was lucky enough to have an Amiga 500 when I was a kid, and my dad even bought a 20MB hard drive for it off a bloke in the pub. It cost him £100, which is insane, and we never used it. I think all you could really do was install Workbench (sort of like the Amiga equivalent of Windows for PC) so that it ran a bit quicker, rather than loading it from disk each time. I've no idea, really. As I believe I've made clear previously, we were awful, ungrateful children.

Many in the UK will remember the 1989 Amiga 500 Batman Bundle – packaging the machine with a great conversion of the arcade game The New Zealand Story, flight simulator Interceptor, graphics editor Deluxe Paint 2 and, of course, the popular Batman game which had been brought to the market by the publisher Ocean. Ocean had established a strong reputation for their mix of arcade conversions of titles such as Pang and Chase HQ*, and licensed titles such as the aforementioned Batman, Miami Vice and Robocop. It was by no means the only publisher existing in this space. US Gold focused on importing successful American games for the UK and European markets. Mastertronic specialised in budget games, retailing for as little as £1.99. This was a market also served by the legendary Codemasters and of course, we can't mention them without also mentioning the Oliver Twins, creators of the ultimate gaming mascot, Dizzy the egg.

Lest you think I'm being sarcastic, let me be clear, I *love* Dizzy. Before I ever set eyes on a digital plumber or hedgehog, Treasure Island Dizzy was my go-to game. I always struggled to finish it though, as it only gave you a single life. Years later,

---

* The Amiga version of The New Zealand Story was also theirs.

when I was lucky enough to interview the game's creators, the Oliver Twins, they shared with me that originally it was intended that you would have three lives, as is standard in most games. However, in the game you could pick up a snorkel so you could go underwater, but if you dropped it while you were underwater you drowned and then, when you respawned back on land, you couldn't get back underwater to pick it up again. As a result, this error made the game impossible to complete. The Oliver Twins wanted to get it on sale quickly to make some sweet dollar though so, rather than amend the game to remove this troublesome piece of logic, they just made it so you have to complete the entire game without dying, and presented this as if it was a deliberate choice. If the Oliver Twins made cars, they'd forget to put two wheels on, then look you dead in the eyes and claim they'd actually made a bike.

Dizzy first found life on the UK's 8-bit computers, the Amstrad CPC, Spectrum and Commodore 64, but from Treasure Island Dizzy (his second adventure) onwards, he could also be found on the 16-bit Amiga and Atari ST. Many games were released for both generations during this transition period, all of which deserve a quick wink; games like Turrican, The Sentinel, Archer Maclean's International Karate + and Barbarian. Some began life on 8-bit platforms and were ported to 16-bit, but this also happened frequently in the other direction. Some titles never made the leap though, with Cauldron, The Way of the Exploding Fist, Jack the Nipper, Spindizzy and Where in the World is Carmen Sandiego? being examples of late-era 8-bit games that stayed where they were, although, as in the case of the last of these, success would mean that later installments would make an appearance on 16-bit computers.

Towards the end of its life, the market for 8-bit games was extended thanks to several companies wringing a bit more money out of older titles by releasing compilations where, for every quality game like Ocean's Hunchback or Quicksilva's Time-Gate, there'd be some shoddy titles they'd managed to get on the cheap. The first company to do this was Computer Records, with a collection called Select 1. Computer Records was actually another name for Telstar, a UK record company that had successfully used the same approach with music compilations: basically, if you're going to get the rights to include Madonna's latest hit on your compilation album, you'll also need a Bucks Fizz B-side to reduce the overall cost.

Another company, Beau Jolly, again founded by some guys from the music industry*, soon did the same, and achieved particular success with their 10 Computer Hits series which featured games like Chuckie Egg and Harrier Attack. Eventually, more established publishers realised they could release compilations of their own back catalogues, making it harder for these upstarts to source quality titles; Ocean, for instance, did well with They Sold A Million which included Jet Set Willy, Daley Thompson's Decathlon, Sabre Wulf and Beach-Head. Not that publishers wouldn't still occasionally release their games for third-party compilations though. The Soft Aid compilation released to support Band Aid featured classics like Ant Attack and Horace Goes Skiing.

---

* Two former K-Tel executives, Nigel Mason and Colin Ashby.

It's hard to overstate just how thriving the UK games scene was in the late eighties and early nineties. Other than Rare, pretty much everyone stuck with computers, and for that we have to be eternally grateful. Psygnosis gave us Shadow of the Beast and Lemmings. Gremlin (not the Sega one) gave us Zool and the Lotus Esprit Turbo Challenge racing series. Team 17 gave us Alien Breed and Superfrog. Core Design gave us Rick Dangerous and Chuck Rock. Sensible Software gave us Wizball, Cannon Fodder and Sensible Soccer,* the last of which was full of humour like the custom 'political' team which featured Hitler on the right wing, and Stalin on the left. The Bitmap Brothers in particular gave us lots to be thankful for, with Speedball, Xenon, Gods, Magic Pockets and The Chaos Engine, plus there were 3D sports titles like Formula One Grand Prix and Archer Maclean's Jimmy White's Whirlwind Snooker doing the rounds, and we've not even mentioned Pinball Dreams, Dino Dini's Kick Off or everyone's favourite Secret Service fish, James Pond†!

Many of the people responsible for these games and others like them had honed their skills as part of Europe's thriving demoscene, which had emerged out of early computer game

---

* And the less-essential Sensible Golf and Sensible Train Spotting, which suggested they may have overextended their brand.

† Electronic Arts did well publishing ports of games like Shadow of the Beast and James Pond on the Mega Drive, but it worked in both directions, as in the case of Desert Strike, which began life on the Mega Drive and subsequently made the move to 16-bit computers.

piracy, where teams of programmers, known as hackers*, would remove copyright protection from games and distribute them via Bulletin Board Systems (a precursor to the internet which allowed people to dial into specific servers using a modem and their phone line). As speeds for this were still very slow, the more hackers could use their skills to compress the games, the quicker they could be downloaded. Over time, hackers began to add personalised 'intros' to these 'cracked' games, as a way of gaining recognition for their work, and these became evermore elaborate – the challenge was to create the most impressive audiovisual experience, in the smallest possible file size. Over time, the scene fragmented into those who cracked games, and those who just wanted to make impressive demos. It's the latter who often went on to become games programmers, having developed skills that allowed them to push the hardware's limits. There are many examples of this stuff, but the one that got passed around at my school was Jesus on Es by Leeds Spreading Division, which crammed a thirty-minute rave on to just two Amiga floppy disks†.

The first time I remember playing a cracked game was on one of the Acorn Archimedes computers at my secondary school. Occasionally you'd log on to one and someone had left a game on its hard drive, sort of like the nerd version of finding gentlemen's art pamphlets abandoned in the woods.

---

* Hackers in the early days meant anyone highly accomplished at programming, as opposed to its modern connotations of specifically using those skills to break through computer security systems.

† The full thing's available on YouTube, and I insist you go and watch it.

Over time I accumulated a whole range of these games on floppy discs so, whenever we had computer classes, my discs would be passed around so people could play games when teachers weren't looking, in exchange for pocket money or sweets. I was like a drug dealer, but one that dealt in copies of Solitaire and Mahjong.

I was having a whale of a time, knee-deep in sherbet and swizzle sticks, but not everyone was doing so well. In particular, the downside of cracking was that the income of game publishers began to significantly diminish. While most people didn't have modems to access BBSs, all it took was one person to copy a game for a friend* and, before you knew it, everyone in the playground had it, and no one had paid a penny. It's estimated for every copy of a game sold there were around ten pirate copies in circulation.

As modems were rare, and BBSs slow, the other way people began to share software was through the postal system. One programmer, Fred Fish, began to collate and distribute floppy disks filled with free software, known as Public Domain, and many other companies began to redistribute these to a wider audience in exchange for a small fee for the cost of the disk and the postage, plus a little bit on top. That's right, young people, our internet used to literally be delivered to us via post. One of the best-known of these companies was 17-Bit Soft-

---

* Xcopy was an early software tool widely distributed which allowed people to easily copy disks, and just the mention of its name has made a bunch of you burst from the flood of memories it triggered. Imagine if I used my power for evil.

ware, whose founders would later form the Team 17 publishing house, after a software development team calling themselves Team 7 approached 17-Bit Software about releasing their beat-'em-up game Full Combat.

It was also around this time that computer viruses began to proliferate. The first was in November 1987, when the Swiss Cracking Association created a program for the Amiga which copied itself onto any write-enabled disks, and then showed itself every fifteenth time the disk was booted, with the phrase 'Something wonderful has happened Your AMIGA is alive!!!' (sic), an adaptation of a quote from the 1986 movie, *Short Circuit*.

In America, 'disk magazines' really thrived. At their peak, the company Softdisk had 100,000 subscribers paying $9.95 a month to receive a disk containing programs for their Apple II computers. Shareware also grew in popularity as a model of distribution around this time. It had begun in the early eighties when Andrew Flugelman, who would go on to be the first editor of *PC World* magazine, gave away a piece of communications software he'd created called PC-Talk, but asked people to send him a cheque if they liked it. Incredibly, hundreds did, and many others began to explore this model as a result. It's hard to imagine this working in any other industry. If Dunkin' Donuts replaced their tills with an honesty box, they'd be bust within a week.

For those who could afford a modem and the phone-line charges, MUDs were still going strong too during this time, and they came in various flavours, just like real mud. Some, such as AberMUD, focused more on the gameplay side of things, whereas Tiny-MUD, created by James Aspnes at Carnegie-Mellon University in Pittsburgh, focused purely on social interaction. There were no games and, as a result, no scores or levels. DikuMUD (created in Denmark by students in the University of Copenhagen's Computer Science department) added many concepts from Dungeons & Dragons to create something with a strong sense of adventure.

To play a MUD, you'd need access to an online network such as The Source, which charged a massive $100 set-up fee, and then $10 per hour for connecting to it. Clearly early online gamers needed a pretty strong income to feed their habit – Heroic Fantasy, a 1982 turn-based role-playing game played via email was $2.50 per *move*. This in particular blows my mind. How is it possible that this game can have been so good that people were willing to pay $2.50 for a single move, yet no one has ever heard of it? The more I learn about early online gaming, the more it feels like the publishers that commissioned me to write this book are trolling me with craftily-placed fake reading materials.

Prior to the internet, which basically allows users to connect to everything, everywhere, online networks like The Source were the way people accessed online content. For modern readers, it's helpful to think of each network more like a website, where you can only access the content that is on that site. Obviously, to compete in the market, these networks had to provide a lot of stuff. The Source eventually got bought out by a network you may have heard of, CompuServe, who in turn began to struggle when America OnLine (AOL) appeared and severely undercut them*. Of course, for all these companies, as they were charging by the hour, the idea was to keep people connected for as long as possible. AOL had previously operated as Quantum Computer Services, and their early network for Commodore 64 users, Quantum Link, found particular success with RabbitJack's Casino, which was great because what this expensive hobby really needed was a way to facilitate gambling too.

Quantum Link really was at the cutting edge of online gaming as, around the same time, they worked with LucasArts to offer their users Habitat, an early MMORPG (massively multiplayer online role playing game), again for the Commodore 64, not necessarily a platform today's gamers would naturally associate with the genre. Habitat was hugely ambitious for many reasons. Firstly, unlike most MUDs, it wasn't text-only, it had graphics. Furthermore, up to this point, most MUDs weren't permanent. Once players had found all the treasure, the game would reset, and treasure would be put in new places. Habitat didn't do this; it was built to evolve. Players could customise their appearance, decorate virtual homes and keep pets. They could trade items, check their in-game finances and even log support issues from within the game. Side-games covering everything from chess to road races were available and this was just as well, as early players completed all the original in-game quests very quickly. LucasArts gave players access to weapons in the hope that

---

* AOL started charging $2.95 per hour, versus CompuServe's $5.

they'd create their own fun while they worked on new quests but, unsurprisingly to anyone who's ever played a game online, the world became lawless: players immediately began to attack each other and steal one another's items. The virtual town Populopolis elected a sheriff in an attempt to restore order and asked LucasArts to grant them special powers. One player formed the 'Order of the Holy Walnut', a virtual anti-violence religion, which is a great idea because religious philosophy never creates escalating tension when discussed online.

Alas, the Holy Walnut never had a chance to become a god to rival our own, as the game turned out to be too ambitious for its own good. The original vision had been for Habitat to support 20,000 players. Given MUDs had tended to support a hundred players at most up to this point, and that was *without* graphics, this was clearly a big ask. The game was shut down in 1988 when it transpired that the beta test of just 500 people had used up one per cent of Quantum Link's entire network capacity.

Sierra Online also attempted to enter this growing market in 1991 with The Sierra Network. It offered online multiplayer card and board games as a way of encouraging social inter-action between senior citizens who couldn't so easily get out and about, which is a lovely thing . . . no, you're crying . . . shut up.

Sadly, despite eventually having 30,000 users paying $2 per hour, it lost millions as it simply cost far too much to maintain. They estimated 50,000 regular users would be needed just to break even and, at this time, there simply weren't enough people with modems that could (and, crucially, would) access the service.[*]

The same year The Sierra Network launched, Quantum Link felt technology had moved forward enough for them to give MMORPGs another go, and commissioned Don Daglow to attempt something similar to Habitat, resulting in Neverwinter Nights. It was the first commercially released MMORPG, and a huge success. By the end of its life in 1997, it had over 100,000 players, some of which even met through the game in real life, and got married. You might be wondering why Neverwinter Nights managed to succeed where its many predecessors had failed, and the answer is a simple one: the internet. Although its forerunner ARPANET had been opened up to businesses in 1988, it wasn't until 6 August 1991 that it was opened up to everyone. AOL, CompuServe and others began to dovetail their existing services into the internet, instantly giving them more capacity and content, while also allowing the companies to offer their products to a global user base. That alone may not have been enough if, two years earlier, Tim Berners-Lee hadn't developed the idea of the World Wide Web. This hypertext-based system made the internet easily navigable by less computer-savvy people, thanks to the introduction of websites, and web browsers. The first browser to really gain widespread usage was 1993's Mosaic, and many of the team involved in its creation were also

---

[*] Sierra sold their network to AT&T in 1994.

involved in the development of 1994's Netscape Navigator, which soon became the market leader.

Clearly, it was an exciting period for anyone with an interest in computer games. It was still a world where anyone with an idea, and the willingness to develop the skills needed to become a competent 'hacker', could distribute their games to people, whether via disk or online. Two Americans in particular were to embrace this ethos and these opportunities, and develop something so successful that it would force the console industry to sit up and take notice. As is befitting of two such heroes, they were both called John.

Our first John, John Romero, had been bitten by the gaming bug as a child in Colorado when he saw Colossal Cave Adventure on a computer at a local college. Inspired, he began to program his own games, and churned them out with impressive regularity. His first sale might not have immediately suggested greatness though: Scout Search for the Apple II was a maze game where you (a dot) collected scouts (several dots), before being attacked by a grizzly bear (another dot). However, while it wasn't much to look at, it was fun*, and he was paid $100 by *inCider* magazine, who published the code for its readers.

Necessary context for the younger people reading: magazines used to publish code for games, and we would then type

---

* Even more so if you're a fan of dots. And who isn't, am I right?! (waits for an eternity for someone to accept his offer of a high five)

them in to our computers ourselves and save the results to a cassette or disk, so we could play the game whenever we wanted. At least, that was the theory. What actually happened is you would spend six hours typing it in, trying to make sure you got every single letter and character from pages of gibberish one hundred per cent correct. You'd then go to run it and it would almost immediately display something like 'line 260 error' and you'd have to work out what you'd done wrong. If I'm honest, as a six-year-old with a bike, I never really embraced debugging.

Romero secured a job at Softdisk but when they began to use him primarily for converting applications for their IBM-PC disk magazine, *Big Blue Disk*, rather than working on games, he became increasingly frustrated. After much complaining, he convinced Softdisk to create a new PC disk magazine, *Gamer's Edge*, and he pulled two guys in to work with him. Adrian Carmack for his artistic skills, and our second John, John Carmack, for his programming talent. Apparently Adrian and John are not related, but how many Carmacks can there be? I've never heard of another one and, given you're unable to reply to me, I'll happily state that you haven't either.

Carmack* had a passion for BBSs that had got him in trouble as a young man. Through them he learned about various nefarious activities, such as phone phreaking (hijacking free long-distance telephone services) and how to make explosives. On one occasion he followed instructions to make a

---

* From now on, if I just say Carmack, I'm talking about John.

thermite paste in order to melt through the glass of a nearby school's window, with the goal of stealing their Apple II computer. The paste worked, but the resulting hole proved insufficient for his overweight friend who reached through the hole to open the latch the old fashioned way. The moment the window was opened, the school's alarm was triggered, and Carmack was sent off to spend a year in a juvenile detention home.

An early issue Romero and Carmack encountered when creating games for the PC was that no one had yet managed to find a way to make graphics scroll smoothly on them. One night, Carmack pulled an all-nighter with a colleague with the aim of solving this problem, which they did by recreating the first level of Super Mario Bros. 3, christening the resulting demo 'Dangerous Dave in Copyright Infringement'*. Nintendo, unsurprisingly, declined the Johns' offer to create a PC version of the game as they were doing quite well without any help, but around the same time the publishing company Apogee got in touch about releasing games via shareware. While shareware had grown as a way of distributing software, it had never really caught on with games until Scott Miller, Apogee's founder, solved this by giving away just the first 'episode' of a larger game. His first attempt, a maze game called Kingdom of Kroz, did so well he began to

---

* A bold move given the 1987 computer game Great Giana Sisters had been the subject of controversy due to it featuring a virtual carbon copy of the first level of Super Mario Bros.

create additional episodes and made over $100,000*. He then began to seek out others who could distribute their games in a similar manner, through Apogee. Ideally, the games would be efficiently coded so that their files were small enough to be shared across BBSs, to widen the audience of potential customers.

When Romero showed Miller Dangerous Dave he was impressed by what Carmack had achieved, and tasked them to create an original game using the same techniques; thus was born Commander Keen in Invasion of the Vorticons, an episodic platform game, the likes of which had never been seen on PC. Working on it in their free time around their jobs at Softdisk, the first episode, Marooned on Mars, was uploaded in December 1990, with the second and third episodes available to buy for $30. Prior to this, Apogee's monthly shareware sales were in the region of $7,000, but this quickly rose to $30,000, helped by Miller hyping it to the heads of BBSs and shareware magazines prior to its release.

As soon as their share of the cash started rolling in, the Commander Keen team immediately quit Softdisk to form their own company, id Software. It was suggested to Carmack that he should patent the engine he'd created which made these smooth scrolling graphics possible, but he was incensed. Carmack, a true hacker, felt that all innovations in programming built on the work of those before them and as such, patenting something which would restrict others' potential to

---

* British developer Jeff Minter also enjoyed some success releasing games in this way, including 1991's legendary Llamatron.

build on your work was fundamentally wrong. You'd struggle to find a clearer difference between computer game creators and the policies of video game titans like Atari and Nintendo. Whether this was admirable benevolence or utter stupidity was the subject of much debate amongst his colleagues.

Not that Carmack cared, as he was already looking ahead to the next technical challenge to be overcome. While his colleagues set to work on more games using the Commander Keen engine, Carmack began experimenting with 3D graphics, having been inspired by Origin's sci-fi flight-sim, Wing Commander. Carmack's frustration was that many early 3D PC games were far too sluggish due to the amount of work needed to render their worlds. He began to solve the issue, and did so with ingenious solutions such as only drawing walls, not bothering with roofs and floors, and using 2D scalable sprites for in-game characters, rather than tying up the processor with rendering 3D models. This was first implemented in his 1991 game, Hovertank 3D, which had a tank driving round a 3D world killing enemies and rescuing hostages, albeit a world where the walls were just single blocks of colour. While the whole thing looked so basic it could have been drawn in about five minutes by a toddler, the game was a huge step forwards, as it offered a far faster-paced 3D world than had been seen in other genres like flight simulators. However, rival companies were pushing forwards too with innovations of their own. A former colleague of Romero's had begun work on a new Ultima game, Ultima Underworlds: The Stygian Abyss. They had found a way to apply wallpaper-like textures to polygons ('texture mapping' as it would soon commonly be known) and, on hearing this, Carmack set to work on adding this to his 3D engine. This was successfully implemented in his next title, the dark fantasy-themed Catacomb 3-D, released later that same year*.

It was the following year, though, when id would really make its mark with this 3D technology. Hovertank and Catacomb had both been viewed by the team as prototypes and were released via Softdisk. Their next game, Wolfenstein 3D, would be a full-blown release via Apogee, and would take inspiration from 1981 Apple II game, Castle Wolfenstein[†], which saw players sneaking through a world filled with Nazi soldiers, viewed from a top-down perspective. The guys felt it was more fun to kill Nazis, rather than just sneaking past them, and refined the storyline to be an infiltration of Hitler's underground bunker. It's worth remembering that before the rise of the alt-right, nobody seemed to think about defending Nazis[‡].

The blend of John Carmack's once-again-improved 3D engine and Romero's level design proved irresistible, and stood in stark contrast to games like SimCity and The Secret of Monkey Island, thanks to the game's unapologetic, even

---

* Influences worked both ways. The 1987 game Dungeon Master on the Atari ST had been inspired by early Ultima games, but Richard Garriott himself cited Dungeon Master as an influence on new elements introduced into subsequent Ultima games.

† There were no copyright issues with this as Muse Software who made the original had declared bankruptcy, and its trademark had been allowed to lapse.

‡ Cut to a shot of me scream-crying into a pillow.

gleeful representation of graphic violence, made all the more vivid with Adrian Carmack's gruesome art*. It wasn't without humour, though. Rather than offering traditional difficulty levels from easy to hard, Wolfenstein 3D offered everything from the beginner's 'Can I Play Daddy?' to 'I Am Death Incarnate'.

In many ways it was a natural successor to games like Atari's Gauntlet† but of course, being in 3D and viewed from a first-person perspective, it was all the more immersive and, thanks to Carmack's refined engine, it was fast. So fast. Carmack had stripped out every element he could that slowed down the game's pace.

Wolfenstein 3D was a huge hit upon release in 1992, the most successful shareware game to date. The original business model was going to be to release a first 'episode' comprised of ten levels for free, then offer two further episodes for a fee. However, when Miller found out the guys could make a new level in a single day, he encouraged them to make six episodes, not three. Encouraging people to dig a little deeper, they could upgrade to the first trilogy for $35, or buy all six episodes for $50. And people did. id Software's royalty cheque in the first month after its release was $100,000. This, for a company with just a few guys and barely any overheads, was an insane

---

* Helped by Scott Miller's advice to use the new VGA (Video Graphics Adapter) standard which allowed 256 colours, instead of EGA (16 colours).
† Or perhaps even Pac-Man – in fact, Wolfenstein 3D includes a secret area which fully recreates a 3D first-person version of that game, complete with ghosts!

amount of money. Not content with making a fortune via shareware, id then also reached an arrangement with the publisher FormGen to release a retail version, Spear of Destiny, which was essentially a prequel to the main story, with entirely new levels*. When Formgen expressed concerns that maybe the game should be toned down, id instead cranked things up, adding the Nazi anthem to the opening sequence, and gruesome replays of boss battle deaths, including a bursting Hitler†.

The game was so successful even Nintendo had to take notice, porting the game to the SNES, although losing the blood and swastikas, and swapping the enemy dogs for rats. In the crazy world of Nintendo, it's okay to kill animals as long as you kill the right ones‡. A second version of the game was also released on SNES; Christian game publisher Wisdom Tree's Super 3D Noah's Ark, which saw Noah throwing drugged food at the more rambunctious animals on his boat, to get them to sleep. Why they felt the need to release this as an alternative to the original I'm not sure as I would have thought Jesus would have been happily *anti*-Hitler. Still, given the number of violent games out there, I guess it's nice to see them attempting to release something with a more positive message. In this case, with Noah's Ark, human-enforced giraffe incest.

---

* They nearly did the deal with Sierra, but it fell through when id pushed for a hefty six-figure advance.

† The best kind of Hitler.

‡ CompuServe had bigger issues with it, eventually choosing to remove the game from their service altogether, due to its use of Nazi imagery, which was illegal in Germany (and, of course, CompuServe was available worldwide because *the internet*).

This bizarre game was made possible because of Carmack's insistence the game engine be made available to other developers rather than aggressively protected as would have been the case at every other company, though he did at least concede to them charging a fee for its use. Carmack was already working on an improved engine anyway, for what would be seen by many as the true arrival of the first-person shooter as a genre, and the dawn of the PC as a gaming platform that could finally challenge the dominance of the consoles: Doom.

Rooms could now have varied heights and curved walls, rather than everything seemingly taking place in rectangular bungalows. There were even stairs! This might not seem like a big deal but, to ensure speed, Wolfenstein had had to play out entirely on the flat. For Doom, lighting effects were improved too, and ceilings and floors could also have textures applied, further enhancing immersion. More than all of this, though, Doom introduced the option of multiplayer 'death matches'. Initially, like with Maze on the Imlac PDS-1 back in the seventies, this was achieved by networking together multiple computers in the same room, but upon its release fans soon modified it to allow for competitions over the internet.

After Wolfenstein was released, some gamers had hacked it to create new versions of graphics and levels. This 'modding' (modifying) would have been opposed by most other companies but, again, Carmack embraced it, so much so that Doom would make its editing tools available for people to do as they wished. Soon after, fans even created the Doom Editor Utility (DEU), providing a simple interface with which anyone with basic skills could begin to create their own levels. Gaming had come a long way since Pinball Construction Set.

Even more generously, id permitted fans to share their levels online, and even sell them, without paying id a penny. However, when id found themselves overtaken in the PC game sales charts by an unofficial CD-ROM containing 900 user-made Doom mods, they realised they may have been too generous, and began to curate and release their own collections.

On 10 December 1993, the night id were ready to release Doom, they were going to do so initially via a file transfer site on the University of Wisconsin's network. It's an incredible approach, as there's absolutely zero distribution cost for the game publisher. They simply upload it, then leave it to the fans to spread it across the internet on their behalf. However, this new way of doing things wasn't without complications. When they went to upload the file, 125 people were already connected to the network in anticipation of its launch. Unfortunately, 125 people was the maximum number of connections available on that network – id couldn't get on! Via a separate chat channel, they had to ask the fans to get off as, if they didn't, they wouldn't be able to upload the game. Thankfully, they obliged, the file was uploaded, and id announced to the world it was done. Then 10,000 gamers immediately attempted to download it simultaneously, and the University of Wisconsin's network crashed. They'd never seen anything like it before. But then, no one had.

If you hadn't already worked it out, Doom was a huge hit, of course. id once again chose to adopt a shareware model, but this time managed things themselves. Not that Miller at Apogee minded, as his company were still making good money from Wolfenstein 3D, and were also doing great with their own original game, Duke Nukem. id didn't bother with a separate retail version this time, but did provide retail stores with disks of the shareware version. Normally a publisher would expect a royalty from the stores for these, but id produced and provided theirs for free. No fee, no royalty, and the retailers were welcome to keep any profits they made from selling the shareware version – naturally, the retailers were delighted! As far as id was concerned, the more shareware copies that were distributed, regardless of how, the more potential there was to convert them into sales of the full game. In exchange, the retailers got given a product that was one hundred per cent profit. And it worked. After Wolfenstein 3D was released, id's monthly royalty cheques were in the region of $100,000. After Doom was released, id were soon making $100,000 a *day*, despite it being estimated that only one per cent of people who played it subsequently bought the full version.

While it was undeniable that, under this model, it was possible for small teams of programmers to make previously unimaginable amounts of money by delivering their games direct to their customers, it was by no means the only business model. As everything we've covered here was happening, there were many others choosing to pour a *lot* more money into their creations. However, as some were about to discover, spending more didn't always equate to more success.

9

MULTIMEDIA AND
THE CD-ROM

In 1987, PCs began to compete visually, thanks to the introduction of VGA (Video Graphics Array) graphics cards which
allowed for 256 colours on screen at once*. In 1988, sound
cards and speakers began to become more common† and in
1990 CD-ROM drives offered significantly more storage,
meaning software could begin to include real music, sound
effects, voice acting and even video footage. All of this led
the industry's key manufacturers to agree a standard for the
Multimedia PC in 1991, as a way of providing software developers with a clear target. Before that, making a PC game that
worked for everyone was comparably difficult to making a
single pair of jeans that would fit all mammals.

The standard also gave manufacturers the reassurance to

---

* In contrast to the preceding CGA and EGA iterations which only
allowed for sixteen.
† Nineteen eighty-nine's Sound Blaster from Creative Labs was the
one that really caught on, leading to 'Sound Blaster-compatible' becoming a prerequisite for sound cards in the same way 'IBM-compatible' was
for PCs.

invest in key components in sufficient quantities to bring down costs and, as a result, the PC began to be a viable challenger to Apple, Atari and Amiga, where gamers had already begun to see the potential that computers offered over their console counterparts. Defender of the Crown (1986) on the Amiga was one of the earliest to demonstrate the potential of 16-bit computers. Set in medieval England, it mixed action scenes of jousting and castle sieges with the aim of securing all of England against the Normans. Its developer, the appropriately titled Cinemaware, approached game development more like a movie studio, storyboarding the experience while considering ways of making the narrative branch in meaningful ways based on the player's actions, thus beginning a journey into the realm of what we would later recognise as 'interactive movies''. The game has always reminded me of an attraction called Medieval Times I went to in Florida as a child where you had a meal and watched things like jousting and stunts on horseback. Even as a kid, it struck me as odd that people would choose to eat dinner in a room that was slowly being filled with horse turds. If you went to Heston Blumenthal's for the tasting menu, and after every course the waiter curled one out onto some straw, you'd be understandably perturbed. Although they'd no doubt do it more posher; they'd probably pair the poos with the food, like with wine.

---

* Of course, 1983's LaserDisc game, Dragon's Lair, gave many people the first experience they might recognise as being described in this way, but that was in the arcades rather than the home.

I digress. Another early game to demonstrate the cinematic potential of games was 1989's Prince of Persia. It utilised a technique known as rotoscoping, where the designer Jordan Mechner traced over film frames of his brother running and climbing, to give the main character in his Arabian Nights-themed game far more realistic motion than had been seen before. Of course, Mechner didn't fly his brother to the Middle East to do this, they'd just scampered around a parking lot in New York. The mystical tone of the game is somewhat undermined when you know it's actually drawings of a kid falling off bins. Meanwhile, in France, Delphine Studios experimented with cutscenes to seamlessly integrate narrative into their 1991 game, Another World, with an aesthetic similar to that of a comic book. They also boldly removed all the on-screen display elements such as score, lives and on-screen prompts, so that nothing distracted or broke the immersion of the game's world. They would go on to refine this approach, and also integrate Prince of Persia's animation style, in their 1992 hit, Flashback.

On PC, 1990's Wing Commander from Origin blended cinematic storytelling scenes and action-packed space battles to give gamers the feel of being involved in their very own *Star Wars*-esque adventure. It raised the bar for computer games, but not necessarily in an entirely positive way. It cost a lot more to make than many of its peers so, when it was successful, rivals had to match them to compete, which, in retrospect, played a significant part in the increasing conservatism of games development – if it's cost a fortune to make it, it better be good and turn a profit, so don't take any risks: just make sure it sells. As we know, that had been the norm in the video game market for some time and, of course, with all these technological advances we've mentioned in computer graphics, sound and storage, there was no way the console market wasn't going to be innovating as well.

Nintendo had a relationship with Sony since the late Eighties, and were working with Sony's hardware designer Ken Kutaragi to develop a CD-ROM add-on for the Super Famicom.

When the relationship began, Sony had no interest in the video game market, but Nintendo increasingly got the impression that Olafsson and Kutaragi were starting to hatch bigger plans. So, Yamauchi instructed Lincoln and Arakawa to make a new deal with the Dutch company Philips that would, with the benefit of hindsight, grant Nintendo the control and reassurances that their Sony deal had not provided. Japanese contracts tend to be shorter, and more open, with a reliance on good faith, so Yamauchi felt he could extricate himself from the Sony deal after all this, without legal action.

And so it was that, the day after Olafsson announced the Nintendo-Sony partnership, Nintendo announced that they would instead be working with Philips on the project, humiliating Sony in the process. But if Nintendo had hoped this would put Sony in their place, they were very much mistaken. As well as the SNES-CD, Nintendo and Sony had intended for a standalone hybrid SNES/SNES-CD console to be released too, which would be dubbed the PlayStation. After Nintendo's snub, Ken Kutaragi requested permission from Sony's bosses to build on his work to date and pursue the creation of a stand-alone, next-generation console that would render the SNES and Mega Drive obsolete. His wish was granted, and he began to solicit the help of engineers on Sony's System G (a $250,000 special-effects engine) to help him design a new system capable of rendering 3D graphics. While he did this, Olafsson began gearing up for the software side of the challenge.

Nintendo never actually released a CD add-on for the SNES, but Philips did release their own system, the CD-i, before the end of 1991 and, as part of their agreement, they were able to release games for it which included Nintendo characters. Development of the games were handled not by Nintendo, but by other third parties and, without putting too fine a point on it, they stank. Hotel Mario, a puzzle game where the main objective is literally to shut some doors, was only saved the distinction of being the worst thing ever seen by a human's eyes by Zelda's Adventure, which chose to cast people who were seemingly allergic to acting to perform in the game's ill-advised Full Motion Video (FMV) cutscenes. At the bargain price of $1,000 when it launched, somehow the CD-i never really caught on.

Earlier that year, Commodore had also attempted to enter the market with the CDTV (Commodore Dynamic Total Vision*), which involved none other than Atari founder,

---

* No matter how many times I read the words behind that acronym, I still can't quite work out what they thought they meant.

Nolan Bushnell. After several failed ventures following Chuck E. Cheese's bankruptcy in 1984, including companies specialising in peripherals, photo booths and printer cartridges, Bushnell had had to sell off many of his assets. This official endorsement of the new hardware would be personally lucrative, but it wouldn't do the system any good. Really little more than a modified Amiga 500 with a CD-ROM drive instead of a floppy one, and without a keyboard or mouse, its asking price of $1,000 was an awful lot for not a lot; in fact the Amiga 500 had only cost $699 when it launched four years earlier. Clearly, hardware manufacturers were betting an awful lot on 'but you can put CDs in it' as a successful wallet lubricant.

You can see the appeal of CDs to game developers – they offered so much more storage, and were much cheaper to manufacture than cartridges – but it seemed no one quite knew what to do with all that space and, as we've seen time and time again, a games console is nothing without good games. Sega hoped this would be the not-so-secret ingredient they could add to the mix, to allow them to succeed where others had failed. The Mega-CD (Sega CD in the USA) wasn't an entirely new console, instead it was an add-on for the Mega Drive* in much the same vein as Nintendo's plans for the SNES but, in contrast to this cutting-edge hardware, the game that was going to really get people to notice it had actually been kicking around for a very long time.

Way back in 1984, Tom Zito was a rock critic at the

---

* It wasn't the first attempt at this. A similar peripheral for the PC Engine was launched in Japan in 1988.

Washington Post who had begun to cover video games as their popularity grew. One of the people he interviewed that year was Nolan Bushnell, who took a shine to him, and several months later Zito was invited to join one of Bushnell's new companies, Axlon Inc, which would be making high-tech toys. Their first project, AG Bear (or Almost Grown Bear) did okay, but might have done an awful lot better if it wasn't for the arrival the same year of Teddy Ruxpin. Ruxpin could tell your children stories, whereas AG could only mumble in response to 'hearing' noises, like a drunk uncle at a funeral. Arguably, the only reason AG sold at all was because Teddy Ruxpin was sold out, so he was a solid alternative for parents who didn't mind their children screaming 'I hate you' on Christmas Day.

Zito was interested in exploring the idea of 'interactive television' and formed a real supergroup of gaming alumni – Steve 'Slug' Russell (Spacewar!), Rob Fulop (Atari, Imagic), David Crane (Atari, Activision) and several more. It transpired that the graphics chip in the ColecoVision* had been built with the possibility of using full video as backgrounds, however it was abandoned due to cost. Zito's team built on this idea and had a prototype up and running, but needed funding to take the idea further. They reached out to the toy company, Hasbro, who funded the project, henceforth referred to as 'NEMO'† but delays eventually led Hasbro to

---

* Yes, we've gone that far back.

† I have no idea why they settled for that name, and I've really tried to find out. If you know, drop me a line, it is driving me *insane*.

issue an ultimatum: either move the project completely over to them and continue it, or stay with Bushnell's Axlon and lose funding. So Zito jumped ship.

Initially, the 'interactive movie' Zito was developing for the system was going to be based on the hit movie *A Nightmare on Elm Street*, but the deal fell through and so he evolved the narrative to be an original story, christened Night Trap. The game allowed the player to view footage of what was going on in each room in a house, and protect the girls having a slumber party there from invaders by correctly timing the activation of various traps. If they were successful, they'd see the invaders getting trapped. If they weren't, the victims would suffer the consequences. The NEMO* technology allowed a single VHS videotape to be split into several tracks using compression. For younger people unfamiliar with videotapes, imagine a plastic bible you can't open with wheels in it that spool magic Sellotape.

The system allowed for five videos to be streamed simultaneously, as well as sixteen audio channels, plus the program code itself. However, the limitation of VHS meant you couldn't simply skip back in time, hence the game's conceit of the whole thing playing out in real time. Getting every scene to line up on a single timeline was *really* difficult, given they were all shot separately, but this didn't put Zito off and he wasted no time in creating a second title too, Sewer Shark; an on-rails shooter set in a series of tunnels. As with Night Trap, the game

---

* Seriously, what does it mean?

required a film crew and actors, and they even brought in John Dykstra (*Star Wars*) to help with special effects. The budget for the game was in the millions which, for the time, was absolutely unprecedented.

Unfortunately, they were struggling to make the hardware, now known as 'Control-Vision'*, financially viable. It would have cost $299 (incredibly high for the time) and the games were so expensive to make that they figured it could never be profitable – each game basically required them to make a really complicated movie. Also, it became apparent from play-testing that, although the novelty factor was high, the games really didn't have much replay value due to their linear nature. In a way it's impressive that they managed to spend so much on it before this occurred to anyone. The whole thing was so expensive – Hasbro spent $20 million on it in total – that the funding was pulled just three months before the system was scheduled to launch. An insane investment, but better to stop there rather than plough another fortune into manufacturing stock they might never sell. Zito briefly explored launching the games on LaserDisc to recoup some of the costs, but that fad soon disappeared too and the whole thing was stuck on a shelf.

Zito bought back the rights to the games in the hopes that someday technology might catch up and he'd be able to do something with them and, in his defence, it actually wasn't that long before Sony began work on the Nintendo

---

* ★★★ Rubbish console name klaxon. ★★★

PlayStation. They heard on the grapevine of Zito's project and signed him up but, before he was able to finish reworking his games for the new CD format, Sony and Nintendo parted ways. What an Unlucky Frye. But still, all was not lost. Sony had a US video game publishing division, Sony Imagesoft, and they and Zito approached Sega to rework the games for the Sega CD. It wasn't a perfect fit. Whereas the SNES could handle 256 colours, the Sega CD was stuck with thirty-two, so the whole thing looked more 'grainy', but they did manage to get it working. Under the terms of the agreement, Sega and Sony would split the publishing of Zito's games; Sega took Night Trap, Sony took Sewer Shark and both were released as part of the Sega CD's US launch in October 1992[*].

One can see how Sony were benefiting hugely from these relationships in the early nineties. They'd had an opportunity to develop hardware alongside Nintendo, and now software for Sega, both of which would put them in good stead for their increasingly ambitious future plans in the sector. In fact, after the Sony-Nintendo partnership fell through, Sega of America's Tom Kalinske had even begun developing their vision for a 32-bit Sega console in collaboration with Sony, but Nakayama vetoed the partnership, as Sega of Japan was already working on its own hardware. So, just as Atari had passed on Nintendo's NES and Sega's Mega Drive, Nintendo and Sega had both passed on Sony's hardware. Sony, who now had the benefit of

---

[*] To place this in context of the previous chapters, this is one month *prior* to the launch of Sonic 2.

insight into both Nintendo and Sega's future plans, would no doubt find this information invaluable, should they ever find themselves in competition with them . . .

Back to the Mega CD, Sony had unknowingly dodged a bullet in opting for Sewer Shark. Night Trap was about to be on the receiving end of some very tricky press, alongside another game that arrived that month in the arcades: Mortal Kombat. The company Williams wanted a rival to Street Fighter 2, and Ed Boon and John Tobias stepped up. As fans of the digitised graphics becoming more prevalent in titles like Narc and Terminator 2, they chose to make a fighting game with digitised actors for characters. Digitised graphics had been creeping into the arcades for some time. Ralph Baer (he of Magnavox Odyssey fame) had developed a tool in 1981 that allowed people that got high scores in arcade games to have their photo taken on an in-built black and white camera, and have that displayed instead of just their initials. When the scoreboard on the prototype cabinet very quickly became filled not with faces, but other body parts, the idea was quietly shelved.

For Mortal Kombat, Tobias and Boon had originally intended to have Steven Seagal or Jean-Claude Van Damme captured for the lead character, but both were already committed to other projects, so Boon and Tobias created their own fictional characters instead, each with their own look and fighting style as in Street Fighter, but more influenced by Tobias's love of martial arts movies. Atari had actually created a game very similar in visual style to Mortal Kombat in 1990, Pit Fighter, but that gained little attention, presumably because by that point Atari were about as cool as your dad when he 'casually' mentions bands he thinks your friends might know.

Street Fighter 2's 'special moves' had a big influence on Mortal Kombat too, but Boon and Tobias took that even further by including a hidden character to fight: Reptile. He only appeared rarely* and led to many people getting grief when their friends assumed they were making it up. As well as each character getting their own moves, they also each had 'fatalities' – gruesome final acts you could use to humiliate your defeated opponent, such as electrocuting them until their head bursts, or pulling their heart out through their chest. These were a badge of honour in the arcades, as you not only had to know the move, you also had to execute it quickly, and correctly, with everyone watching. Do them, and you were a hero. Fudge it, and you'd have been better off losing.

I have a very close personal relationship with the game Mortal Kombat, though not necessarily in the way you might expect. Yes, it was a pivotal game released just a month after I became a teenager, but it's not the game itself. Reader, I had my first ever kiss behind a Mortal Kombat arcade cabinet, on roller skates, at the rink in Milton Keynes my dad was a DJ at. There's a lot to unpack in that sentence but I think the takeaway is that, if the soundtrack to your first kiss was provided

---

* To fight him, you need to get a Double Flawless victory in single player mode. You have to do this on the Pit stage. You have to finish the match with a fatality, and you have to do all this without blocking. Not only that, it'll only work if there's a silhouette flying past the moon, which only occurs in one in six games. So don't bother trying.

by a parent while a machine screamed 'Finish Him', be prepared for that to be a dominant theme in future conversations with your therapist.

Anyhoo . . . Just as with Street Fighter 2, Mortal Kombat was going to be an important weapon in the ongoing Sega vs Nintendo home battle. Acclaim had acquired rights to the home versions, and had managed to get Nintendo's blessing for them to release it on both consoles simultaneously. This was partly down to Nintendo's increasing relaxation of their licensing rules, but equally (if not more so) a result of Nintendo's Arakawa and Lincoln witnessing Acclaim's execs surviving a car crash on the way to their meeting, and feeling that arguing over video game release dates might seem somewhat trivial under the circumstances. Whatever the chain of events that led to it occurring, Mortal Monday*, as it was dubbed, was going to be a huge event, seeing the simultaneous launch in America of the game on Sega and Nintendo's consoles. It was released on the Game Gear and Game Boy too but those are probably best avoided unless you're a fan of stop-motion animation made by preschoolers.

On console, while the SNES version was graphically superior, Nintendo insisted they toned the game down, despite Acclaim's advising to the contrary. Blood was replaced with grey 'sweat', and the fatalities were swapped out in favour of more sanitised 'finishing moves'. The Genesis version, on the other hand, had all the fatalities, and the blood could be

---

* 13 September 1993.

unlocked through the inputting of a secret code using the controller's buttons – ABACABB – so chosen as a witty wink towards the band Genesis' album *Abacab**, although it would have been wittier if they'd spelled it correctly. Unsurprisingly, the Genesis version of Mortal Kombat sold way more as a result of being the 'complete' version of the arcade experience, and it did nothing to change people's perception of Nintendo as being way less cool than Sega.

This was not without consequences. As concerns rose over the escalating violence in video games, it was perhaps inevitable that politicians would need to weigh in and, in 1993, hearings were conducted to evaluate the issue†. Much attention was given to Mortal Kombat and Night Trap at these hearings, but no game was safe. Even the cute puzzle-platformer, Lemmings, was called out for the use of 'satanic imagery' in its lava levels, which tells you something about the general level of discourse surrounding the hearings.

Dr. Eugene Provenzo, Jr. reported that, having looked at the forty-seven most popular games in America‡, forty had

---

* While we're on the subject of cheat codes, I can't in all good conscience deliver this book without including the early 'Konami Code' first seen in Gradius but used in many of their titles since: Up Up Down Down Left Right Left Right B A Start. People literally have tattoos of this. What a wonderful world.

† Some claim Nintendo hired a lobbying firm to alert politicians to the growing violence in video games (particularly on their rival's system) but I can't verify this and I don't want to go to prison, so let's go with 'allegedly'.

‡ No idea why he went with forty-seven and not fifty – surely that in and of itself would be enough to make anyone question his judgement?

violence as a central theme, and thirteen involved kidnapping of women, versus only eleven being sports-themed. Whatever your position on this issue, it's fair to say that, as the wider population discovered what was going on in video game land, these were worrying figures. Robert Chase of the National Education Association further made the argument that because games are active, rather than passive, they not only risk desensitising children to violence but actively encouraging it through rewarding such behaviours in games. A defence often cited is that people play these more violent games precisely because they're fantastical, allowing people an escapism into situations they would never dream of actually being part of in real life, but is the reverse also true? Is there a bunch of guys out in Afghanistan letting off steam by playing Ecco the Dolphin? I'm joking, of course. No one wants to play Ecco the Dolphin.

At the hearings, when it was time for the companies to testify, Howard Lincoln was more than happy to point out the ways in which Nintendo's policies protected consumers from the types of violence peddled by Sega. Sega responded with research showing the higher average age of their consumers, and the fact that they alone had already implemented a rating scheme for games sold on their systems. Nintendo then offered proof that Sega had actually only implemented the rating system *after* they'd had a backlash – the launch release of Night Trap, for example, didn't have an age rating on it. Things soon degenerated into a very public airing of both companies' dirty laundry, not helped by the fact that speaking for Sega was Bill White, who had left Nintendo of America as their director of advertising and PR only several months earlier, as the result of a fallout. Mud was slung in both directions and eventually the hearing was adjourned on 9 December 1993, with the industry tasked with creating a satisfactory ratings system in the interim, or else risk government involvement*. This directly led to the formation of the Interactive Digital Software Association (IDSA), a body created to represent the games industry. One of its first acts was to create the Entertainment Software Rating Board (ESRB) in the USA†.

If the hearings were designed to increase censorship, in some regards, they had the opposite effect. With the new rating system in place, everyone felt free to let loose. Nintendo allowed Mortal Kombat 2 to be released complete with all the blood and violence, and game creators no longer felt pressure to self-censor, though Mortal Kombat 2 did have its own tongue-in-cheek response with the addition of new types of 'fatality': friendships triggered end moves like cake baking and disco dancing, while Babalities literally turned your opponent into a blubbering baby.‡

Even during the hearings, Sega actually did quite well from the controversy. The old saying 'any press is good press' seemed true when Night Trap and the Sega CD received a

---

* Fun fact: after all this furore, Doom was released the very next day.

† Similar bodies would soon follow in other territories, both for video games and computer games.

‡ Some developers did change tack. Rob Fulop (Night Trap's designer) went on to create the most inoffensive game possible as a response to all this, resulting in the long-running Petz series of virtual pet games.

sales boost from the coverage. However, upon its conclusion, some retailers did choose to bow to pressure from customers, and removed the offending products from the shelves. This can't be blamed for the Sega CD's relatively rapid decline though. The additional cost of new hardware to play these games was prohibitive for many and, anyway, there really weren't that many games people felt were worth the investment. Development kits hadn't found their way to third-party developers until relatively close to the system's launch, which meant for the first eighteen months there was little being released, and the stuff that was rushed out wasn't great. This in turn led to sales of the system dropping off, which in turn led some developers to abandon projects. The importance of a strong line-up of games proved pivotal for the Sega CD, and it wasn't long before it could be found in bargain bins around the country.

So, the video game industry still hadn't managed to make a success of CD-ROMs, but one person who many expected to crack it was Trip Hawkins. In 1991 he left the company he founded, Electronic Arts, to form The 3DO Company*. The philosophy behind the 3DO Interactive Multiplayer, or simply 3DO as it's more commonly known, was that the hardware would be defined as a standard, but then any third party could license the right to make it, in much the same way as was the case with CD players or VCRs. This comparison is the reason

---

* Though he left EA, he remained on the board there until 1994, but was no longer involved in the running of the company.

the 3DO is so-called – third in the list of AuDiO, ViDeO, 3DO. I've promised myself I won't swear in this book and, as a result, I've not found a single appropriate way of expressing how much I irrationally hate this non-word. The suffix of 'Multi-player' is supposed to reinforce the machine's ability to play music, games and photographs from CD but, of course, Multi-player isn't a word either, so that didn't help.

Its creators, RJ Mical and Dave Needle, weren't short of relevant experience. As you'll remember, the pair had worked on the development of both the Commodore Amiga and the Atari Lynx. At first, they approached Sega of America with the system during Michael Katz's tenure (he had, after all, been supportive in the development of the Lynx) but as with the later hardware offer from Sony, Sega of Japan vetoed it. Mical and Needle shopped it around elsewhere, eventually finding a partner in Hawkins. The first company to launch the console, in October of 1993, was Matsushita (aka Panasonic) and, while many other companies such as Samsung, Toshiba and AT&T also took on the hardware licence, none of them ever actually released their own versions as it didn't take long at all for it to become apparent that it was yet another stinker. A version of the violent biking game Road Rash made at least some impact, thanks to it being one of the first games to use licensed music in-game, in this case a soundtrack by bands like grunge pioneers Soundgarden, but a conversion of a three-year-old Genesis game wasn't enough for many people to justify buying a piece of hardware that, at $699, was around four times the price of Sega's system.

It really didn't help that, as there was no single company with a primary incentive of selling the system, there were no first-party games created as system-sellers. The assumption that third parties would fill that void just didn't hold true. Hawkins' old company, Electronic Arts, tried to help it along with established titles like Madden and FIFA, and even the first instalment of a new racing franchise, The Need for Speed, which has managed to continue to the present day despite the original version being criticised for the complete lack of speed its title claimed to need. Even accurate sampling of the sound made by the featured cars' gearsticks couldn't save that one. I wish I was joking. There could be few clearer differences in game design philosophy than between Carmack's approach with Wolfenstein 3D of 'take out anything that slows it down' and EA's 'sure it's slow, but we recorded some noises from an actual car!' Yes, EA were demonstrating the potential of what the hardware could do, but it just wasn't impressive enough for people to make the expensive leap to the 'next generation' of gaming. The 3DO struggled on for a couple more years, and had a final hurrah with the platformer Gex the Gecko, voiced by stand-up comedian Dana Gould, but the writing was on the wall.

Undeterred, Commodore had *another* go at the market in 1993 with the European launch of the CD32 (based on their Amiga 1200 computer this time) but, as a result of missing a deadline to pay for the use of another company's patent in its design, their American launch that autumn was delayed when an injunction was filed. The stock sat in a warehouse and, before the matter could be resolved, Commodore filed for bankruptcy in April of the following year. At this point, it seems like every previously successful company was trying to outdo each other in the 'Worst Console Ever' awards, yet we're still not finished.

Step forward, Atari!

Surely this would be a winner. The legendary company must have learnt from their mistakes by now. They've stuck with cartridges instead of CDs, and gone straight for 64-bit rather than 32-bit*. It's going to change the very nature of gaming!

Nope. Also arriving in that autumn 1993 period where seemingly every month saw the release of a new console, the Atari Jaguar did very little business, thanks again to an absence of games that anyone could possibly care about. At launch, there were only two games available, one of which – I kid you not – was called Trevor McFur in the Crescent Galaxy.

Christ.

At least the console was only $250. But $250 is still a lot of money for something that would have been more use as a clay pigeon than a games console. The following year, Jeff Minter gave the Jaguar its most praised game, Tempest 2000, but for all the bells and whistles it was really just an update of a thirteen-year-old arcade game. Another Brit, Andrew Whitaker, gave the system Alien vs. Predator – a graphically-impressive

---

* There's some contention about whether this was accurate, with Atari doing some PC Engine-esque massaging of the truth to justify the claim.

platform-exclusive, first-person shooter that landed *before* the release of Doom, but that still wasn't enough to make a difference. The lesson is simple. First the Lynx, then the Jaguar: you can name things after wild cats all you want but it won't automatically make them desirable. This is further proven by the surprising lack of responses I've had on the dating app Tinder, where I go under the name 'The Leopard'*.

While the video game industry was still struggling with how to make the most of the latest advances in hardware, 1993 saw several flagship computer games which made CD-ROM drives feel like a must-have for many. The first, Myst, did so well it held the title of bestselling PC game for nearly ten years. Its creators – the brothers Rand and Robyn Miller – described their games as 'interactive worlds', with a strong focus on exploration. In Myst's case, this took the form of a deserted island populated solely by puzzles to be solved by 'The Stranger'. The master stroke was to build the game's world in 3D software on much more advanced computers, then take photos of each game 'screen' and port them to the consumer systems. This allowed the game to have far better graphics than could have been possible on the release platforms. This wouldn't have been possible at all without significant funding from Sunsoft, Japanese electronics manufacturer Sun Corporation's video games brand. However, they weren't interested

---

* For the love of God, won't someone swipe right?

in PC gaming and, in exchange for funding the project, they got the rights to the game on CD-ROM *consoles* only, and we all know how well those were doing at this time. The Millers retained the PC rights and therefore ended up with the lion's share of the profits. Awkward.

Another game that year to dazzle everyone was The 7th Guest, the first CD game to sell over a million copies. We're firmly into 'interactive movie' territory once again with this one. It took inspiration from the TV show *Twin Peaks* and set players the challenge of solving puzzles in a haunted mansion, using video footage throughout as the narrative emerged. The game's development was led by two guys, designer Rob Landeros who'd worked previously at Cinemaware on Defender of the Crown, and programmer Graeme Devine who'd worked for the budget label Mastertronic. Mastertronic had merged with Virgin Interactive in the late eighties and, in fact, both men worked for Virgin Interactive when they pitched the idea for the game. Virgin was so excited by the idea that it fired them both immediately.

That's not as bad as it sounds, as the reason for the official 'firing' was so that a new company, Trilobyte, could be formed specifically to develop this ambitious new game. Despite a budget in excess of half a million dollars, the game's creation was by no means straightforward. Production ran over, and the budget grew accordingly. Put simply, these guys didn't know what they were doing – rather than approach this like the making of a film, as Zito had done with Night Trap and Sewer Shark, this was very much game developers learning how to make a movie 'on the job'. The blue screen they filmed their actors against turned out to be the wrong shade of blue, making it impossible for them to seamlessly transpose the video footage over the game's 'virtual scenes'. The solution was to leave in the resultant blue borders on people and explain them away as ghostly 'auras'. Teething problems aside, you couldn't argue with their work ethic. Landeros once left a meeting for fifteen minutes to get married.

Just like Sunsoft with Myst, Nintendo paid the game's creators an unprecedented $1 million for the CD console rights to The 7th Guest though, in this instance, they never had any expectation of making their money back, having already given up on the SNES-CD. Their motivation for this was simply to make it impossible for Sega to have this flagship CD-ROM title appear on the Sega CD, lest it turned around dwindling sales figures for the hardware.

While the game was undoubtedly well received, it did have two common criticisms. The first was that the game struggled to decide what it was: was it a horror story being interrupted by puzzles, or a puzzle game being interrupted by a horror movie? Either way, many found the two elements didn't quite gel as much as they would have liked. The second problem was that, for all the good work that had been done in defining a standard for Multimedia PCs, there were still occasional compatibility issues due to the vast number of interchangeable components on the market. For example, a particular brand of sound card was unable to render the in-game digitised speech, essential if the player hoped to progress further. Others found that their computers, while meeting the 'minimum required specifications' to play the game, couldn't necessarily play it in anything approaching a smooth manner and it is for this reason that, to this day, consoles are universally recognised as superior to PCs for gaming in every regard*.

The third big game in 1993 to be exclusively released on CD-ROM was LucasArts' Star Wars: Rebel Assault. Taking sound and video from the movies themselves and integrating it with 'on-rails' space battle sequences, it allowed players to have the closest experience yet to what it would actually be like to be in *Star Wars*. Obviously, it was a huge hit for precisely that reason, but many nevertheless felt that the game was to some extent a triumph of style over content. It was impressive, sure, but the compressed video and audio were often of less than desirable quality, and gameplay sometimes strayed to the simplistic, or repetitive. If you're struggling to picture it, imagine a game that looks like a bootleg copy of itself filmed in a drive-through cinema through a sock.

Clearly it was going to take the industry a few more years before the hardware could deliver on the promise multimedia offered but, in the meantime, while the eventual success of CD-ROMs as a storage medium seemed inevitable given the

---

* Obviously that's not true, but it's fun to troll PC gamers. They're prickly.

benefits they offered over traditional cartridges or floppy disks, the video game scene had another innovation it wanted to explore.

Move over CD, here comes 3D.*

---

* I am disproportionately happy with myself for noticing this chapter could end with a segue from the focus on CD to the next chapter's focus on 3D. I couldn't find a phrase to do this without it feeling crowbarred in and incredibly naff, but I'm damned if I'm not doing it anyway.

10

3D: 50 PER CENT BETTER, BECAUSE MATHS

From 1991 to 1993, a *lot* happened in games. So much so that I've essentially covered that period three separate times in the last three chapters. You'll just have to trust me that, when I tried to write this book purely chronologically, it was absolute chaos. You'd better be on board, because we're going to cover that period one more time in this chapter, before pushing forwards into Britpop* but, before we do that, it's worth recapping the key things we've seen in the last three chapters to contextualise what follows.

1991:

— Failed launches of CDTV and CD-i

— Sonic the Hedgehog on Genesis

— Super Mario World on SNES

---

* We're not actually going to cover Britpop. All you need to know is that Oasis were better than Blur until they had one too many special nose drugs, but Radiohead were much more betterer than either of them.

1992:

— Sonic the Hedgehog 2 on Genesis

— Street Fighter 2 on SNES

— Wolfenstein 3D on PC

— Night Trap on Sega CD

1993:

— Failed launches of CD32, 3DO and Atari Jaguar

— The 7th Guest, Myst, Star Wars: Rebel Assault and
  Doom on PC

— Mortal Kombat on Genesis and SNES

— Hearings into game violence

3D rose in prominence around the same time as all the above, partly due to one of the key benefits of traditional game cartridges over CD-ROM. They offer the ability to add new hardware within the cartridge itself, to enhance a console's capabilities. Nintendo's Super FX chip did precisely this, and helped them to continue to be seen as innovative while everyone else was falling over themselves to release expensive CD-ROM-based paperweights.

The Super FX chip didn't begin life at Nintendo, though. It actually owes its existence to a British company, Argonaut Software, run by Jeremy 'Jez' San. Two teenagers who worked for the company, Giles Goddard and Dylan Cuthbert, had a minor hit with a wireframe 3D computer space adventure, Starglider, and, as an experimental bunch who were always keen to push technology, they set themselves the task of trying to get 3D working on the NES. When they managed to achieve this – no mean feat given the hardware's limited capabilities – they pushed themselves even further, trying to do the same for the Game Boy. Incredibly, they were also successful with this and, upon demo-ing the results to Nintendo in 1990, Miyamoto and co. were so impressed that they bought the rights to the game and released it on the Game Boy as 'X' in Japan, in 1992. I'm not sure why they chose not to release it globally, given how groundbreaking it was but, having had a look at a few videos of the game, I'd hazard a guess that it was because X was execrable. To quote the great Dr. Ian Malcolm: '[They] were so preoccupied with whether or not they could, they didn't stop to think if they should.'

At that 1990 meeting, Nintendo also showed Argonaut a prototype Super Famicom, which had its 'sort of 3D' capability in the form of Mode 7, and discussed how they might be able to work together to improve the 3D effects on the system. Nintendo had originally hoped that Argonaut might be able to squeeze more out of the console using their expertise, but Argonaut pushed for the need to develop custom hardware. In partnership with a company called Flair Technology, they set to work on the Super FX chip – so much more powerful than the SNES processor that they joked the SNES was essentially just a box to keep the Super FX chip in.

Originally, Argonaut wanted to make a new Starglider game using the chip, but Miyamoto instead worked with them to create a new title. Argonaut weren't really game designers like Miyamoto; they were programmers that liked pushing hardware to its limits. As with Donkey Kong's successful collaboration between Miyamoto and Yokoi, this new partnership allowed both parties to build on each other's strengths. One early choice by Miyamoto was to make the game 'on rails' as opposed to allowing players to fly wherever they liked. This gave the game, now christened 'Star Fox'*, enough structure and focus to allow a narrative to be played out alongside the action, rather than the less story-focused 'just fly and shoot things' previously more associated with the genre. With the characters Falco Lombardi, Slippy Toad, Peppy Hare and the eponymous hero Fox McCloud, the game was injected with a charming personality that helped it to become hugely success-ful upon release in early 1993.

Of course, the game wasn't released in a vacuum. There was increasing interest in 3D generally, in part thanks to Sega's success in the arcades the previous autumn with Virtua Racing, developed by Yu Suzuki, who had already established a reputation with previous games like the Hang On, Space Harrier and Out Run series. In fact, 3D in the arcades goes all the way back to Atari's ambitious 1983 I, Robot and continued to rear its head from time to time, such as with Hard Drivin' (also by Atari) released in 1989, incidentally the same year the Amiga saw 3D games like Indianapolis 500: The Simulation and Stunt Car Racer.

It wasn't just racing games that took advantage of 3D though. 1991's Virtuality series of arcade machines, the first of

---

* Rechristened 'Starwing' in Europe, to avoid confusion with the German company StarVox.

which were powered by an Amiga 3000*, offered many gamers their first opportunity to don a helmet and experience Virtual Reality. Their first game, 1991's Dactyl Nightmare, allowed four players to fight each other with guns in a virtual world, while trying to avoid being caught by pterodactyls, which makes it sound far better than it actually was. A number of other titles followed from the company, including a 1996 VR version of Pac-Man, but their life was limited. The arcade machines were huge, and incredibly expensive, both for operators who had to staff them to ensure the expensive tech was used correctly, and for gamers who were charged a premium for using them. Also, they had a tendency to give people headaches or make them want to vomit, not traditionally experiences humans want to pay for.

Back to Virtua Racing. Sega were of course keen to bring the experience to the home, but the Genesis simply wasn't up to it. In much the same way that Nintendo added the Super FX chip to the Star Fox cartridge, Sega developed the SVP (Sega Virtua Processor) chip. Originally, the intention was to develop the technology in a modular fashion, whereby gamers would pop a new 3D-enabling add-on into the Genesis' cartridge slot, then dock the game cartridge into that, but this was soon dismissed due to the cost of manufacturing. So, charmingly, they instead decided to let the consumer dig deeper, retailing Virtua Racing in March 1994 as one supersized cartridge costing a terrifying $100, a number even more

---

* A higher-powered successor to the Amiga 500.

terrifying when you realise the game had just three different race tracks. That didn't matter so much in the arcade where you could give all three tracks a go for a credit each but, at $33.33 per track for the home version, that's a bit harder to swallow, no matter how many goes you get.

Although Sega had abandoned the idea of putting the SVP chip in a separate add-on, they did still like the add-on idea, and chose to implement a variation of it for their next two Sonic the Hedgehog platformers, 'Sonic the Hedgehog 3', and 'Sonic & Knuckles'. Originally these two games were intended to be just one, but the game had ballooned in size (the complete game would have required a huge 34-megabit cartridge) and was behind schedule. To combat both issues, it was agreed the second half would be kept back to give them more time to work on it, while the first half of the game, Sonic the Hedgehog 3, would be released in time for their targeted launch date of 2 February 1994: Groundhog Day (rebranded, naturally, Hedgehog Day). Given their obsession with renaming days at this point, you can't help but wonder if they didn't hold the game back past Christmas solely so they could unleash their latest pun on the world.

Regardless of the reason, they were going to miss the 1993 Christmas season, and so two franchise spin-offs were hastily released to plug that gap. Both managed decent sales, as by this point Sonic was consistently beating Mickey Mouse and Mario in awareness and popularity polls; people simply couldn't get enough of the blue hedgehog. The first game,

Sonic Spinball, was a mediocre pinball game with the hedgehog replacing the ball. While they'd swapped Sonic from being a rabbit to a hedgehog during his inception, it seems they were less concerned about a strong rationale for in-game logic when churning out filler for festive sales. The second game was the more enjoyable Dr. Robotnik's Mean Bean Machine, a reskinned version of the popular Tetris-like Japanese puzzler, Puyo Puyo, although the wording in its manual leaves something to be desired. In two-player mode, if you're doing well, a bunch of beans will be 'dumped' into your opponent's screen. These beans are a different colour to the other beans. The term used to describe them? Refugee beans.

To quote Sega: 'Refugee beans don't come from Beanville, and can't be grouped with any (other) clan'.

I'm not saying the current toxicity surrounding the debate on immigration is *entirely* Sega's fault, but a lot of our current politicians were in their twenties when this game came out . . .

There was in fact a third Sonic game released in 1993, and it was a platformer, like the other core Sonic titles. It was a really good platformer, actually. Sonic CD for the Sega CD is considered by many to be the equal of the main franchise entries, despite being created by the members of the 'Sonic Team' that had been left behind in Japan when Yuji Naka moved to America. However, the Sega CD's lower user base meant it didn't do as well as it perhaps deserved and, of course, most people were happy to wait for the imminent release of the sequel proper, Sonic 3, on the Genesis, plus Sonic & Knuckles would be along soon too.

When Sonic & Knuckles arrived in October 1994, Sega's Lock On Technology was finally a reality. By inserting Sonic 3 in the flap on the top, you would unlock the full original game, as intended. But that wasn't all. If you put Sonic 2 in it, you'd get Knuckles the Echidna in Sonic the Hedgehog 2; the original Sonic 2 game but with Knuckles as the playable character instead. If you put the first Sonic game in, it displayed a screen that said 'No Way', implying there was no additional content. However, if you then pressed the A, B and C buttons simultaneously on that screen, a new game known by fans as Blue Sphere appeared which would offer randomly generated 'Special Stages' like those seen in Sonic 3 & Knuckles. Quite a lot of levels, actually – 134,217,728 levels, to be precise. Why you'd go to that much trouble and then hide the thing behind a secret code I've no idea. Perhaps they were embarrassed about its repetitive nature: 6,201,728 of its levels are duplicates so it actually only had just over 128 million original stages. Lazy.

Sega weren't the only ones getting people to plug things into other things. Pass-through cheat cartridges such as Action Replay and Codemasters' Game Genie that allowed players to modify their games were hugely popular in the early nineties and, in June 1994, Nintendo released the Super Game Boy. This $60 device allowed SNES owners to play Game Boy games on their TV and yes, you're right, that is a waste of time and money. By 1994, you could buy a Game Boy for less than that, and you'd have been well advised to do so. No other handheld could come close to the level of success the Game Boy enjoyed, and with new games based on established franchises such as Zelda, Mega Man, Mario* and Metroid (all of which continued to do well on the SNES as well), it had a vast back catalogue. Sega's Game Gear, in the meantime, mostly survived on a diet of Sonic and Ecco the Dolphin ports and spin-offs.

An entirely new franchise that would go on to have a long life with Nintendo also began on the Game Boy: Kirby's Dream Land. Created by Satoru Iwata at the developer HAL Laboratory, so called because 'each letter put them one step ahead of IBM', the game did well enough to warrant a sequel in 1993, which incredibly was released not on the SNES, but the NES. One of the last great games on that platform, it wrung every last drop out of the ageing hardware. It was this second game on the NES that saw the introduction of Kirby's now-famed copy ability, where enemies would endow him with new abilities if he sucked them into his mouth, and swallowed . . . We'll leave that there.

Increasingly, with the relaxing of Nintendo's licensing restrictions, many more battles were fought based on cross-platform releases† and, of course, publicity was often largest around these titles due to the larger markets they were able to reach as a result of their availability on more than one console. Platform games like Cool Spot, Earthworm Jim and Aladdin all vied for attention during this period, the latter

---

* Including our introduction to Mario's latest nemesis, Wario.
† Not to say there weren't still platform exclusives, of course. Gunstar Heroes, for example, a run-and-gun title for the Mega Drive, still appears on lists of the best games of all time to this day.

of which sparked particular debate as Disney film had been adapted by different companies for the SNES (Capcom) and Genesis (Virgin Games). In retrospect, even the SNES version's designer Shinji Mikami conceded the Genesis version was better, benefiting from Disney's help with the animation, and the addition of a sword. Swords, you see, are cool. All these platform games – Cool Spot, Earthworm Jim and Aladdin (the Sega version) – have a similar feel, and that's no coincidence. Northern Irish game developer David Perry was involved in all three and gained a reputation as a golden boy of the genre, richly deserved given he even managed to make a game about the circle on a can of 7-Up feel playable.

Sports games also played a huge part in the Sega-Nintendo battle. Arcade basketball hit NBA Jam launched on consoles on 'Jam Day'* which, I think we can all agree, isn't a thing. This habit of renaming days tended to tail off after this, and it's not hard to see why. There's a Wikipedia page solely about 4 March, which contains over 300 entries of things that happened on that day and, at the time of writing, Jam Day isn't one of them†. So there is some justice.

Electronic Arts was by now delivering annual releases of many of its core franchises, such as Madden NFL (formerly known as John Madden Football), which introduced official teams in Madden NFL '94 (released in November 1993 just to

* 4 March 1994.
† Of course, the moment this book is released, one of you is going to add it on there, thus giving it precisely the recognition I'm arguing it doesn't deserve. You utter swines.

make this paragraph more confusing) and official players*
in Madden NFL '95 (released in November 1994)†. After that,
they've continued with their annual release schedules where,
other than updating team rosters, the amount of change year-
to-year makes me, someone who doesn't really play many
sports games, question why they need to be a full price release.
It's not as if football changes unrecognisably within a twelve-
month period, is it? Yes, before high-speed internet was a
thing, buying a new game was the easiest way to get the latest
features, but surely today if you already bought the main
game, you should just have to pay a little upgrade fee to
update the teams, rather than pay $50 just so you get the new
version with improved sock animations, or whatever the
latest unnecessary thing is. Given EA entered the video game
market reluctantly *because* of the greedy practices of companies like Nintendo, it's amazing to see how happy they are
now each year to reach deeper into fans' pockets. Not a joke,
just annoyed. I see you, EA.‡

November 1994 was a huge month for video games for
several reasons, the first of which was a new game from Nintendo and their long-term collaborators Rare which would
prove the SNES still had plenty of life left in it. Rare had
been busy at work with some high-end Silicon Graphics work-

---

* The first game to introduce real players, though not teams, was actually 1989's Tecmo Bowl on the NES.
† Its FIFA series introduced the same innovations for British Soccerball a
year later than Madden.
‡ And don't get me started on the whole 'packs' thing in FIFA 19. Just
open a casino and be done with it.

stations, generating pre-rendered art. 3D models of characters and scenes would be created, then the designers would scan in images of things such as leaves and shovels to give them realistic textures. In the same way as with Myst on PC, the resulting images could then be exported to the SNES and used to dazzle the children of the nineties who loved nothing more than scanned images of garden tools and litter. When Rare demonstrated the results to Nintendo's execs, they kept looking under the table, refusing to believe the graphics they were seeing were on a SNES, rather than running off a hidden workstation. So impressed by what they had achieved, Nintendo gave Rare their blessing to create a new game using their oldest mascot, Donkey Kong. Miyamoto provided concept art to inspire them, but they were given free reign to evolve the ideas as they saw fit.

On 21 November 1994, Donkey Kong Country was released to critical acclaim and instantly became the fastest-selling game in history. If there had been any doubt before, it was clear now that Rare would be a vital part of Nintendo's strategy going forwards. The same day it was released, Sega of America also had a big launch. Not for a game, but for hardware. The 32X inserted into the Mega Drive's cartridge slot, much like had originally been envisioned for the Sega Virtua Processor dock, and then 32X cartridges plugged into that. Rather than a simple chip though, the 32X upgraded the Genesis to a 32-bit system, and gave it the ability to competently render 3D graphics. It was intended as a way to give Genesis owners a lower-cost way of entering the next generation but, at $159 without a game, it was by no means cheap. Launch titles were a version of Doom, and a conversion of Sega's Star Wars Arcade*; an improved version of Virtua Racing didn't quite make the launch date, but was available in time for Christmas.

The system struggled from the beginning. Stung by the poor games line up for the Sega CD which had been released in the US only two years earlier, many were reluctant to adopt another piece of add-on hardware until they saw if software support was strong enough to justify the cost. Many more had already grabbed the $100 Genesis version of Virtua Racing just nine months earlier and could hardly justify $229† for two more tracks and a choice of cars. In truth, Sega of America were inclined to agree. The 32X had never been their idea. Sega of Japan had presented two systems they had been working on to the American team: the 32-bit CD-based Saturn and the 32-bit cartridge-based Jupiter. When America suggested the Jupiter was really little more than an unnecessary upgraded Genesis, not dissimilar to the SVP chip they were working on at the time, they somehow found themselves tasked with reworking it as an add-on, referred to internally as 'Mars' to maintain the planet theme‡, while Japan forged ahead with the Saturn.

---

* Not dissimilar in gameplay to Atari's 1983 version, though obviously far more advanced graphically.

† $159 for the 32X, $70 for the game.

‡ Seeing the Genesis as Earth, the Planets code name for systems

Sometimes, when my daughter has got tired of playing with her toys, she'll point out to me that it's got very messy, and suggest I tidy them up, which I'll all too often concede to, for the sake of a quiet life. This is basically what happened to Sega of America, who found themselves having to salvage a product they didn't even want or ask for in the first place. The difference is, my daughter's only three. I really should stand up to her.* What really doomed the 32X wasn't the previous failure of the Sega CD though, or the high cost for early adopters. It was the fact that, just one day after its release in the USA, the Saturn was released in Japan. Knowing it would soon be making its way to the USA, both consumers and developers alike saw little point in the 32X. The truth of the matter was the Genesis never really caught on in Japan, so Sega of Japan wanted to push ahead with the next generation in the hopes of benefiting from being first to market. Meanwhile, in America, the SNES and Genesis were both doing well enough to not need mid-generation upgrades. And, for those who'd continued to be loyal to Sega, purchasing the Genesis, Sega CD and 32X, they were almost $650 deep on hardware costs (over $1,000 at today's prices) and that's before you bought any games to take advantage of it all. To say your choice was

---

expanded in two directions: towards the Sun for handhelds (Game Gear was Mercury and the Nomad – a US-only Mega Drive handheld released in 1995 – was Venus) and from Mars outwards for consoles. Neptune was briefly used to refer to a projected new 32-bit console based on the 32X/ Genesis combo (which, itself, as mentioned above, was spawned from the Jupiter).

*   But I totally won't.

limited would be somewhat understating things: only six games were ever released that took advantage of that full rig. All of them were merely enhanced versions of Sega CD games and one of them, Surgical Strike, was only released in Brazil. Once you factor in flights there and back to buy it, even the most ardent Sega-phile would have to begin to question whether the company's heart was really in the right place.

All this aside, the Saturn's Japanese launch was a success, thanks to one title in particular, a version of Yu Suzuki's smash-hit follow-up to Virtua Racing, Virtua Fighter, which again offered gamers the chance to experience a 3D polygon world. It had to be purchased separately for an equivalent of $80, as the console came without a game but still pretty much everyone bought it, despite the hardware alone costing the equivalent of $469. I suppose compared to $650 for the Sega CD 32X, it looked like a bargain. Anyway, the Saturn immediately sold out.

One thing that always surprised me about two-player fighting games in the arcade was the politics of it all. If someone was playing single-player on Virtua Fighter, perhaps having got quite far through the campaign as a result of feeding the machine with coins, you could rock up, slam in a single credit and suddenly you'd hijacked their journey and they had to compete against you instead. Then, if you won, they had to put money in to fight you back. Of course, anyone in their right mind would respectfully wait in this situation until the cabinet became available, though I did on one occasion see a younger kid do this to a much bigger one. I think it was only sheer shock at the audacity of it that prevented the older one from attempting to recreate the game's special moves in real life.

Less than two weeks after the Sega Saturn launched in Japan, Sony launched their new system, the PlayStation, for $50 less than their rival. As they weren't established in the industry, demand was lower, but to avoid leaving anything to chance Sega tactically released a second wave of Saturns to retailers on the same day. As a result, the Saturn edged it over the PlayStation in 1994, but many began to murmur that it looked like Sony might have the better machine. Sony had been building up to this moment for years, of course. From the beginning of their relationship with Nintendo in 1988, through their work on software for the Sega CD, they were focused on learning all the right lessons from their rivals. Kutaragi, seeing the future as 3D, built a system well-equipped to handle this. Sega, on the other hand, had initially intended the Saturn to be a 2D powerhouse and it was only the success of their own Virtua series of arcade games that forced them to amend the console's architecture relatively late in the development process. Not only were Sega's American and Japanese divisions at loggerheads, but the business team responsible for hardware development seemingly lost sight of the importance of strong arcade ports, which had been so helpful in the early days of the Master System and Mega Drive.

This attempt to integrate 3D so late in the development of the Saturn led to a fudged solution which made it far harder for software developers to make the most of the Sega hardware than was the case with Sony's. Olaf Olafsson had even acquired the Lemmings creators Psygnosis for the newly formed Sony

267

Computer Entertainment (SCE) division, and tasked them with building development libraries and tools to offer to third parties, making it far simpler (and therefore more appealing) to develop for their console. Favourable licensing agreements and a commitment from Sony to an aggressive marketing campaign further sweetened the deal. Clearly, Sony weren't playing games*.

Psygnosis also worked on early titles for the PlayStation, most notably Wipeout, with its impressive soundtrack of artists like The Chemical Brothers and Orbital and its less impressive cars which steered like 300-mile-an-hour shopping trolleys. Psygnosis were hugely valuable to Sony, but the key third party in the early life of the PlayStation was undoubtedly Namco, who made the leap from Nintendo in the hopes of a more equal relationship. With a knack for 3D arcade games that could rival Sega's, they gave the PlayStation the perfect response to everything Sega threw at them. Virtua Racing and Daytona USA? Ridge Racer. Virtua Fighter? Tekken. Virtua Cop? Time Crisis[†]. In fact, Namco's System 11 arcade board on which Tekken ran was a modified version of the PlayStation hardware developed for the arcades.

May 1995 saw the formal USA launch of both Sega's Saturn and Sony's PlayStation at the inaugural Electronic Entertain-

---

* I've waited over 250 pages to use this turn of phrase. A Herculean feat of self-restraint, I'm sure you'll agree.

† Personally, I always preferred Atari's Area 51, and this footnote was the only place I could find to mention it. So that's why this is here. My wife likes it too. Bye!

ment Expo (E3). Founded by the Interactive Digital Software Association (four words which seem to have been chosen specifically to make playing games sound as un-fun as possible), the event aimed to give the games industry its own showcase for forthcoming releases. Previously, they'd shared the Consumer Electronics Show (CES) with everything from phones to fridges.

I've never really understood why everyone looks forward to E3. It's become a huge event in the gaming calendar but, when you were a kid, if your parents had sat you down in the summer and played you videos of all the toys you wouldn't be getting until Christmas, you wouldn't have been excited, you'd have beaten them to death with a Boglin.

Prior to the event, Sega had announced the Saturn would launch in the USA on 2 September – a Saturday, or 'Saturn Day'* as it would be known – but from the stage Kalinske announced that, while that would still be the official launch date for the $399 Saturn, 30,000 systems had already been distributed to key retailers like Toys R Us and Electronics Boutique, and were available to purchase immediately!

This was a huge surprise for everyone in attendance. Steve Race, the president of the newly formed Sony Computer Entertainment of America (SCEA)†, would struggle to top it. This wasn't his first rodeo though. He'd been VP of Atari's

---

* For the love of God, make them stop.

† Sony Imagesoft (the label behind Sony's Sega CD games) was folded into this new company. And, while we're here: ★★★ Boring company name klaxon. ★★★

European Division during the VCS era, co-founded Worlds of Wonder (the NES's distributors in the USA) and been engaged by Kalinske as a marketing consultant for Sega during many of the Genesis' key campaigns. When he was introduced to the stage by Olafsson, he appeared with his sheets of notes in hand. Arriving at the podium, he simply said one thing – '$299' – and left, to much applause and whooping*.

Not only had Sega's early launch reveal been blown away, their choice to bring it forward ended up doing more harm than good. Many smaller retailers took offence at not being included in Sega's early stock allocations, so they chose to drop support for it before they'd even begun stocking it. There were very few games launched during the interim period between May and September, as it had caught third-party developers off guard, so they weren't too impressed about being kept out of the loop either. If you're confused by this poor series of decisions taken by Sega of America, it's because they were actually being taken by Sega of Japan. Ever since the very public flogging Sega had received during the hearings relating to Night Trap and Mortal Kombat, Japan slowly began to take back control, feeling the damage done to the brand was a sign that Kalinske had been given too long a leash. Whether this damage was real or imagined on the part of Sega of Japan is a point of contention and certainly there's a cultural factor at play but, either way, Japan had the final say and, emboldened by their strongest market performance to date, were determined to push forward with their plans for the Saturn.

---

* Footage of this exists online. It's pretty cool.

Sega of America did manage to release a couple of key titles during that summer. Daytona USA offered a notable graphical upgrade over Sega's previous driving game, Virtua Racing, and Panzer Dragoon was a well-received on-rails fantasy shooter, harking back to the gameplay of Space Harrier. Dragoon is often assumed to be a misspelling/translation of Dragon*, given you ride one in the game but a dragoon is actually a term used to describe a class of mounted infantry who used horses to get around, then dismounted to fight. Panzer is a German word for armour, and your in-game dragon is indeed armoured. So, what we're actually dealing with here, is some advanced wordplay where your 'dragoon' protagonist is riding an armoured (i.e. 'panzer') dragon. As if that wasn't enough, the term dragoon takes *its* name from a weapon known as a dragon, which was a handgun version of a blunderbuss used by French army dragoons. And I appreciate all this might not sound funny but, in my defence, it isn't.

Just to complicate matters, Knuckles Chaotix was also released around this time for the Mega Drive's 32X. It's a particularly odd one, being essentially a Sonic game without Sonic in it, created without Yuki Naka's input, as he was working on another project for the Saturn. The game had an infuriating mechanic that involved tethering the player to a second character, who could either be controlled by a second player, or the computer, and they then had to work cooperatively to get through the levels. The experience was akin to attempting to break the 100 metre sprint world record while

---

* Much like the confusion surrounding the name of Donkey Kong.

tied by a bungee rope to a friend that had wandered off to get crisps. Although some people appreciated the attempt at innovation, most felt it just slowed up the gameplay, because it did. Also, at a time when everyone was excited about the move to 3D, another 2D platformer just felt old hat.

When the PlayStation launched in September in America, the first 100,000 sold out immediately, giving them a 30,000-unit advantage over the Saturn, despite Sega's head start. The following month, Sega of Japan's Nakayama decreed that Sega would cease work on everything except Sega Saturn worldwide. This strategy wasn't without merit. Sega was increasingly spreading its focus very thinly across many products. Not only hardware such as the Game Gear, Genesis, Sega CD and 32X, but also a growing number of tangential endeavours such as the Japanese amusement park, Sega Joyopolis, the Sega Foundation, which was created with the noble goal of funding access to the internet for the underprivileged, and the Sega Pico, dubbed 'The computer that thinks it's a toy!' Even the least academically-minded child knows full well that anything that describes itself as 'edutainment' will offer a lot of 'edu' but zero 'tainment', and it never stood a chance.

By the end of 1995, Sega of Japan was still doing well thanks to Saturn releases of its hit arcade titles. Sega Rally Championship benefited from the expertise of Kenji Sasaki, who had been poached from Namco's Ridge Racer team, Virtua Cop successfully added light gun shooters to the genres covered by the growing Virtua brand, and Virtua Fighter 2 was an improvement over the original in every regard. These were all released in America that year too, but it wasn't enough. For many US consumers, this decision to focus solely on the Saturn was the final straw. The 32X was less than a year old, and the Saturn's full nationwide launch had only occurred the previous month. It was simply too soon to abandon the 16-bit market. Sega's Nomad, a handheld version of the Genesis, was literally released in America the same *month* as the Saturn-only announcement.

By 1996, Sony was outselling Sega two-to-one in the USA and Sega of America had to make significant redundancies as a result of their downturn in performance. It was no surprise when Tom Kalinske resigned; he no longer had the freedom he'd insisted on when he'd been poached from Mattel, and it was clear the choices Japan were making made it impossible for the American division to thrive. David Rosen, with the company since its inception in 1965, soon followed, as a way of expressing dismay at the way Kalinske and co. had been treated. Nakayama stepped down too, though only from his involvement in Sega of America; he would remain at Sega of Japan for several more years. As with Atari the previous decade, another giant seemed to be falling.

You might have thought things couldn't get any worse, but Sega's abandoning of 16-bit had also served to strengthen the position of their other rival; Nintendo virtually had the whole market to themselves. In 1995, twenty per cent of the US market for video games was in 32-bit consoles, versus sixty-four per cent for 16-bit. Sega of Japan might as well have handed Nintendo of America a massive bag of cash.

Nintendo may have lost some fans to Sony by delaying their own transition to the next generation, but this late period in the SNES's life saw many of their most successful titles. Killer Instinct was Nintendo and Rare's* response to Virtua Fighter and Tekken, and employed the same graphical trickery used to make Donkey Kong Country look so good. Initially a 1994 arcade game, the 1995 SNES conversion was celebrated on launch, despite having to make so many compromises in the transition that the end product was more diluted than the free orange squash you get at a school fete.

Yoshi's Island, a sequel to Super Mario World, saw the dinosaur take centre stage alongside a baby Mario, and made subtle use of an upgraded version of the Super FX chip† to achieve it's beautiful 'pop-up book come to life' 3D effects. The game was initially rejected by Nintendo for looking too much like Super Mario World at a time when they were moving towards the more realistic graphics seen in Donkey Kong Country, but Miyamoto rebelled by pushing in the opposite direction, making it even more cartoony. He felt Donkey Kong Country was an example of how 'players will put up with mediocre gameplay as long as the art is good'. Shots fired! Gamers clearly disagreed though, and two Donkey Kong Country sequels, Diddy's Kong Quest and Dixie Kong's

---

* And Williams, who signed a deal with Nintendo to develop arcade games such as Killer Instinct using Rare/Silicon Graphics technology (referred to at the time as 'Project Reality').

† This Super FX 2 chip was also used to bring Doom to the SNES.

Double Trouble did great business, as did the Game Boy spin-off Donkey Kong Land series.

Platforming was making the transition to the next generation too, with Ubisoft's 1995 hit, Rayman. Initially developed as an exclusive for the Atari Jaguar, PlayStation and Saturn versions were quickly created when it became apparent that the Jaguar was rubbish. If you've ever played Rayman, you'll have noticed he doesn't have any arms or legs. This was because the animators found them too hard to animate. He's still got hands and feet, but they float nearby, disembodied. It just doesn't make any sense. Rayman's hardly photorealistic. All he needs for an arm is two lines drawn between his body and his hand, then a bit of colouring in. How did they get away with it? There's no other job where you can just refuse to do some of the job. If you went to a car mechanic and he said 'I don't do engines, so I'll just cut a hole in the floor and you can move it round with your legs like the Flintstones' you'd be well within your rights to find someone else who could actually fix cars.

Back on the SNES, Dragon Quest and Final Fantasy* continued to do the business in Japan, and 1995's Chrono Trigger gifted the SNES an incredible JRPG which saw Final Fantasy's Sakaguchi collaborate with Dragon Quest's Horii and Toriyama. This was made possible as Horii and Toriyama were freelance, rather than committed exclusively to Enix, so could freely work with Sakaguchi for Square. Given the

---

* And its spin-off, Secret of Mana, which had originally been planned as a launch title for the aborted SNES-CD.

amount of rivalry we've seen throughout the history of games, this spirit of cooperation is a cause for much celebration! Square even found time to make a brilliant Super Mario RPG, Legend of the Seven Stars, in 1996, a year which also saw the first appearance of the successful farming RPG/sim, Harvest Moon.

Sega had managed a couple of final 16-bit hits in 1995, in the form of innovative beat-'em-up Comix Zone which sees you navigate through the panels of a comic book, and the colourful platformer, Ristar. Ristar's particularly good, because the main character has arms. Stretchy ones. You could literally use his arms on Rayman, and no one would even notice. The whole thing's a farce.

Though Nintendo were still doing well with the SNES, they were struggling with a new piece of hardware. The Virtual Boy was the latest innovation from Gunpei Yokoi, and was billed as the successor to his Game Boy. Placed on a tabletop, the player would place their head up to the visor, and two screens (one for each eye) comprised of red LEDs would give the player the illusion of 3D. Why red? Because full-colour screens were too expensive, and the colour red apparently uses less battery than any other colour. This is why teachers use red pens to mark homework*.

While everyone else was content to create 3D models in normal games, Nintendo was pushing to provide an authentic 3D experience. The tabletop stand was chosen over head-

---

* I'll level with you – I was really tired when I wrote that. It's wilfully nonsensical and you deserve better.

mounting to remove the issue of motion sickness common with movement tracking in VR, but users still reported headaches, dizziness and even cases of epileptic seizures. Given the system had the potential to make people shake uncontrollably and lose consciousness, it hardly seems necessary to mention the Virtual Boy also had a lack of quality games. But it did. In fact, it had a lack of games, full stop. Only twenty-two were ever released, and what few there were didn't seem that much improved by being in 3D. The industry wasn't impressed, and neither was the buying public. Released in Japan in July 1995, it had been discontinued by December.

Despite having been involved in the creation of Donkey Kong, the Game Boy and so many other things that defined the very essence of Nintendo for millions of gamers across the planet, after the failure of the Virtual Boy Yokoi found himself an outcast in the very company he'd helped to build. The following year, after thirty-one years with the company, he left Nintendo. But he wasn't beaten. By 1997 he was working with the company Bandai to create a new handheld, the Wonder-Swan.

Sadly, Yokoi never saw its release as, on 4 October 1997, while driving on the Hokuriku Expressway in Japan, he drove into the back of a truck. Upon leaving his vehicle to inspect the damage, he was tragically hit, and killed, by a passing car.

Just like Frogger.

11
ALL CHANGE

Back in computer land, Microsoft were about to take centre stage, and do their part in cementing PCs as the primary computer for gaming. On 24 August 1995, Windows 95 was released and soon afterwards Microsoft introduced DirectX, a technology that made it easier for games to reliably run on the new platform, rather than requiring users to exit to MS-DOS and tinker with settings*. Of course, it was by no means perfect at first, and it was still nowhere as easy to run games on computers as it was on consoles, but it was a vital step in the right direction.

Computers were still very confusing around this time. By 1995, the Pentium series of processors was well established, but my family still had a 486 DX2 66 – I'd love to tell you what that meant but in those days you worked out how good your computer was solely based on what other computers were called. A 486 was definitely better than the 386, and much better than the 286, and the fact the DX had a 2 next to it

---

* Although, actually, many programmers preferred to do that, due to the increased control it afforded them over a user's hardware.

probably meant it was twice as good at whatever DXs did. The 66 was the biggest number you could get with one of those. The 486 wasn't as good as the Pentium, which was really a 586 with a less confusing name in the hopes of making all this less baffling, but it was still a solid computer. Probably.

As sales pitches frighteningly close to the above paragraph took place in electrical goods retailers across the planet, Windows 95 found itself embroiled in what became known as the first 'browser war', thanks to the inclusion of Internet Explorer* with most versions of the operating system, thus removing the need for people to install Netscape separately. Whereas Internet Explorer was provided free to all users, Netscape derived its income from business use of its software and IE's release decimated Netscape's income. In 1998 this was recognised as illegal, monopolistic behaviour and Netscape's new owners, AOL, received a substantial settlement of $750 million. While describing this whole thing as a browser *war* might have been a linguistic stretch, it was indisputable that the internet was now big business.

Back when Windows 95 launched, to demonstrate its potential a team at Microsoft successfully ported a version of Doom to the operating system, and even shot a promotional video to demonstrate the power of the new platform, superimposing Microsoft CEO Bill Gates into the game, and literally showing him killing a man with a gun. Unfortunately, he delivered his performance with all the pizzazz of a geography

---

* Built on the work of Mosaic, Microsoft having licensed the rights to it from its creator, Spyglass Inc.

teacher trying to sell a room of teenagers on the beauty of oxbow lakes. Doom wasn't the first game to appear on Windows, of course, but prior to this they tended to be simple puzzle or card games like Minesweeper and Solitaire. Occasionally slightly more 'gamey' games would appear, such as downhill sports sim SkiFree, which I recently discovered to my cost was nowhere near as popular as I thought it was, when I attempted to use it as a reference point at a comedy gig.

Doom's sequel, Doom II: Hell on Earth (released in 1994) went straight to market as a full commercial release published by Good Times Interactive (GTI), a company founded by one Ron Chaimowitz. Chaimowitz might not seem an obvious partner for one of the biggest game releases of the year as, prior to this, his CV mainly consisted of nurturing Hispanic music acts like Gloria Estefan and Julio Iglesias for CBS Records in Miami, and founding a company called Good Times which sold budget releases of public domain movies and Jane Fonda workout tapes. However, as the games market had opened up, he'd created Good Times Interactive as a separate division, which had a focus on securing budget rereleases of games from companies like EA and Broderbund, in much the same way he'd done for films in the home VHS market.

As he'd made good money from this endeavour, he soon wanted to find his own new games too, and looked to the shareware market for possibilities. At the time, id, having separated from Apogee, didn't have a traditional retail plan for Doom. In the end, rather than release a parallel version comprised of new levels as they'd done with Wolfenstein, they agreed that GTI could release a new set of Doom levels, but it would be billed as a straight sequel. This meant Carmack was once again free to develop a new game engine, while the id team created Doom 2's levels. Unsurprisingly, Doom 2 was a massive hit, and played a significant role in the growth of 3D graphics cards for PCs, as people wanted to get the best performance possible.

Two years later, id released its follow-up, Quake. Critically acclaimed, and with a soundtrack by the Nine Inch Nails' Trent Reznor, the game again was a huge success, in no small part due to its fast-paced sixteen-player online deathmatches. It wasn't long before teams began to form and compete in tournaments, foreshadowing the eventual emergence of eSports. Good players began to gain fame online, and even got sponsorships from companies like Microsoft.

Quake wasn't without issues, though. id chose to release the game's shareware version on disk to allow them to bypass the publisher GTI – there was no need to share the profits of a retail version because people could buy an unlock code to activate the full game, which was actually also encrypted on the shareware disk. However, their greed was to be their downfall as hackers wasted no time in hacking the disk and unlocking, then self-distributing, the full version for free. Having spent so many years giving so much to the hacker community, this must have been a bitter pill for Carmack to swallow. Moreover, it was a financial disaster and, as a result of the fallout, GTI and id separated*. And it wasn't the only

---

* In the meantime, Doom's previous publisher, Apogee, was doing great with their own game, Duke Nukem 3D – some called it the 'Quake killer'.

fallout. After the release of Quake, Romero was fired for not pulling his weight, Carmack feeling that Romero had spent far too much time enjoying the celebrity which came with their success, but far too little time actually working on the game. During production, an active member of the Doom mod community, Tim Willits, had even been employed by id to design levels for Quake, to plug the hole left by Romero's regular absences.

Although it was true that Romero had been living the good life, he had also been busy helping Raven Software develop their own game – Heretic* – using the Doom engine, and he was still very driven. Upon his dismissal from id, he wasted no time in forming a new company, Ion Storm, and was soon proclaiming to everyone that his new game, Daikatana, was going to be superior to everything that had come before it. Securing a vast amount of investment for his new company, he failed to deliver on his many promises, which increasingly seemed like hollow boasts. A key part of the problem was that his plan relied on developing his new game using Carmack's Quake engine. Which, of course, he could. Carmack's game engine was once again available to everyone. Unfortunately for Romero, while he was developing his new game, Carmack was developing a far superior engine for Quake's sequel, designed to make the most of emerging hardware such as 3dfx's Voodoo graphics cards. By the time Quake 2 was unveiled to the public, Romero's team were deep into development using the earlier engine and, though Romero made the

---

* And its subsequent sequel, Hexen.

choice to get his team to rework the game on the newer, more impressive, engine, the complexities of migrating over led to countless delays*. While Romero struggled to create a working game, Quake 2's success poured daily salt into his wounds.

This isn't to say the original Quake's tools weren't impressive, and fans were once again making the most of the generous access Carmack gave them. He offered up the game's custom programming language, QuakeC, which meant people could now create not only their own game maps, but whole new engines. After just a few months, three fans had worked together to create a mod which became known as Team Fortress – a great game in its own right, which allowed teams of soldiers with varying abilities to compete in multiplayer 'escort' and 'capture the flag' missions. If you've ever had abusive language screamed at you by an anonymous child over the internet, it's likely it was on one of the many subsequent games that took inspiration from these new styles of gameplay.

Another group of fans used Quake's 'record' feature to make their own short movie, adding dialogue to footage shot entirely in-game. While simple, this Diary of a Camper was the first example of what would evolve into a whole new style of in-game movie-making which would become known as 'machinima'.

Another game that owed a debt to movie-making was the sequel to The 7th Guest, The 11th Hour, although it would have far less impact. The 7th Guest had so much buzz surrounding it that The 11th Hour was already being made before

---

* The game wouldn't actually see the light of day until the year 2000.

the first title was released, but it was made without Devine's involvement. As with Carmack and Romero at id, Devine and Landeros had a falling-out over their approach – in this case, Devine disliked the more violent and smuttier tone the sequel seemed to be adopting. By the end of 1996, the pair were no longer on speaking terms and Trilobyte's board made the decision to fire Landeros. Devine sided with them, not his friend, a choice which would continue to haunt him for a long time afterwards but, lest you think it's all doom* and gloom during this period, Myst's 1997 sequel Riven was released to positive reviews and strong sales. One of its creators, Robyn Miller, did leave the company after its completion, but this was entirely amicable.

The same could not be said for Bullfrog though. Following 1994's release of the successful funfair management sim, Theme Park, and fantasy-shooter, Magic Carpet, Bullfrog was acquired by Electronic Arts and Molyneux became a VP there. By late 1996 his increased corporate responsibility had him yearning for more active involvement in game development, and he made the decision to resign. He chose to stay on until the completion of the devilish management sim, Dungeon Keeper, in 1997†, although development of the game had to be moved to his house when EA banned him from entering the offices after his resignation. Soon after Molyneux left, others

---

* No pun intended. I wish I was good enough for it to be intended. But it wasn't. At least I'm honest. As if that's worth anything.

† Theme Hospital, Theme Park's spiritual successor, was also released by the company earlier that year.

followed, citing a change in culture after EA's acquisition. Bull-frog had always been a company that celebrated innovation and originality but, after EA got involved, many felt it became more like a production line. I'd imagine them literally not letting the guy who was making their next hit game in the building put a bit of a downer on the general vibe of the place too.

Nineteen ninety-seven was also the year Electronic Arts bought Maxis, so clearly EA weren't short of cash or struggling to survive after the exit of founder Trip Hawkins. Maxis had done well with SimCity sequel SimCity 2000 in 1993, but since then had struggled to follow it up with another hit with the same reliability that Bullfrog had, despite having a clear formula – see if you can spot it: SimAnt, SimFarm, SimEarth, SimLife, SimTower, SimIsle. That's right – all the games' titles have vowels in them.

EA's punt on Maxis eventually proved wise though. While it's slightly outside the timescale we're looking at in this book, it would be remiss of me not to mention that, in 2000, Will Wright delivered the first instalment of his latest game for Maxis, the phenomenally successful The Sims.

In case it wasn't already apparent, the games industry was entering a significant period of consolidation through acqui-sition. Sid Meier's company Microprose was acquired by Spectrum Holobyte in 1993, but Meier happily stuck around for several years while his team created a bunch more great games, including a sequel to Civilisation and the first instal-ment in the brilliant X-COM sci-fi strategy series, UFO: Enemy Unknown.

The French company Infogrames acquired Ocean Software, GTI and eventually Hasbro Interactive, which itself had acquired what was left of Atari Corporation by that point, and MicroProse. The company rebranded and began to use the Atari name.

AOL bought CompuServe and merged with Time Warner, which itself was a merger of Time Inc. and Warner Communications (the old Atari investors). The whole thing would eventually be purchased by AT&T. Prior to that, Time Warner had sold Atari Games to WMS Industries, a company that was a result of Williams purchasing Bally/Midway in 1988. In 1998, WMS spun-off all those video game bits as a new public company, which adopted the name Midway (this then held Midway, Williams and Atari Games' rights). That was eventually acquired by Warner Bros. in 2009, a subsidiary of – you guessed it – that same Warner merger mentioned above.

Given we've drifted quite far into the future, I might as well tell you that the companies Square and Enix merged in 2003, and acquired Taito and Eidos Interactive (which, in turn, owned U.S. Gold and Core Design amongst others). Eidos Interactive was then rebranded Square Enix Europe.

The mid-nineties really was a period where everything just seemed to balloon in scale. There can be few clearer examples of this than when Roberta Williams decided to revisit the game that had started it all for Sierra, Mystery House, having grown bored after nearly ten years of success with the King's Quest series. However, this time, rather than the simple Apple II game whose code had been cobbled together by her and her husband in a few days, Phantasmagoria took four years to make, and cost $4 million. Its creation involved shooting 800 scenes across a 550-page script, and a 135-person Gregorian choir singing in Latin. I'll be honest, it feels like savings could have been made. If the Gregorian Choir had been, I don't know, just eighty people, can you honestly say you'd have noticed the difference?

Released on seven CDs, clearly they'd wasted no time in working out what to do with all that extra storage space, though some people still had trouble understanding the differences in file size. When Trilobyte had delivered the game The 7th Guest to the publisher, for example, they actually requested a floppy disk version.

While Phantasmagoria was criticised by some for being derivative of horror movies, and by others for having puzzles that were too easy, it arrived at precisely the right time. In 1995 the Multimedia PC was must-have hardware, and the game sold over a million copies in its first six months. That same year, Sierra's Gabriel Knight series had a critically acclaimed sequel, The Beast Within, which employed live action throughout*. Though it couldn't match Phantasmagoria for sales, it did beat it in one regard: its script ran to 900 pages[†]. Clearly things were starting to get out of hand and by the time Phantasmagoria's sequel, A Puzzle of the Flesh, was released the following year, the initial excitement over the

---

* Its predecessor had made tentative steps into multimedia, with a separate CD-ROM version that included voice acting by the likes of Tim Curry and Mark Hamill.

† Zero musical monks though, so, swings and roundabouts.

genre's novelty was already fading. 'Interactive Movies' were beginning to be seen as the worst of both worlds – all too often just a bad movie with shallow gameplay, rather than an immersive, evolving narrative where the player had a true sense of being in control of the story. The genre was losing favour with game developers too as it was very restrictive – you can't easily or cheaply get actors back for reshoots if you decide to make changes, so the finality of filming scenes was actually hampering their creativity.

Still, the bubble hadn't burst yet. In 1996, Ken and Roberta Williams sold Sierra On-Line for $1.5 billion (so they probably could afford all those Gregorians, to be fair). Roberta stuck around for two more years to finish King's Quest: Mast of Eternity, but the new owners didn't really respect her approach and she felt undermined. The game ended up selling poorly compared to previous instalments and she left shortly after. But don't feel too sorry for her. She and her husband had just made one-and-a-half *billion* dollars*. She'll probably be all right.

Meanwhile at Origin, they had also suffered disappointing sales. Nineteen ninety-four's critically-acclaimed, first-person action-adventure System Shock would be hugely influential on the action-based story games that would rise to prominence in the years to come but, in spite of that, it failed to do much more than wipe its face financially. The publisher didn't

---

* And, as an extra sweetener, the company's new owners became embroiled in an accounting scandal which led to its CEO and Vice Chairman going to prison. Lovely stuff.

have all its eggs in one basket of course, and founder Richard Garriott was hard at work creating the ambitious Ultima Online, which would stand on the shoulders of earlier endeavours like Habitat and Neverwinter Nights. Origin was yet another company to have been acquired by Electronic Arts (in 1992, in their case) and that was just as well, as Garriott needed their help in funding the development of this latest idea, such was its scale.

Garriott and his team toiled away at developing the game world, creating various roles players could inhabit, an economy, shops, bars to hang out in and even an ecosystem. For example, the in-game wolves ate the in-game rabbits. If the rabbits vanished, the wolves died off. The complexity of it all was staggering. After four years, in 1996 they were ready to do a prelaunch beta test, and asked willing participants for just $2 for the CD needed to play the game. At this point, the most popular online game had managed to grow to 30,000 players; Ultima Online had 50,000 people sign up almost immediately. Part of the appeal was that, in the intervening years, bandwidth costs had sunk, and so Ultima Online was able to adopt the relatively new business model of a monthly subscription which allowed unlimited connection to the game, rather than an hourly fee.

The moment the players arrived, they broke the game. They killed the rabbits, because it was easy, and they could. Soon the wolves died, and there was nothing left to kill. So they started killing each other. Higher-level players killed lower-level ones. More strategic players would hide outside mines and ambush anyone that emerged with treasure.

Garriott's vision for a truly immersive online world had become little more than an anarchic, corpse-looting simulator. On one occasion, when he was in-game as his alter-ego, 'Lord British', he encountered a thief robbing a new player. He told them off and they gave back the items and promised not to do it again. Then they immediately did it again. And again. In Garriott's words:

'I said okay that's it, I've warned you twice. You did it three times in a row so I'm about to ban you from the game forever.' The thief then drops character and goes 'Okay, Richard Garriott, if that's who you really are, I'll have you know that I'm only playing the role as you defined it in the game. I'm playing a thief and I'm using the thieving skill that you put in the game and if you are a thief and the king of the land comes and tells you not to steal of course you're going to tell him you won't, before going somewhere else and getting back to thieving because that's what you do.'

This was a real moment of clarity for Garriott: the player was right. There's no point blaming players for doing things the game allows them to do. From then on Origin went to great pains to develop the interpersonal elements within the game, adding features such as reputation scores, safe zones and even virtual jails. A new role, community manager, was also created to manage player relations in-game. As well as making the game better, this also had a strong commercial imperative – if players felt cheated and quit the game, Origin wouldn't get to keep taking their monthly subscriptions. As

---

*   Donovan, T.: *Replay: The History of Video Games* (Yellow Ant, 2010).

a result, these sorts of games have to evolve via a symbiotic relationship between gamers and the developer.

On another occasion, the day the beta version of the game was to close, Garriott was going from community to community in-game to thank people for participating. Things were going fine, though participants were being a little mischievous. In one town a player cast a spell which created a wall of fire near where Garriott was standing. Unphased, given his character's immortality, he stepped into the fire. And promptly burned to death, as he'd forgotten to switch his immortality on. Garriott's associate producer, Starr Long, stayed in character and began to punish the people for killing their leader, conjuring countless devils, demons and dragons. Unable to cope with the large amount of data required to render the ensuing chaos in which most of the game's players were killed, the game became slower and slower, and eventually crashed. Thus the beta ended not with a fond farewell, but with an almighty massacre; a glorious testament to the extent to which the players' choices informed the game world's narrative.

The game was a huge hit on release, and is still going strong today, over twenty years later. Not only did it represent a watershed moment in online gaming, it gifted gamers with many words they use commonly today, like raids, griefing and nerfing – the latter so-called because at one point Origin reduced the damage swords caused to the extent that players felt it was more like attacking each other with soft foam 'nerf' bats.

During this time, LucasArts continued to release graphic

adventures using their SCUMM engine – titles like Full Throttle and The Curse of Monkey Island – but it was the 1998 release of Grim Fandango that, for many, was seen as the pinnacle of LucasArts' adventure games. Directed and written by Tim Schafer, who had been involved in many of the SCUMM hits, sadly its commercial performance fell short of what it deserved and, as a result, the graphical adventure genre began to decline. However, just like Origin, LucasArts had spread its risk. They did incredibly well in the mid-nineties with their PC Star Wars games in the X-Wing, Rebel Assault and Jedi Knight series*.

So far this chapter, we've focused on the fates of the key computer game companies we've met on our journey but, as the PC gaming market expanded and evolved, many new companies and franchises appeared that would take the baton passed to them (whether willingly or not) from those who came before, and companies that had been lurking in the shadows refined their work and reached a bigger audience. Revolution Software stood on LucasArts' point-and-click shoulders with Beneath a Steel Sky and Broken Sword. The guys behind Dune 2 had continued to help grow the popularity of Real Time Strategy games from 1995 with the Command & Conquer franchise, and it was that same year that saw the founding of Ensemble Studios, who would offer the genre a more historical approach with their 1997 debut, Age of Empires. Not all games were quite so serious though. Team 17

---

* Prior to this, they also had success with a trilogy of SNES games based on the original movies.

released the turn-based tactical game Worms in 1995, which owes its cartoonish art-style to the fact that the original development version literally ripped graphics straight from Lemmings. My favourite character in Worms is the old woman. Sure, she might look harmless, but she can be just as deadly as any of the other weapons available; a highly satirical reminder that, if we assume all terrorists conform to one particular ethnicity or gender, we risk exposing ourselves to attack while our eyes are off the ball. Worms began life on the Amiga in 1995, a year that also saw the brilliant Super Skidmarks take the spirit of Atari's Super Sprint series and give it a contemporary sheen.

Video games had always looked to the past for inspiration, but it was around this time that it began to do so with nostalgia. Nineteen ninety-three's Microsoft Arcade offered PC and Mac users a chance to play Atari games like Missile Command, Asteroids, Centipede, Tempest and Battlezone, but presented them from a historical perspective, its accompanying manual even including histories of how the games had been developed. Activision released their own Atari 2600 compilations for PC and Mac in 1995, and Midway and Williams both did the same with their arcade titles in 1996, even going so far as to include video interviews with their games' designers. Similar offerings also began to appear on console, for example, Super Mario All-Stars revamped Mario's NES titles for the SNES, and Namco Museum, which brought Pac-Man and more to the PlayStation. It went the other way too, with Sega developing a relationship with Microsoft and beginning to port Saturn games to Windows 95, lest you were in any doubt as to how dead the Saturn console was by this point. And 1995 even saw an early example of homebrew, with Ed Federmeyer's brand new Atari 2600 game, Edtris 2600.

Before we head back to consoles though, there's three more companies we simply must mention, as they would each go on to have a huge influence on gaming in the years and decades that followed. The first, Bethesda, had actually been kicking around since 1986, when they created the first physics-based sports simulation, Gridiron. However, they subsequently became embroiled in a legal tussle with EA, who purchased the rights to the console versions of the game but then never released any. Bethesda believed they only did this to get their hands on their Gridiron code, for appropriation in EA's Madden series. The matter was eventually resolved out of court.

What really brought Bethesda to everyone's attention was The Elder Scrolls RPG series, beginning with 1994's cult hit, Arena, so called because the game had begun its development as a medieval gladiator game. By the time it was finished all elements of that had actually gone completely but apparently the publicity materials had already been made and, as we all know, you can't unprint things. So, the name stuck, despite no longer bearing any relation to the gameplay, but it didn't seem to do any harm. The scale and depth of the world gained particular praise and its sequel, 1996's Daggerfall, found even more widespread appeal.

Bethesda would also see success in the twenty-first century with the Fallout franchise, but the first two titles in that series, which were released during this period, were 2D isometric turn-based RPGs by Interplay Productions, rather than the 3D real-time adventures which would follow when Bethesda acquired the IP from them.

Interplay had also published a couple of fun console games in the early nineties by a company known as Silicon & Synapse* who, by 1994, had renamed themselves Blizzard Entertainment and were set to release their breakthrough RTS hit on PC, Warcraft: Orcs & Humans. While it had a single-player campaign, it opened the door to wider acceptance of multiplayer gameplay in the genre and a sequel in 1995 improved on every aspect. The future legacy of the franchise can't be overstated, with the third instalment boasting a mod, Defense of the Ancients, which inspired League of Legends and eventually led to an official sequel, Dota 2 – two of the biggest titles in eSports today. Another eSport, Hearthstone, would be born from Warcraft, as would the most popular MMORPG ever, World of Warcraft.

You'd think that'd be plenty for one company but 1996 saw the release of another hit franchise, the action role-playing, hack-and-slash, Diablo. Its next major franchise launch would eclipse even that, though. Nineteen ninety-eight's sci-fi RTS, StarCraft, was the bestselling PC game that year, and a single country was responsible for half the copies sold. It's not nec-essarily the country you'd expect, though. In fact, it's not a country we've mentioned a single time so far. Time for a brief history lesson . . .

Japan annexed Korea in 1910 and, after World War Two,

---

* Puzzle-platformer The Lost Vikings, and Rock n' Roll Racing.

surrendered the country to the USSR in the North, and the USA in the South, as these were the allied forces operating in each area when the war ended. As the Cold War escalated, rather than a unified Korea as was originally envisaged, the area was split in two. Good old America and Russia; using their power to increase global stability and help the planet be awesome.

South Korea had banned the import of Japanese goods after the war, which seems fair enough given they'd caused their country to be chopped in half. This policy remained mostly enforced until the late 1990s and, as a result, video games and consoles were scarce. However, the rise of PCs as a gaming platform gave people a new way to play. The games industry struggled to establish itself there at first, though, as piracy was rife. What changed things was the internet. In 1995, the South Korean government announced a plan to develop the country as a 'knowledge-based society', built on widespread access to broadband at a time when dial-up was still the cutting edge in most places. However, by 1997, South Korea was struggling. Their economy had shrunk by a third but the government doubled down on the 'knowledge-based society', offering subsidies to anyone creating businesses in associated industries. This led to a proliferation of internet cafes with high-spec computers, and these outlets were known as 'PC bangs', which is also the first two words of any Google search by people who find the police sexy.

By 1998 there were around 3,000 across the country. A lot of people were unemployed, and had little to do during the day. PC bangs offered a cheap way (around $1 per hour) to kill time playing computer games. The country discovered StarCraft, and the nation of sci-fi lovers adopted it as their own. By the early twenty-first century it was a national sport, with events in arenas watched by hundreds of thousands on TV and online. The rise of eSports was now undeniable, and unstoppable.

Other online games did well in South Korea too, such as the MMORPG's The Kingdom of the Winds and Lineage, both created in the country by Jake Song. Online gaming had helped tackle the issue of piracy for many local developers as, even if people weren't willing to pay for a game, they weren't able to connect to an online server without paying the required fee. By 1999, thanks particularly to StarCraft and Lineage, the number of PC bangs had risen again from 3,000 to over 15,000. For many, not just in South Korea but across the planet, the line began to blur between reality and fiction as well. People began to sell virtual items for real money. A house in a good area of the game Ultima Online could retail for as much as $10,000 which, I'm sure you don't need to be told, is insane.

Of course, that was very much the exception. To afford something that extravagant, you'd have to be as rich as Bill Gates, or his ex-employee, Gabe Newell. Who's Gabe Newell? I'm glad you asked. This is a segue and it is happening to you right now without you even noticing.

Gabe Newell dropped out of Harvard in 1983, but somehow that didn't stop him finding employment at Microsoft where he worked closely on the development of Windows, acting as producer all the way back on its very first public release, version 1.01, in 1985. Ten years later, when they needed to port Doom to Windows 95, it was Newell that was given the important task of leading the team that created a version of the hit game and would demonstrate Microsoft's latest operating system was *the* gaming platform for computers. Having enjoyed the process, and inspired by a colleague who'd left to work on Quake, he made the similarly bold leap of forming his own company, Valve, with another colleague, Mike Harrington. They managed to secure a licence for the Quake engine before the game had even launched thanks to their personal contact, although by the completion of their own game they'd modified seventy per cent of it in order to be able to create the game they envisioned. As with id, Valve would go on to provide these development tools to the community, to allow them to create their own mods, such as Counter Strike*. Some were also developed internally, like the Quake mod update, Team Fortress Classic†.

Valve's first game was published by Sierra‡ on 19 November 1998. Initially, Half-Life might not seem like much of a game at all. In the first ten minutes, you do little more than get the protagonist Gordon Freeman to take a monorail journey and head in to work. There's no traditional action to speak of; indeed, it's little more than a commuter-sim at first which, on

---

* This would evolve into its own series, and its fourth instalment, Counter Strike: Global Offensive, established itself as a popular eSport.

† Valve hired the creators of the original mod.

‡ It was the last publishing deal Ken Williams would sign before he left after selling the company.

the face of it, is rubbish, but all is not as it seems. The game subtly begins to drop hints at something darker taking place at the Black Mesa Research Facility with its 'show don't tell' approach to narrative. Rather than cutscenes, the game chooses to have events trigger in-game which progress the narrative, which also means the player never has control removed from them, increasing the sense of immersion. The player is free to choose *how* they observe events as they unfold before them and, rather than discrete levels, the whole thing unfolds as one continuous experience, bar the occasional few moments for loading. The environment is also used to subtly help tell the story, with things like a blood-stained wall that suggests something sinister has occurred here before you arrived. Okay, granted, that particular example's not *very* subtle, but it illustrates my point, albeit with the grace and delicacy of someone burping on public transport and then shouting 'I burped!'

Arguably, the game warrants the term 'interactive movie' far more than any of the titles that thought passively viewing Full Motion Video was the way to make a game filmic. However, to be fair, it was only thanks to the recent progress made in the quality of 3D graphics on PC that they were able to share their fictional world with the player without resorting to filming studio sets. Half-Life was undeniably the culmination of much that had come before, and it didn't hurt that the game arrived at a time when first-person shooters were very much in vogue. For example, Epic Games' Unreal* had also

---

* Which gifted developers the Unreal engine.

been seen to breathe new life into the genre when it was released earlier that year. But even if first-person shooters had been the least popular game genre on the planet, it's impossible to imagine how Half-Life could have ever been received with anything other than open arms. The game's frequent integration of puzzle elements really helped to give the player's actions a sense of purpose seldom found in other examples of the genre such as Doom and Quake. To this day, Half-Life frequently appears on polls of the greatest games of all time.

With Half-Life, gaming had grown up.

12
HEY! LISTEN!

Half-Life heralded a grittier, more mature approach to game design, but that didn't mean games couldn't still be colourful, family-friendly and unabashedly joyful, and no company represented that approach more than Nintendo. Despite their early collaborations with Sony and Philips, they had ultimately decided to stick with cartridges over CDs for their next console, the Nintendo 64, arguing that the absence of loading times was essential for the most satisfying possible experience. Of course, the fact that cartridges allowed them to continue to exercise control over manufacture was entirely coincidental*.

Sticking with cartridges meant that N64 games would necessarily be smaller, although Nintendo claimed they were working on compression techniques to circumvent that issue. Regardless, while they might not have had the storage capacity of CD, they did have something the others didn't – instead of a 32-bit processor, Nintendo went 64-bit. And

_____

* It wasn't.

proper 64-bit too, not the half-way house fudges we'd seen before with systems like the Turbografx-16 or the Atari Jaguar.

Understandably, given their success on the SNES, much was made of the fact Rare were onboard to create games for the new platform. Acclaim were another early party to come on board with Turok: Dinosaur Hunter, highly anticipated thanks to the N64 hardware having been developed with Silicon Graphics, whose workstations had been used for the dinosaurs in the *Jurassic Park*[*] movie. Silicon Graphics had actually met with Tom Kalinske about a potential hardware collaboration shortly after Sega of Japan had vetoed Sega of America's dalliance with Sony, but Nakayama vetoed that too, despite the fact their chip would have been faster, more powerful and cheaper than what Sega of Japan were making. By that point Kalinske had had enough and, just like when Ralph Baer had grown frustrated with Magnavox's handling of the Intellivision hardware and tipped off Coleco about the AY-3-8500 chip, Sega's Kalinske put Silicon Graphics in touch with Nintendo's Howard Lincoln.

Prior to launch, a lot of attention was actually focused on the N64's controller, which notably had more handles than you have hands. Unless you have three hands. I guess you might have, I've not met you, but I'm happy to play the odds on this one.

The controller certainly looked different to everything that had come before, but the reason soon became clear. It had a

---

[*] Another iconic cinema moment, the transformation in *Terminator 2* was also done on their hardware.

D-pad on the left-hand side and buttons on the right, as was standard by this point, but in the centre there was an analogue stick, which would allow console gamers a greater degree of control than ever before. The further you pushed it from its centre, the faster your character would move. People forget now that the Saturn and PlayStation both shipped with conventional D-pad controllers at launch. Sony only introduced the Dual Analog Controller after the N64's launch, and only released the second revision, the DualShock, after Nintendo released their vibrating Rumble Pak add-on for their own controller*. Though the dual analogue stick configuration of Sony's final offering certainly took things further and would become the future standard, Nintendo's many innovations often get forgotten because they're not 'cool'.†

The N64 launched in Japan in June 1996, and in the USA three months later. Released for $250, Sony once again chose to compete on price, and reduced the PlayStation to $199. Nintendo and Sega duly followed, but the move hurt Sega more, as their system was more expensive to manufacture. In Japan, Sega managed to continue to perform well, but the country was very much Nintendo territory, and it wasn't long before the N64 overtook both them and Sony. The N64 sold out on launch, with two-thirds of its 300,000 day-one customers grabbing a copy of Pilotwings 64. But that wasn't the reason they'd bought the console. There was only one game that really mattered: Super Mario 64.

---

* Inserted into the controller's 'memory card' slot.
† Can you tell that I was very much Team Nintendo?

In fact, Miyamoto's newest game was the reason the N64 didn't release until 1996. The hardware was ready to go the previous year, but he felt he needed more time to make the best-possible game. It was worth the wait. To say the game hit the ground running would be an understatement. It immediately defined 3D platform games with its pitch-perfect gameplay and made incredible use of the console's new analogue stick. The blend of puzzle and action elements was perfect and it cemented Miyamoto's reputation as a true genius. However, if you ask Jez San from Argonaut, the game's inspiration actually stems from a prototype 3D platformer on the SNES his team presented to Nintendo which had Yoshi scampering around thanks to their Super FX chip, prior to Nintendo ending their agreement with Argonaut.* Whatever the truth behind all this, Nintendo had successfully migrated their mascot into the third dimension. Sega, on the other hand, still hadn't brought Sonic to the party.

Yuji Naka was instead focused on his new action game, Nights into Dreams. It wasn't bad; in fact it was very good, but compared to the 3D worlds on offer elsewhere it simply didn't compare. It did employ 3D graphics, but gameplay was still very much only in the 2D plane, leading to the coining of the term 2.5D to describe it and similar titles. Sega's other main releases in 1996 were yet more arcade conversions: Virtua Cop 2, an expanded version of Daytona USA, and Fighters Megamix, a ridiculous but fun fighting game which included

---

* The game was eventually reworked and later surfaced on the Play-Station in 1997 as Croc: Legend of the Gobbos to little fanfare.

unlockable characters such as Deku, the Mexican green bean; Hornet – literally the car from Daytona USA, punching and kicking with disembodied tyres à la Rayman; and the palm tree from the developer AM2's logo. To unlock that last one, all you had to do was play the game for eighty-four hours.

Clearly Sega had lost their minds and, in the absence of a blue hedgehog to keep Mario on his toes, Sony offered a similarly odd animal that would prove to be a more than adequate replacement.

In 1994, under the guidance of Mark Cerny (former founder of Sega Technical Institute), the company Naughty Dog* began to develop a platform game which would make the most of the new generation of hardware. Positioning the game's camera behind the main character meant that for a while the developers referred to the game as 'Sonic's Ass Game' but thankfully the guys eventually settled on an identity for their protagonist. They opted for a bandicoot on the basis that it was a lesser-known creature, so people could associate the word Bandicoot with their game's lead character (christened 'Crash'), not the animal. It's a great sleight of hand, the name 'Crash Bandicoot', because it's not actually anywhere near as unusual or wacky as it sounds. In the same way that Sonic the Hedgehog is simply a fast hedgehog, Crash Bandicoot is just a bandicoot that crashes into things. Sneaky Cerny.

During Crash's development, programmer Andy Gavin

---

* Naughty Dog would become a vital partner for Sony in the years to come, with franchises like The Last of Us and Uncharted.

reverse engineered the PlayStation as he was unhappy with the tools provided by Psygnosis, feeling they were insufficient for him to realise his vision. When they demo-ed the game to Kelly Flock, a Sony executive, she was impressed, right up until she found out the way they got their game to work was by accessing the CD-ROM drive far more frequently than the official tools and rules would encourage, to constantly pull data up as needed. The problem was that, at the rates Naughty Dog were thrashing the hardware, it would have worn it out in about three weeks. The game would literally break PlayStations. But the game was undeniably good so, while Naughty Dog worked on the game, Sony's engineers improved the hardware.

Crash Bandicoot was eventually released the same month as Super Mario 64. Miyamoto was dismissive of the game, feeling it only created the *illusion* of a 3D world. It was very linear, and far more reminiscent of the 2D platformer Donkey Kong Country with its crate smashing and riding on animals, albeit with a clever 3D twist, rather than an innovation in the way that Super Mario 64 was. Nevertheless, it was fun to play, and people bought it in their millions*. No doubt its success was also helped by a brilliant advertising campaign which saw an actor in a Crash costume calling out 'plumber boy' Mario outside Nintendo's Washington headquarters until security escorted him away. In the same way Sega had set itself up in competition with Nintendo, Sony was now doing the same,

---

* Sequels would follow in 1997 and 1998, as would the by-then ubiquitous platform game Kart spin-off in 1999.

while Sega's neutered American division stood by and wondered how it had fallen so far, so fast. Crash was never the official PlayStation mascot – he wasn't made by Sony themselves and Kutaragi himself wasn't really a fan – but to many gamers, he served precisely the same role.

Mario, Nights and Crash were all very cartoonish visually, but that autumn Core Design offered console gamers a more mature art style, combined with the 360-degree freedom Miyamoto was so proud of in Mario 64. Tomb Raider wasn't a platforming game, more an action adventure, but its impact on people playing it for the first time was similar to the wow factor of Mario, perhaps even more so because of the more realistic art style. Earlier that year, Resident Evil* had impressed on PlayStation too with similar graphics, but that game opted for fixed cameras and a control system which received criticism. Should there be an ill-timed change in camera angle you could end up doing the opposite of what you intended. I actually like the control system, because it far more realistically reflects how you'd behave in that situation. If I'd just walked round a corner and seen a zombie eating someone's face, I wouldn't calmly retreat, or shoot it. I'd struggle to use my limbs properly and end up running into a wall.

The game is also noted for its exceptional(ly bad) dialogue. In the 2008 Gamers Edition of the Guinness World Records, Resident Evil secured the coveted honour of 'Worst Game

---

* Infogrames' 1992 game Alone in the Dark is an obvious forerunner to Resident Evil, similar in many ways but, in fact, Resident Evil was an attempt to create something similar to Capcom's 1989 game Sweet Home.

Dialogue Ever' thanks to gems like this one: 'Jill, here's a lock pick. It might come in handy if you, the master of unlocking, take it with you.' Yet, despite its flaws, the game is still incredibly effective in creating unease in the player. There was one moment in it where a dog jumped through a window that was so scary, I didn't so much poo myself as leap up so quickly that the poo didn't have time to travel up with me.

Both Resident Evil and Tomb Raider were notable in having female lead characters, Jill Valentine and Lara Croft, respectively. Before we get too carried away with our praise for the Super-Feminists at Core Design though, it's worth pointing out that they initially only made Lara a woman because the original character looked too much like Indiana Jones and, given the gameplay, they were convinced they'd be sued. Regardless of their motives, the game was well timed. The summer of 1996 saw the arrival of the pop group the Spice Girls, so another strong British woman (albeit a digital one) was seen to tap into the zeitgeist of the 'Girl Power' movement, which helped in the game's promotion.

There's probably no clearer indicator of the decline of Sega's Saturn than the fact that the first Tomb Raider was released on Saturn and PlayStation, whereas its second and third instalments in 1997 and 1998 were only on PlayStation*. Enthusiasm for the N64 was also in danger of tailing off as, other than Wave Race 64 (or 'F-Zero on Water' as it became known) there was a far less steady release of new titles for

---

* For the sake of the pedants, they were also released on Windows and Mac OS.

Nintendo's hardware towards the end of 1996. It also didn't help their argument that 64-bit was so important when cross-platform games like Mortal Kombat Trilogy were released that autumn and the 32-bit PlayStation's version looked and sounded better.

The other big thing that happened in 1996 was, surprisingly, a new Game Boy game. At this point, the hardware was seven years old, but it would survive for many more thanks in no small part to a game which Game Freak had been developing since 1990: Pocket Monsters. Or, to give it its Western name, Pokémon*. It was released in two versions, Red and Green†, each of which had a few exclusive Pocket Monsters. This meant that if you wanted to catch all 151 of them, which I gather is very much the point, you had to swap with friends who owned the other cartridge. This novel approach appealed to Miyamoto as an interesting use of the Game Boy's link cable, and also no doubt did its bit for childhood obesity, as children set out to each other's homes to do swaps.

Though it was released in 1996 in Japan, it would be two-and-a-half years before the game would make it to the West. A big part of this was due to the fragile nature of the code, as a result of its protracted development. Seemingly minor amends could mess up the whole thing and so the game had

---

* Renamed to avoid infringing on the Monster In My Pocket toy range, Japan eventually adopted the shorter name too.

† The Blue version was also released later that year in Japan, and would be utilised in the Western release, where the two versions were dubbed Red and Blue.

to be completely rebuilt from scratch. It was also dialogue-heavy, and not only did the dialogue have to be translated, but there were 151 Pokémon to be creatively named in English (and trademarked!) without losing the spirit of the original – the dragon-esque 149 was named Dragonite, suggesting that they might have been phoning it in a bit by the end. In the meantime, the whole thing really took off in Japan. Cartoons, trading cards, toys and all manner of other merchandise spawned from this surprise hit. It even led to the planned Game Boy follow-up, the Game Boy Color, being pushed back for another couple of years*. What this meant was that by the time they were ready to launch in the USA in late 1998, the campaign was immense. Pretty much everything landed at the same time, and the relentless onslaught of Pokémon-related things had the desired effect. Despite doubts as to whether or not a Western audience would take to it, Pokémon became a hit practically overnight.

America had heard of Pokémon once before when, on 16 December 1997, an episode of its cartoon was broadcast in Japan that caused over 650 viewers to have epileptic seizures. Whoops. Luckily for Nintendo, the show was still called *Pocket Monsters* in Japan so, when 'Pokémon' launched in the West, most people didn't make the connection†.

---

* They did launch a revised Game Boy, the Game Boy Pocket, in 1996 – it was slimmer and smaller overall, but with the same size screen, albeit a better one with proper black and white instead of green/grey. It also only needed two AAA batteries instead of four AA ones.

† And, obviously, they didn't air the offending episode there, because of

Before Pokémon arrived in the West, Bandai's 'loveable egg'* Tamagotchi got people fired up over nurturing digital creatures. It was a simple handheld on a keychain with a dot matrix screen, with buttons to let you feed and play with it. If you didn't, it died. This also happened if bullies stole them and held them to ransom, but this definitely didn't happen to me and I'm absolutely not still sad about it.

For a short while, *everyone* had one, and Bandai couldn't keep up with demand. Many other companies were more than happy to create their own versions to plug the shortfall, including Nintendo, who released their own version, a pocket Pikachu (the most popular Pokémon). Theirs also had a pedometer in it, which earned you one 'watt' every twenty steps, to exchange for treats for your pet. Incredibly, even this seemingly unrelated sub-industry had a negative impact on Sega. They'd been exploring a merger with Bandai around this time but, during the same period Tamagotchi filled Bandai's coffers, it also became clear that Sega were on a downward trajectory they'd struggle to pull back from, and Bandai lost interest. Sega couldn't catch a break.

In 1997, as Sega clung to home conversions of their mercifully successful 3D arcade games, Nintendo could barely put a foot wrong. They had two great sequels with Star Fox 64 and Mario Kart 64, and Rare filled out the roster with Blast Corps, Diddy Kong Racing and Goldeneye 007, giving the N64 five

---

the *massive amounts of epileptic fits it caused*. How was that a thing that could happen?!

* Not as rude as it sounds.

much-needed exclusives. All of these games were hugely well received, particularly Goldeneye which eventually became the third highest-selling N64 game of all time, behind only Super Mario 64 and Mario Kart 64, ending any debate as to whether first-person shooters can work on consoles. Goldeneye had actually taken huge inspiration from Sega's Virtua Cop, and was originally intended as an 'on-rails' shooter. It was certainly a far more mature, violent game than would normally be associated with Nintendo, and was held up as proof that the company were finally willing to cater to an older demographic. The game's more realistic style, and the extent to which it adhered faithfully to the movie's plot, foreshadowed the type of narrative-led gameplay we'd see the following year on PC with the release of Half-Life. But it wasn't all good news for Nintendo.

Namco had been a big loss when they'd chosen to work with Sony from the PlayStation's launch onwards, but arguably the damage to Nintendo was even larger when, in 1997, Square Soft's Final Fantasy VII was released exclusively on Sony's console. Until then all the previous instalments had been on Nintendo systems, but the series creator Hironobu Sakaguchi felt he needed the space of CD-ROM to give him the creative freedom necessary for his vision, and he really did make the most of the medium. With cinematic cutscenes and a symphonic soundtrack, the huge game (in length, not just data) simply wouldn't have fit on cartridge. Doubly upsettingly for Nintendo, Final Fantasy VII was a breakthrough in the West, the first of the series to sell more there than in Japan.

Triply upsetting, the game also helped Sony to finally overtake Sega in Japan and, quadruply upsetting, Dragon Quest VII also made the leap from Nintendo to Sony. Quintuply upsetting, I've really cluttered this paragraph with all these ascending prefixes.

The platformer Oddworld: Abe's Odyssey did good business for Sony in 1997 as well, but the game that really got people talking was a very untraditional one. No evil baddie to kill, no princess to rescue, just a simple tale about a dog that was in love with a sunflower.

In the eighties, Masaya Matsuura was in a successful J-pop band called Psy · S. After they split in 1996 he began to focus full-time on creating software. He'd been dabbling in that field for some time and had always had an interest in computerised music so it was somewhat inevitable that, once he was able to give it his complete focus, he would apply everything he'd learnt to date to create something that would allow people to press buttons in time with the rhythm of his music, in order to make a paper-thin dog called PaRappa rap. PaRappa was a play on the Japanese word for paper-thin, a nod to the game's art style of 2D characters in a 3D world, developed by New York artist Rodney Greenblat for the game, PaRappa The Rapper. The game could have easily just felt like a modern version of the old Simon (or, more correctly, Atari Touch Me) game, but the stroke of genius was to have the game's environment change based on how you were doing. Miss the beat, and the backing music would drift out of tune, or the other characters might fall asleep instead of dance.

PaRappa became the face of PlayStation for a while in Japan due to the game's success, which also inspired Konami to create some new, unique experiences for the arcades. Just as well, as Konami had begun to struggle as the latest generation of consoles narrowed the gap between the home and the arcade. Beatmania offered gamers the chance to perform to anyone within earshot on a video game version of a DJ turntable, while the following year's Dance Dance Revolution allowed people to show off their moves. Simple to pick up – just move your feet to correspond with the on-screen directional arrows – the game soon became an art form, with two distinct styles: 'Perfect Attack' (no mistakes) and 'Freestylers' (add elaborate, unnecessary flourishes to your dancing while still playing the game). Lots of people found these games great fun to play and they were good at drawing a crowd too, as people gathered to watch. What's more, with Dance Dance Revolution, you could finally count gaming as exercise! It wasn't long before competitions began to take place.

Personally, I'm of the opinion that the people who use these games to show off are the worst humans ever and, should overpopulation continue to be a problem for the planet, might I humbly suggest rigging these machines with trap doors above fires, as a way of efficiently harvesting meat?

Let's pull this back. By the end of 1997, Sonic had finally made some appearances on the Saturn, though not necessarily in the way gamers might have hoped. Sonic R was a so-so racing game, Sonic Jam was a repackaging of Sonic 1, 2, 3 and Knuckles, and Sonic 3D Blast was a port of a 1996 isometric game originally just intended as a swansong for the Genesis.* Where was the 3D Sonic game everyone was expecting? Well, it's complicated . . .

Not long after Naka moved to America to work on Sonic 2, divisions began to grow between the Americans of Sega Technical Institute and Naka's Japanese Sonic Team. After the completion of Sonic 3 & Knuckles, Naka moved Sonic Team back to Japan to work on Nights into Dreams, while STI† began work on another Sonic game (they'd previously been the ones that did the Sonic spin-off, Sonic Spinball).

Originally intended as a 2D game for the Genesis, it fairly rapidly was moved to the 32X, then the Saturn after briefly being considered for the vague 32-bit cartridge-based Neptune system. It was then switched from 2D to 3D. With so many changes, it was bound to be a bit of a mess, and so the team split in two to try to hurry development along; one working with the engine used on games like 1996's Panzer Dragoon sequel, the other working on PC with the intention of porting to the Saturn later.

This fragmenting of the team eventually led to a rivalry between the two Sega of America sub-teams, exacerbated

---

* The work for both Sonic R and Sonic 3D Blast was outsourced to the developer Traveller's Tales. Sonic 3D Blast wasn't the first isometric Sonic game – look up the rarely spotted 1993 arcade game SegaSonic the Hedgehog.

† I've just realised what an unfortunate acronym that is. Crikey.

when Sega of Japan visited and didn't like the look of the PC stuff, which had been poorly ported to Saturn by a third party for the purposes of demonstration. Before that team could show Sega of Japan the original PC stuff, Sega of Japan went and saw the other team's work, preferred it, and instructed the former to move their development over to the latter. By now it was March 1996, the game had to be ready for release before Christmas, and the goalposts for what the game was even meant to be had changed significantly at least six times.

In an attempt to help move things along faster, the STI team requested Sonic Team's 'Nights' engine, which was well suited to their needs but, after barely two weeks spent migrating the game to that, Yuji Naka insisted they cease all work with his engine else he would quit; Sonic Team were working on their own 3D Sonic game and didn't care for STI hijacking their engine for a competing, and what they perceived would be an inferior, product.

Bear with me, I'm nearly there, although it doesn't get better.

By May, one of the programmers, Chris Coffin, had worked himself so hard (he had literally been living in the office) that he got severe pneumonia. Another, Chris Senn, was told he had six months to live*. With the project in turmoil and two key members of the team out of action, the decision was made to pull it. STI was disbanded soon after and, with the Saturn struggling, it was soon agreed that Yuji Naka's 3D Sonic game

---

* Thankfully he survived.

would be moved over to Sega's next console, in the hopes of a fresh start all round.[*]

Basically, Sega were admitting defeat and would just keep the Saturn ticking over with a few more sequels and arcade conversions like The House of the Dead and Sega Touring Car Championship until it was all over, with one key exception: 1998's Panzer Dragoon Saga. Making the not-so-obvious genre leap from on-rails shooter to RPG, it became the most critically acclaimed game on the Saturn but, due to its appearance so late in the console's life, most people were looking elsewhere and its relative scarcity means it commands a high price to this day among collectors.

Sony weren't averse to banging out the sequels either. Wipeout, Tekken, Crash Bandicoot, Tomb Raider, Resident Evil and Ridge Racer all received prompt follow-ups to keep things moving, but there were new titles too. Gran Turismo brought something new to the racing genre at the beginning of 1998 with its absolute commitment to realism, allowing the player to not only drive over a hundred real cars, but earn credits to purchase new parts, and tinker with the tiniest of settings to enhance the car's performance. As someone who's never really had an interest in cars beyond their ability to move me between places faster than legs, I hate this side of car simulations. I'm good at games, but bad at cars. Please don't make me be bad at games because I don't understand the impact a

---

[*] A glimpse of its Saturn prototype can be seen in Sonic Jam, as 'Sonic World' a 3D interactive museum/lobby which allowed players to browse concept art, manuals and so on.

change in my suspension configuration will have on a car's torque. I'll be honest, I don't even know if suspension has got anything to do with torque, I just have a vague memory that torque is a car word. This is why I've never had a car pass an MOT – they can smell the stupid on me.

Nineteen ninety-eight saw the release of another game I didn't like but that everyone else has agreed was good: Metal Gear Solid, a sequel to Hideo Kojima's late eighties' Metal Gear games. An action adventure with an emphasis on stealth rather than combat, Kojima was also committed to realism with the goal of immersion, going so far as to uniquely model individual desks within the game which was, of course, a massive waste of effort. Professional voice acting and cinematic cutscenes built within the game's graphics engine to ensure a smooth flow from gameplay to exposition all served to further create a cohesive experience unlike most before it. As I say, a lot of people love it but personally, if I fancy a game of hide-and-seek, I can just start counting to ten when my daughter's around, and it doesn't cost me fifty quid.

More up my alley was the first instalment of Grand Theft Auto, unusual in console gaming in that it was released in Europe before other territories thanks to the developer, DMA Design, being based in Scotland. Making an appearance on the PC a couple of months before it arrived on PlayStation, it had evolved through a number of different iterations before the final game emerged and was, by their own admission, a buggy mess for ages as a result. One bug in particular led the police to try to drive through you when in pursuit, the outcome of which was that they seemed to be trying to ram you off the road. They liked that and it stuck. When Gary Penn joined the team after working on the sequel to Elite, Frontier, the mechanic of doing jobs to earn money found its way in, albeit in a city rather than outer space. When it was finally released it wasn't the 3D open-world title fans of later instalments might be familiar with, but a top-down 2D affair, which felt quite old fashioned in comparison to most other games of the time. What gave it its appeal though was its shameless amorality.

The PlayStation really did cater for every sort of gamer. At one extreme you could be reversing over Hare Krishnas for cash in Grand Theft Auto, at the other you could go on colourful adventures with a friendly purple dragon. Spyro the Dragon, produced by none other than Mark Cerny who was now at Insomniac Games, was a deliberate attempt in 1998 to show that the PlayStation was just as capable of catering to younger gamers as Nintendo, though with games like Yoshi's Story (a sequel to the SNES's Yoshi's Island) and the brilliant Banjo Kazooie from Rare, Nintendo were still very much leading the charge.

By contrast, Nintendo wanted to demonstrate it could appeal to older gamers and did so with titles like 1080 Snowboarding and F-Zero X, both of which had been produced by Shigeru Miyamoto but, in truth, none of these games could hold a candle to the final game we're going to look at in this book.

The Legend of Zelda: Ocarina of Time was developed alongside Super Mario 64, but intended to be a launch title for the N64's future Disk Drive add-on, the 64DD. Repeated delays in the release of the hardware* meant the game eventually launched on a massive 256-megabit cartridge instead†. Just like Mario, Link made the transition to 3D flawlessly. It was Miyamoto's final game as a director, before switching solely to producer for future titles, and he really made sure he went out with a bang.

Beginning in the Kokiri Forest village, the game initially keeps you close to home, exploring the interior of the Great Deku Tree while you get used to the core mechanics you'll be using on your adventure. But then, when you finally venture out to Hyrule Field and the world stretches out before you, your breath is taken away. It's hard to explain to a modern gamer the sense of scale you felt the first time you saw Death Mountain in the distance as you ventured towards Hyrule. Exploring this seemingly vast world was a huge part of the joy of the game. Granted, its scale pales in comparison to modern open-world titles, but at the time it was unique. Its time travel mechanic added an extra dimension to things, forcing you to consider how actions in the present might help you in the future, and Koji Kondo once again provided a score that complemented every corner of Hyrule.

Two technical innovations in particular were so fundamental that they would be appropriated by virtually all games that followed. Firstly, the targeting lock, which allowed you

---

* The 64DD was eventually released in Japan only in December 1999 and was a total flop.

† In much the same way the original Zelda bypassed the Famicom Disk System for its US launch on the NES.

to maintain a focus on an enemy of your choice while you engaged with it and, secondly, the context-sensitive A button, which would switch its behaviour to suit your current situation. We take both of these things for granted today, but you'll do well to find a single review from the period that doesn't sing their praises loudly and vociferously.

Released on 21 November 1998, the very same week as Half-Life on PC, computer and video games were clearly both in good form. Zelda received perfect scores from scores of publications[*] meaning that, even twenty years later, it still holds the title of highest rated game of all time, despite the endless witterings of Link's 'assistant', Navi the Fairy[†].

As if all that wasn't enough, it gave Ocarina sales a real boost.

---

[*]   Finally, some solid wordplay.
[†]   Who kindly gifted this book its title.

EPILOGUE

Sega's Dreamcast, which launched in Japan just six days after the release of Ocarina of Time, was to be their final console as a result of disappointing sales, though they did continue as a game developer. By the time the Dreamcast appeared, engineers within Microsoft's DirectX team were already tinkering with laptop PCs to assemble a prototype of what would become Microsoft's entry to the home console market, the Xbox – the X a hangover from its working title, the DirectX Box (yet another interesting fact you can tell at parties so that people will find you impressive).

From the Xbox's launch until today, the console market would primarily become a two-horse race between Microsoft and Sony, with Nintendo choosing to follow their own path, innovating in ways other than being the fastest or most cutting edge. This was really nothing new for the company as, ever since the Game & Watch, Yokoi's philosophy for Nintendo had been 'Lateral thinking with seasoned technology', meaning making the most of established, older hardware. This was never more clear than the Nintendo Wii which, despite being the technical inferior of the Xbox 360 and Play-

Station 3 in virtually every way, sold more units thanks to the 'Wiimote', which opened up gaming to an audience that had increasingly shied away from it as game controllers grew ever more complex. While Yokoi may no longer have been with us, his influence on Nintendo would be forever felt.

Microsoft purchased Rare in 2002, ending the developer's close relationship with Nintendo, but the new partnership failed to yield comparable successes. Nintendo remained undefeatable in the traditional handheld market: the Game Boy Advance, DS and 3DS beat off all-comers with ease, though the arrival of smartphones, with their intuitive touchscreen interfaces, opened up that market in the same way the Wii had for consoles. Mobile phone gaming had already made its first tentative steps before our tale ended, in fact, with the 1998 release of the Nokia 6110, and the planet's gradual reintroduction to the game Blockade, soon to be ubiquitous as the rechristened Snake.

Arcades didn't die, but they undoubtedly became a more niche concern, and their focus shifted. With the home market advancing so rapidly, increasingly elaborate (and expensive to manufacture) cabinets were needed to draw people in. Over time, the ratio of video games to claw toy-grabbers and the like would slowly shift in favour of the latter, returning amusement arcades to something more akin to the Midways Nolan Bushnell had worked on before Pong even existed.

Meanwhile, the PC continued its assault, and cemented itself as the platform where you could experience the most impressive games available, if you were willing to pay the price for the most high-end hardware. It even finally offered a Virtual Reality experience that began to deliver against the promise that it had made many years earlier.

The internet of course benefited every area of gaming, but the PC truly embraced it with Valve's Steam platform for video game distribution and the emergence of eSports as a legitimate competitive endeavour that, at the time of writing, is soon to confirm itself as a billion-dollar industry.

From the first computer, the 30-tonne ENIAC, to an arcade version of Pong, took twenty-six years. From that simple game of 'one ball, two paddles and a score' to The Legend of Zelda: Ocarina of Time took another twenty-six years. When you take a step back from the individual games themselves, it's staggering to consider just how rapidly things advanced in such a short space of time. I was lucky enough to be born just in time to experience Home Pong, and have had a relationship with games ever since and yet, when writing this book, I discovered so many more that I had been unaware of, which had played a vital part in inspiring the forerunners to games I enjoy today.

I'm completing this book almost exactly twenty years since Half-Life and Ocarina of Time first went on sale. It's always dangerous to predict the future when it comes to technology, as the reality almost always ends up being something different to what simple extrapolation would expect. Nevertheless, in conducting the research for this book (which was way too much work for the fee, and I regret the whole endeavour – turns out there's *loads* of games) I feel I've learnt enough to be able to make some reasonable assumptions about what we'll have by the time that third twenty-six-year block has passed. I'll leave you with these.

STEVE'S 2024 PREDICTIONS:

— PlayStation 5
— Another Mario game, probably a platformer
— Complicated hardware stuff will get smaller *and* better
— Virtual Reality still a faff
— eSports in pill form

Afterword

by Ella, aged two-and-three-quarters

As dictated:

'I think I should write my bit first.

Nin-ta-noo ta-na!

Potato for dinner.

The fairy likes to eat chocolate cake. She likes to
   eat something else after her chocolate cake –
   strawberries!

Blah, blah, blah, blah, blah, blah, blah.

And again!

Blah, blah, blah, blah, blah, blah, blah.

Toddler Time.

Teddy.

Toodle pip!

Your book has to end with the words "The End".'

Acknowledgements

I owe so much to so many people, without whom I would never have been able to reach the point where this book could become a reality. Of course, that's of no interest to anyone other than the people listed below so, unless you know me and you're wondering if I remembered to say thanks, you can probably skip this.

Thanks to:

Mum and Dad, for always making sure there were video games in the house, and to Paul for playing them with me.

Matt Holt and Brendon Burns, without whom I might have been stuck just trying (and failing) to be a 'proper' actor.

Jan Spaticchia, for employing me while I pursued this ridiculous career, and being unreasonably cool about whether I actually showed up to work or not.

James Neal, Chris Bond, Simon Longden and Adam Mason, for taking a punt on me and making me look good on the first video-gaming TV shows I was let loose on.

Sam Pamphilon, without whom *Go 8-Bit* would never have existed.

Paul Foxcroft, Richard Soames, Guy Kelly and Will Hartley, without whom the original *Go 8-Bit* live show would have been rubbish. Every comedian that was ever a guest. Beth O'Brien, Rachel Semigran, Nicola Lince, Alex Hall, Mickey Carroll, Abi Dalit Symons and Katie Storey for organising all the vodka, paddling pools and tuna. Ryan Taylor and Henry Widdicombe for letting us ruin their lovely venues. Gareth Swann, for making sure the right industry people saw what we do.

Rohan Acharya, for sticking with the show when no one wanted it. Dara Ó Briain for coming on board so they'd let us all play games on telly. Simon Lupton and Iain Coyle at UKTV for taking the punt. Paul Byrne for keeping me sane. Nick Ranceford-Hadley for making the best of a bad deal.

Rob Sedgebeer: All Hail King Rob. Martin Davies, for making the Royal Institution feel like *WiFi Wars'* home.

Richard Roper at Headline, for his kindness when my year fell apart and the book simply wasn't written.

My incredible Discord community, without whose support I'd have never been able to make the leap to doing my own thing on Twitch and YouTube. John S. Reid, for creating the place where I met them.

Chris Slight, for showing me how it all worked.

Tina, for her endless support and patience while I did all the things that got me to this point that didn't make *any* money.

Ella, for reminding me what's important.

And, lastly, everyone that ever made a video game.

Further Reading

This book is silly, and very brief. If you want to find out more, these are the giants' shoulders I stood on to write this nonsense:

Donovan, T.: *Replay: The History of Video Games* (Yellow Ant, 2010)

Goldberg, H.: *All Your Base Are Belong to Us* (Three Rivers Press, 2011)

Hansen, D.: *Game On!* (Feiwel and Friends, 2016)

Harris, B.: *Console Wars* (HarperCollins, 2014)

Herman, L.: *Phoenix IV: The History of the Videogame Industry* (Rolenta Press, 2016)

Kulata, K. et al: *Sega Arcade Classics – Volumes 1 and 2* (Hardcore Gaming 101, 2012/2016)

Kent, S.: *The Ultimate History of Video Games* (Three Rivers Press, 2001)

Kohler, C.: *Power-Up* (Brady Games, 2004)

Kushner, D.: *Masters of Doom* (Random House, 2003)

Pettus, S.: *Service Games: The Rise and Fall of Sega* (Pettus, 2013)

Szczepaniak, J.: *The Untold History of Japanese Game Developers – Volumes 1, 2 and 3* (SMG Szczepaniak, 2014/2016/2018)

FURTHER READING

Sheff, D.: *Game Over: Press Start to Continue* (GamePress, 1999)

Wilkins, C. & Kean, R.: *Ocean: The History / The Story of U.S. Gold / The Story of the Oliver Twins* (Fusion Retro Books, 2013/2015/2016)

Wilkins, C.: *The Story of the Sinclair ZX Spectrum in Pixels – Volumes 1, 2 and 3 / The Story of the Commodore 64 in Pixels / The Story of the Commodore Amiga in Pixels* (Fusion Retro Books, 2014/2015/2015/2016/2017)

And a whole tonne of random Google searches and Wikipedia stuff that might be total nonsense.

Index

INDEX

The End